To Tim Pinsters,

Best wishes (and)

Roll Tide!

Mike Bynum

# BEAR BRYANT'S BOYS OF AUTUMN

# BEAR BRYANT'S BOYS OF AUTUMN

*by*

## MIKE BYNUM

Autumn Football, Ltd.

*Tuscaloosa, Alabama*

Grateful acknowledgment is made for permission to reprint excerpts from the following:

Lines on pages 192–195 from *He Ain't No Bum* by O. A. "Bum" Phillips and Ray Buck. Copyright © 1979 by O. A. "Bum" Phillips and Ray Buck. Reprinted by permission of Jordan and Company, Publishers, Inc.

Lines on pages 178–190 from *Blanda—Alive and Kicking* by Wells Twomberly. Copyright © 1972 by Wells Twomberly. Reprinted by permission of Nash Publishing Company, Inc.

Lines on pages 215–217 from *"Pat Dye: New Life on the Plains"* by Clyde Bolton are from *Lindy's S.E.C. Football Magazine.* Copyright © 1982 by D.M.D. Publications, Inc. Reprinted by permission of D.M.D. Publications, Inc.

Jacket Cover Design: Dennis Luzak, Redding Ridge, CT.
Book Design: Kingsport Composition, Kingsport, TN.
Book Lithograph: Fairfield Graphics, Fairfield, PA.

FOR LISA, WHO WAS THERE DURING THE
FOURTH QUARTER CHEERING FOR VICTORY.

# CONTENTS

# BEAR BRYANT'S BOYS OF AUTUMN

# *Foreword*

*It is an attempt to portray an unique story about a great coach, his prize pupils, and the football dynasty that they built together. . . . It is a book filled with both glory and heartbreak, the past remembered and the present faced.*

It was late November 1982, and the book, *Boys of Autumn,* was being previewed at the University Club in Tuscaloosa. Nearly one hundred and fifty local townspeople, university faculty and administrators, and former players braved the chilling rain to be in attendance. And the white pillared mansion, which had once served as the home of Alabama governors during the mid-1800s, was aglow with the festive marches provided by pianist, George Washington.

Those assembled huddled in the mansion's formal parlor to anxiously flip through the pages of the rough draft copies of the book, and view for the first time the varied collection of memorable photographs and emotion-packed stories of Bryant and his winning football men. *Boys of Autumn* had recently been the basis for a one-hour documentary entitled, "Bear Bryant—Countdown to 315," which was narrated by Joe Namath and aired nationally on NBC, therefore there was a lot of interest to see firsthand the same story retold in print.

Initially, *Boys of Autumn* was scheduled to be released in December 1982, prior to the Christmas holidays, however, the announcement of Coach Bryant's retirement prompted the Publisher to make a management decision which was based, "out of sheer respect and common courtesy for Bryant," and rescheduled the book's release for the first week of February 1983.

Then in late January, the football world was dealt a tragic blow when news began to hit the wire services that Bryant had died in a Tuscaloosa hospital after suffering a sudden, yet massive, heart attack. The funeral and mourning that followed was much like that reserved for presidents and kings. It was a proper farewell tribute to a great football coach, a great man and, no doubt, a great American hero.

*Boys of Autumn,* as you read today, is a re-edited version of the original manuscript that was to have been published and released in December 1982, and later scheduled to be released in February 1983. The actual interviews with the thirty-one former players were conducted prior to Bryant's death. The surrounding text and appendix, however, has been updated to include the events leading up to Bryant's death in January 1983.

It must be noted that several of the former players, themselves, have recently made some alterations in their career plans since the original interviews took place. For example, John David Crow resigned as head coach and athletic director after building a successful athletic program at Northeast Louisiana University to return to his alma mater, Texas A&M, to become Associate Athletic Director. Jack Pardee, who was in the same backfield with Crow at Texas A&M, was voted the NFL's Coach of the Year in 1979, only to be forced out as head coach following the 1980 season in a power struggle with team management. Following a brief stint in 1981 as Offensive Coordinator for the San Diego Chargers, Jack returned home to Texas to take a job as executive vice-president of the highly successful Runnels Mud Company in Midland, Texas. Then in 1983, he was selected to become head coach of the Houston Gamblers of the USFL. Marvin Tate, who was the Athletic Director at Texas A&M resigned in the Fall of 1981 to enter the booming real estate development business in Bryan-

College Station, Texas. Dennis Goehring, having built a financial success as president and chairman of the board of the Bank of A&M in College Station decided in 1981 to sell the bank to financial heavyweight, Republic National Bank of Dallas, for a reported two times book value. Today he is developing the industrial park in Bryan-College Station and monitoring his varied investments. Bobby Lockett, whose "gosh-darns" reminded me of a typical Texan has left the energy conglomerate, Sun Oil Company, to make his own fortune as an independent oilman. And Babe Parilli, a guy whom I have grown close to in recent years, left the Denver Broncos in 1981 and has since joined the Denver Gold of the USFL as an offensive assistant coach and was recently selected to be inducted in the 1983 class of new members in the College Football Hall of Fame by the National Football Foundation, along with two of Bryant's other former players—Lee Roy Jordan and Charlie Krueger.

It is hopeful that in the pages that follow that you will enjoy this inspiring, perhaps heartwarming, story about Paul Bryant and his Boys of Autumn. It is, without a doubt, a very real attempt to portrait an unique story about a great coach, his prize pupils and the amazing football dynasty that they built together, as seen through the eyes of a young author who traveled across America in search of his boyhood heroes—men whose struggles to succeed in football and life made them champions.

*Boys of Autumn,* however, is much more than that. It is a book about some young men who grew up learning to play football in the 1940s, 1950s and 1960s in such places as Beaver Falls, Pennsylvania; Cristoval, Texas and Springhill, Louisiana, and then went on to play on some of the most exciting teams that college football has ever fielded—the teams at Maryland, Kentucky, Texas A&M and Alabama—the teams that were coached by Paul "Bear" Bryant, the biggest name that football has ever known.

*Boys of Autumn* is also a book by, and about, a young student football manager for Bear Bryant's Crimson Tide, who grew up in the 1960s and 1970s being nurtured in the adventuresome tales of King Arthur and Mark Twain, who as a youngster often escaped to see his heroes play at nearby Legion Field, and later, while in college, set out on a quest that would eventually cover 125,000 miles attempting to observe, and to understand, the mystical success formula that Bryant had taught his winning football men.

Finally, and most importantly, this book is a book about what has happened since to George Blanda, Heisman trophy winner John David Crow, Jack Pardee, Joe Namath and the many others, no longer boys but men in their middle years with their glories laid behind them.

*Boys of Autumn* is the story of those incredible ball players as they were then, and as they are now. It is a book filled with both glory and heartbreak, the past remembered and the present faced. And it all revolves around a central figure—the godfather of this memorable football family—Paul "Bear" Bryant.

*Boys of Autumn* is, perhaps, one of the best football books ever written dealing with people, but it is more than that. It is a book about life, and what life does to us all.

The Partners of
Autumn Football, Ltd.

# 1

# *In Search of Camelot*

> *"In the early morning hours before the battle is to begin there is always a calmness that settles in around you. Men who have gone to war and have laid it on the line when everything counted most, they have known this feeling. It is a special time."*
>
> —Johnny Musso

The concrete pathway that is Interstate 10 between New Orleans and Baton Rouge is probably the loneliest seventy miles of highway in America. Especially on an autumn evening.

Massive Lake Pontchartrain, which once served as a haven for French pirates, is always filled with fog, some days just gloomier than others. And there are the bayous which hug both sides of the road giving you only a brief glimpse of the many untold mysteries that lay just behind the moss covered trees. It's almost as if there is a haunting feeling which follows you, causing one to look over their shoulder, nearly every mile along the way.

It was during one of these late night lonely trips in October 1981, while returning to Baton Rouge from a recruiting visit in the Crescent City, that my good friend and head football coach at LSU, Jerry Stovall, gave me a keen insight to the answer of a question which I had traveled so long and so far to find. Suddenly, it all seemed too simple.

He shared with me that the real success which Coach Bryant and his winning men have enjoyed evolved from a philosophy in football that the great coaches—Knute Rockne, Frank Leahy, Paul Brown and Vince Lombardi—have always preached and, most importantly, always put into practice.

Jerry explained further. "In football there is quite often a fine line that makes the difference in winning and losing a big game. And with Coach Bryant, there's a fine line that distinguishes between so called *winners* and a real *champion*. For one must understand that a so-called *winner* is someone who is content in doing great things most of the time. Unfortunately, he is not dedicated to his cause one hundred percent of the time. A *champion,* however, is always willing to pick himself up one more time than he is knocked down. A *champion* wants to win and win badly, all of the time, no matter how great the obstacle."

Continuing, the LSU coach summed it all up. "Mike, in Coach Bryant's way of thinking, the price one must pay for victory is so very expensive that only champions will pay the tremendous price to achieve it."

Shifting in my seat, I glanced outward toward the dark and empty void which was just beyond my grasp. So here it was, I thought, the long awaited answer to a question which I had traveled over 125,000 miles seeking to find. In a flood of emotion my mind began to wander, remembering all of the wonderful people that I had encountered along the way in this sometimes lonesome quest. They were the great heroes of yesterday—George Blanda, John David Crow, Jack Pardee, Joe Namath and the many others. For they had been a part of this privileged few.

Along the way, I have noticed several facets of Bryant's intriguing character which best describe the man within, the *jev vil ud,* attempting to reach the pinnacle of success that only a handful will ever achieve.

As a youngster Bryant used to sit on the loading dock behind the Kilgore General Store watching the trains go through town, waiting one day for the chance when he, too, could hop one of them and leave behind that mule, that plow and that poor-boy existence. In 1946, Bryant began to take his first step toward destiny when he flew all night after the College All-Star game in Chicago in an effort to be in school president Curley Byrd's office by eight o'clock the next morning to get his first coaching job at Maryland. Winning, however, had a price tag. At Texas A&M, Bryant faced his biggest gut check. In coping with the pressures of the job, he and assistant Elmer Smith, being ex-farmboys and early risers, would always take a daily pre-dawn drive on the Old Wellborn Highway, heading out of College Station, to discuss an upcoming game or recruiting strategy all in an effort to overcome the restless, queasy stomachs that always troubled them.

These are but mere examples to explain the tremendous drive in Bryant, both the man and the great football coach. Yet, they explain the *why*. Why he had to take his first Aggie squad to that war camp at Junction. Why he had to return to Alabama, his alma mater, and rebuild them into the championship teams that he had once been a part of in his younger days. Most importantly, it explains why he stood there on the sidelines of Legion Field on November 28, 1981 watching his Alabama team (along with a nationwide television audience) as they defeated cross-state rival Auburn to give him his 315th coaching win and forever a special place in history.

So often when I think of Bryant, I am always reminded of his tower on the sidelines of the Alabama practice field. No players. No coaches. An empty field. Just the tower.

It is the tower which Bryant had climbed countless times to look out over yet another Alabama practice session, observing every play of the day's drill with cold, knowing eyes, looking for satisfaction, or a source of dissatisfaction.

God knows how many times he climbed those steps . . . how many steps . . . how long it takes to get to the top? How about hundreds of times . . . thousands of steps . . . forty-seven years? But Bryant atop this tower in Tuscaloosa may just have been the quintessential ikon of collegiate football . . . There he comes again, starting the day's climb . . . but the slow ascent up those steps is just part of the route that Bryant has taken in becoming the winningest coach of all time in a sport that has captured the minds and memories of millions of fans in a way that no other sport had taken hold of them.

So at a point in life when one is through with boyhood, but has yet discovered how to be a man, it was my great fortune to have been a part of this great football dynasty led by Bryant. Remembering and appreciating the time, which was not so long ago, I have found myself wondering more and more about Bryant's boys. Most of them are retired athletes now, but not old. They are scattered wide, but joined by a common memory. How are the years with them? What past do they remember? Have they come at length to realize what they once had?

Unlike most, an aging football player must confront two deaths. First, between the ages of thirty and forty he perishes as an athlete. Although he looks trim and feels vigorous and retains unusual coordination, the superlative reflexes, the *competitive* reflexes pass on. At a point when many of his classmates are newly confident and rising in other fields, he finds that he can no longer throw the big block or stride downfield past an unsuspecting defender. And when one reaches the age of thirty-five, he is experiencing the truth of finality. As his college or professional career is ending, all things will end. However, he sprung, he was always earthbound. Mortality embraces him. The golden age has passed as in a moment. So will all things. So will all moments. *Memento mori.*

"In the early morning hours before the battle is to begin," Johnny Musso once explained to me, "there is always a calmness that settles in around you. Men who have gone to war and have laid it on the line when everything counted most, they have known this feeling. It is a special time.

"For those who have been fortunate to be a part of this dynasty and have known these meaningful moments when purpose and desire and courage become one—it leaves a lasting impression."

This book, *Boys of Autumn,* is about those men—those privileged few.

With the simplicity that comes with hindsight, we recall the games memorable and the players famous. We recite plays and statistics and the final scores.

This is the easy part.

But what of these men—as men? While Bryant's legacy begins to grow in our memories, the players, themselves, take on a wooden sameness as good soldiers who made those mock battles come out as they did. We forget that they still think and feel, and that they were alive long before, and long after, they signed on for four years of Bryant's tutorledge. For those at Maryland, Kentucky, Texas A&M and Alabama, who lined up for him, they probably could not forsee the significance this coach would play in the history of college football. They were concerned with the future of college football only as an assembly-line worker might view the future of the steel industry.

These men would later become working men, tradesmen, glamerous only when compared with the miners and factory workers who were their fathers and brothers. They were men without great expectations. But they were hungry, hungry enough to hide serious injuries so as not to place their positions in jeopardy. They were individualists, but they submerged their identities for the sake of the team.

"We got along so well," said Ray Perkins, the former head coach for the New York Giants and Bryant's successor at Alabama, "because there was a deep and real respect among us, each for the other. Things were so special then . . ."

Today they are people of middle age. Today they are just men, not superstars. They are prey to the same doubts and problems that mark our own lives.

I asked them to look back at their careers and at Bryant, to look back to what they were in that time and place. They judge those memorable college days not only by Bryant's impact on themselves, their teammates, the games won and lost, but moreso by their personal successes and failures, then and later. Many of them profited from football's burgeoning popularity, but only one, Joe Namath, got rich as a player. The rest simply paved the way for a new era and a new type of athlete. Since leaving the playing field they have faced the ego-binding shock of becoming has-beens. Thrown into the more conventional world, many were ill-prepared. When football values no longer mattered, some could not cope. Several took up coaching, but very few of them still possess a direct tie to the game.

Now, in middle age, their memories are mellow, sometimes somber, often frankly nostalgic. They are no longer young, no longer perfect physical specimens with football talent beyond the rashest dreams of the sandlot player. And football is no longer what it once was in college. Their youth and the games will not come again.

These thirty-one players were participants in a small piece of history—many from different generations but all linked together by Bryant, the godfather of this memorable clan. And by telling us how it looks now through their eyes, they help to fix the moment in a way no one else could. They are, by and large, proud to have played under Bryant, proud to be able to say, "It was mine, I was there." But they are clear eyed, and they also tell us what Bryant was not, as well as what he was.

I have indeed been fortunate these past five years, being able to seek out these heroic athletes who, many of which are now in their forties and fifties, in lairs from Texas to New England, and to consider them not only as old athletes but as fathers and as men, dead as football players to be sure, but still battling, as strong men always battle, the implacable enemy—time.

This story, then, is about men, more than about football. It is an attempt to re-create a dynasty through the memories of its participants. And it is a study of middle age, of a group of men who achieved a kind of fame early in life and for whom the middle years have been a time of adjustment, different from yours in degree, but not in kind. They are presented here not as heroes larger than life, but as witnesses. They are men with human flaws and failings, but men deserving of respect and sympathy.

Most of them have drifted quietly out of the fan's range of view. Like other players, before and since, only a few were lucky enough to become professionals, who in the end would eventually come back to training camp a step or two slower and lose their job to a younger candidate. Or they would get hurt and never fully recover. Or they got traded. Except in the memories of the hard-core faithful, they just faded away.

Today, out of uniform and out of the spotlight, some of these men seem different; others are nearly unchanged. But they are still vividly alive men of middle age with experience and maturity that make them more interesting now than they might have been as winning football men under Bryant. Time dulls the reflexes and slows the legs, but it can sharpen the mind and round out the character. These men may have faded away as football players. However, as men they are still very much here.

They are a diverse group, these Boys of Autumn, fighting as you and I against the intrusion of years. They have attempted to relive what was, for most of them, a better time.

There is sadness here, but a sadness familar to all of us. We can none of us win the war, defeat the calendar. Time is always a mightier opponent.

These men are different now, diminished. The arrogance and nerve of youth has been tempered by the advent of middle age, the forced acceptance of change. They have a tendency to look back, perhaps too often, to remember the glory and the cheers. It is a happier alternative to accept the reality of now.

When once they never thought of anything but life, they must admit that death has made its way into the inner reality of now. Bryant, their great teacher and coach . . . is it really true that Father Time has finally called for him?

Years whirl past faster than we can know, and where we were and where we are is separated by a blurring, fading vortex of half-membrances. Our images are colored by sun, not shadow. We see what we would rather see.

But it is this way for all of us, and has always been. Old men remember each other as classmates, and refuse to see each other as old men.

Many years ago, Oliver Wendell Holmes was asked to deliver the welcoming address for the fiftieth reunion of his Harvard class, a class special for the prominence of its members. He chose to compose a poem.

As he looked out at the audience, he saw gray heads and white beards. Also, he saw empty chairs. And he asked in his poem (as we ask of the men in the book) if these gray heads could be the boys he once knew. He concluded:

> *Then here's to our boyhood, its gold and its gray.*
> *The stars of its winter, the dews of its May!*
> *And when we have done with our life-lasting toys,*
> *Dear Father, take care of thy children, The Boys!*

It has been said "sooner or later society beats down the man of muscle and sweat." Surely these fine athletes, these Boys of Autumn have found their measure of ruin. But one does not come away from visits with them, from long nights remembering the past and considering the present, full of sorrow. In the end, quite the other way, one is renewed. Yes it is fiercely difficult for the athlete to grow old, but to age with dignity and with courage cuts close to what it is to be a man. And most of them have aged that way with dignity, with courage and with hope.

They've paid the price, Paul Bryant's winning football men. In full.

# 2

# *The Test of Time*

*Football is emotion—and, possibly, more than anything else, football is believing. Believing in self. And believing in a man who helps mold that self. On hundreds of American campuses, that man is the football coach.*

When it comes to the business of manufacturing heroes, Americans are a breed apart from all other nations. No other country has sired such a variety as those who have made an impact on our lives and times. Statesmen and men on horseback; inventors and politicians; scoundrels and criminals; movie stars, comedians, athletes, rock stars and cultists.

Oh, we put them up there indeed, on pedestals, in Halls of Fame; inking their names onto miles of headlines. Some with just transitory impact or flare. A rocket of brilliant hue, up just once, quickly, and down, soon nothing more than a dim visual memory on the national retina. Some we establish in heroic perpetuity. Lasting. Legendary. Leaving their mark indelibly.

Leaving a mark is the test of time . . .

And some of these have been football coaches. Say again? Football coaches? You mean you don't think for a moment that as long as Americans play or watch games, they won't forever recall such names as Pop Warner, Amos Alonzo Stagg, Knute Rockne, Fielding "Hurry Up" Yost? And, more recently, Woody Hayes and Paul "Bear" Bryant? Names like that have staying power, a piece with the institutions they served. Far beyond, in fact, that of the men who headed those institutions. Quick now, who was president of the University of Chicago when Stagg ruled the Midway? Who can recall Warner's boss at Stanford? For a million bucks, now, could you come up with the name of the guy who okayed Yost's pay check at Michigan? Rockne's under the Golden Dome? Who was Ohio State's prexy when they sacked ol' Woody? And do you know who Bear's boss was at Alabama? Not to denigrate all those fine and illustrious educators, but it's just a point being made here.

Football, more than any other sport, spawns giants among its coaches. Why football? For a variety of reasons. If you take all its ingredients, put them in a gigantic shake-well and pour out the mix, you've got a multi-faceted but remarkably adhesive phase of the American way of life.

Football is the All America and the scrub third-stringer. It's the Rose Bowl with 105,000 wildly partisan fans, and its the raggedly kids on a vacant lot, pounding away with a well-patched ball. It's a field in Colorado ankle-deep in snow and another in Florida, sun-baked and shimmering with heat.

Football is a magnificent college band drilled to splendiferous perfection. It's lithe, leaping cheerleaders and bouncy pom-pon girls; colorful homecoming floats and old grads returning to relive precious moments and scenes of their youth. It's tail-gate parties, booze and barbeques; *GO IRISH, ROLL TIDE* and *GO BIG RED* buttons worn proudly on wool caps and scarves. It's streamers and cowbells. It's a crisp fall day holding a sense of anticipation unique to the season. It's the horrendous traffic jam at the end of a two hundred mile trip, with nobody really caring because everyone's a veteran at making the kickoff, and time has been allotted for every contingency.

It's high drama and the pits of despair. Exhilaration and shock. It's sport's biggest platoon of zebra-striped officials running a shocking, bruising contest with cool, iron hands. A game where action is stopped by the ubiquitous mutt wandering into the defensive backfield, or the celebrated drunk trying to take a place on the line of scrimmage. A game conspicuously suited for youth with wide shoulders and bulging muscles.

College football is the Great American Novel, with chapters built on Frank Merriwell, the Bible, Teddy Roosevelt and Jack the Giant Killer. Football is the ineluctable memory of Jim Thorpe, Red Grange, Bronko Nagurski, and O. J. Simpson, Mr. Inside and Mr. Outside, the Four Horsemen and the Seven Blocks of Granite.

Football is Walter Camp, the MVP, Hall of Fame and yellowed clippings in a treasured scrapbook. It's Old Glory painting the breeze and fans actually singing the words, probably more so than at any other sporting spectacle. Women who don't know a quick kick from a winged-T shriek with excitement and pound the stranger next to them, because that's football. Football is love, hate, fear. It's courage, tragedy and comedy. It's a game of grace, strength and consummate strategy. It's the Great Autumnal Madness, as Westbrook Pegler once described it—and, above all, football is *American*.

There are those who predict (a pox upon them!) that soccer will ultimately replace football as America's leading sport. No, no, *no!* Let us fall prey to any number of national catastrophies. Tell us the Russians are surely coming. Tell us our air is beyond redemption. Tell us they're going to clone 100 Farah Fawcetts. But don't tell us soccer will ever replace football in America's affection.

Sure, there are the headlines: SOCCER FEVER SWEEPING THE COUNTRY, WORLD CUP HYSTERIA IN ARGENTINA. SOCCER GOING BIG-TIME ON TV . . . The phys ed people read it all smugly. They're enamored of the idea that all you have to buy for a soccer squad are some flimsy shirts and shorts. No expensive pads or macho training equipment. Just put the kids in skivvies, toss them a relatively inexpensive ball and let 'em go. On the cheap.

Oh, sure the aficionados would have us believe it takes the skill of a Nureyev to do what these guys do with their feet, or that game strategy is straight from the playbook of Von Clausewitz, Napoleon or Lee.

Replace football? With the most un-American of all sports? In soccer, for God's sake, you're not even allowed to use your hands which is un-American to begin with. Not using your hands in sports is fine for—well, for Argentines, Germans, Greeks, Poles, Britons, whatever, but not for Americans.

Replace football? Listen—do you know what football really is? Football is the ultimate test of athletic courage and sacrifice. It's the most American of sports. It takes a particular and peculiar appetite to play it. In fact, football is—well it's an *attitude*. The desire and willingness to commit the body at all times with absolute, fearless and reckless abandon. Sacrifice? I forget exactly who said it (maybe Lou Holtz) but the guy proclaimed that if you want to do murder and then hide with perfect anonymity, just jump into somebody's offensive line as a guard or tackle and nobody'll ever know you're there.

Just about all civilized people of the world are into basketball, track and field, boxing, tennis—you name it. But except for our Canadian cousins, nobody—not even the Russians, the Great Imitators—have had the gumption to try football. If you could somehow put together a Russian all-star football team, even one of our lower-level Ivy League clubs would knock their socks off. Attitude would do it for the Yanks. American football stands alone. It is ours. Notably and spiritually ours alone. And if American kids ever lose this desire to hit—and their willingness to be hit—we will come unstuck at some of our strongest national seams.

Football, more than any other American team sport, is the concept of *winning*. Football is emotion—and, possibly, more than anything else, football is *believing*. Believing in self. And believing in a man who helps mold that self. On hundreds of American campuses, that man is the football coach. And the one who doubtlessly evokes more *believing* than anyone can imagine, has been Paul Bryant.

But before we approach those who believed most, it would be useful to back off and take a brief look at him—at Paul William Bryant—quite simply known as The Bear.

# 3

# *Bryant Through the Years*

*Suddenly Bryant yanked off his suit jacket, flung it to the floor and stomped it. Next, he took off his tie and stomped on it. As he rolled up his sleeves in front of the mike, the place went bonkers. A message had been sent and well received . . .*

It wasn't Bear Bryant who invented the double wing. That was dreamed up by Pop Warner in his early coaching days at the Carlisle Indian Institute. Bear Bryant didn't invent the backfield shift. That was Dr. Henry Williams at Minnesota. Bear Bryant didn't invent the screen pass, the lateral pass or the first huddle behind the line of scrimmage. That was the work of Bob Zuppke of Illinois. Michigan's famed Fielding "Hurry Up" Yost invented the Statue of Liberty play, the roving center on defense and the man-in-motion.

Bear Bryant didn't invent the T-formation. That was Clark Shaughnessy's development at Stanford. Bear Bryant had nothing to do with the invention of the wishbone offense, the nickel defense, the tackling dummy, pom-pon girls or Howard Cosell.

So, what's the big deal, then, about Paul "Bear" Bryant having been the most successful coach in football if he never invented anything, huh? Ah, but he *did*. Paul Bryant, for all intents and purposes, invented *winning*—and the Care and Feeding thereof.

The width and breadth of Paul Bryant's winning ways is more than just a mere recital of statistics. But that's where you have to start—establishing the face value of the numbers. For it was during the 1981 season that Bryant's varsity presented him with a particular number that only one football coach in America could own. It was 315—marking Bryant's 315th college football victory, putting him one up on the immortal Amos Alonzo Stagg as the winningest ever among all coaches.

Along the way to number 315, Bryant had won 14 Southeastern Conference titles (13 at Alabama, one at Kentucky); one Southwest Conference crown at Texas A&M; had produced 65 All America players (more than any coach in football); and his record at Alabama, alone, dwarfs anything any coach will ever remotely approach. With the Tide he had won six national championships, had been Coach-of-the-Year three times and had Alabama in a bowl twenty-four straight seasons beginning in 1959. Overall, he sent more of his players and assistant coaches into important coaching posts than anyone who has ever scribbled X's and O's on a blackboard. He had exactly one losing season in 38 years as a head coach at four major schools—Maryland, Kentucky, Texas A&M, and Alabama.

Okay, so much for the numbers. The numbers don't tell *how* he did it. And although the rest of the Bryant story is not as precisely defined, it's as visible as any other public monument south of the Mason-Dixon line. Anyone who doesn't see it that way doesn't know a football from a pumpkin, and those so afflicted—at least in the state of Alabama—are so few in number that a cure isn't worth looking for.

What Paul Bryant won with, was his personal hold on people. Shucks, says the conventional local wisdom, *anybody* can coach big, strong, fast kids, but Ol' Bear, he turned 'em into an extension of himself, complete with all the psychological stuff and motivation, and hung up on a savage refusal to fail. As Jake Gaither, the one-time Florida A&M coach used to say: "I've watched Bear enough to know one thing about him . . . He can take his'n and beat your'n—or he can take your'n and beat his'n."

That probably says it all. Well, not *really* all. Maybe it starts with that *look*, that *presence*, that palpable feeling that, yes, by God, that truly a *legend* was standing there talking to you, or getting you to do something you never thought you were capable of doing.

Ever since Stagg's time, up through Rockne and beyond, college football has had a number of almost deified coaches. None has had the documented reverence of Bryant. Apparently none has invested the game of football and its players with a greater need for redemption, salvation and, yes, even a bit of vengeance.

Newspapers have run tricked up photos to show Bryant walking on water, and it always drew the expected knee-slapping guffaw from readers, but as one admirer insisted gravely: "It ain't true. Nobody really believes Bear can walk on water, but we'd all bet our last buck that he knows where every submerged rock is hidden."

George Blanda, the one-time perennial indestructable of the NFL, who played for Bryant at Kentucky, puts it another way. "He'd blow that whistle, you'd all gather around him, you'd look up at him, and what you'd see was the face of God. Oh, were you ever ready to listen!"

"When he entered a conference room," says another ex-player, "he never had to say: 'Now, pay attention everybody.' He already *had* your attention with his first step into that room."

With the reverence and recognition cloaking Bryant, the Man and/or the Myth, must there have been a Catch 22, or 23? That some place in the Bryant scenario there was surely the obscure evidence that he could have been a closet sonuvabitch? That there are people and players here and there who still hate and detest him? That he was known to have played favorites, pulled strings and kicked a crutch from underneath an old widow lady?

The cynic who believes any of this could make a career of trying to fit fact to wishful fantasy. You want to cut Bryant down to mortal size, you've got to find another way.

Paul "Bear" Bryant—anyplace—whether in a conference room or on a practice field, was a tall (6'3") loosely, but heavily strung (210 pounds), handsome man with the craggiest face this side of Mount Rushmore. He spoke in a slow rumble that seemed to start somewhere near his shoe-tops and took its time coming north and out of his mouth. The syntax was rarely perfect and was mostly down-home and colloquial. But the meaning was never misunderstood. You dug The Bear first time around. If he could have walked with a swaying motion, knees slightly in, he'd have been a good double for John Wayne.

All in all, his presence was stern and demanding, though on a one-on-one basis he could be an avuncular pussy-cat. His charisma was unique in the football coaching business, as was his ability to push his players harder and further than they ever imagined they could be—and still leave them loving it and respecting him for the prodding. Steve Sloan, one of Bryant's great quarterbacks and now head coach at Duke says: "And yet he had this mystic way of making each guy feel he was the only person in the world who mattered at the moment. It kind of gave you little goose bumps."

An alumnus in Birmingham shakes his head deferentially. "Since Bear's been building that gaudy win image for us, a whole generation has grown up with no earthly idea of what a losing season is like—but with the unknown fear that everyone will be smitten and scourged if it should happen. I tell you, we wouldn't know how to live with it if it does."

This constant state of Holy Way in Alabama takes many forms. When Bryant's boys beat Penn State in the Sugar Bowl, New Year's Day 1979, they did it with a dramatic four-shot goal line stand, turning back the Nittany Lions on the final fourth-and-one that could have produced the winning touchdown. Within a few weeks an artist re-created the final play in vivid color and Alabama fans bought up thousands of the reproductions at almost $100 apiece for their dens and rec rooms.

You would think at first impulse that the most important article of clothing in Bryant's life would have been the familiar black and white houndstooth checked hat he wore on the sidelines at Alabama football games. No. Not so. As famous though it may be, Bryant's hat trails in personal significance to a pair of shoes he wore decades earlier as a boy in Arkansas.

He was just thirteen and had never owned a pair bought for him new. Always he'd had to make do with battered, scuffed hand-me-downs from an older brother. But finally his mother decided that raw-boned Paul, sprouting signs of manhood, was entitled to something he could cherish above all imagined treasure—his own pair of shoes.

She knew the silent torment young Paul had endured for years as the object of derisive ridicule in the eyes of more fortunate kids in Fordyce, Arkansas. Ridicule tinged with contempt for a boy from a small, poor, dirt farm a few miles down the road in an implausibly named spot (located on no map whatsoever) known as Moro Bottom. Population, maybe 30; probably fewer because census takers didn't bother much with Moro Bottom. A couple of share-croppers missed here and there—big deal.

Ida Kilgore Bryant, mother of eleven, with Paul the second youngest, went to the rickety dresser drawer one day in August just before school started, took out a faded, velvet lined box and extracted exactly two dollars and forty cents, leaving very little in the box. She told young Paul to hitch up the wagon. It was the wagon she and Paul always used to peddle part of their crop of vegetables to families in Fordyce. The boy always hated those trips because they exposed his poverty. Before the family moved to Fordyce he always dreaded the possibility that a friend would see the four-room shack his family lived in, and where he was born in 1913.

From the time he was six, young Paul Bryant had chopped cotton, raked hay, harvested vegetables and milked cows. There would come a day when he would confess, as an adult, that his greatest fears, often actually in his dreams, were that he'd fail as a football coach and would have to go back to chopping cotton.

On that hot August day in Fordyce, Arkansas, his mother took him to Mr. Clark's shoe store and Mr. Clark fitted Paul with a pair of hightop, black shoes. They gleamed in the sunlight as he left the store, walking on air. He would wear these proudly, now, to school, to church, to town. They would be off his feet only when he slept.

It would not be quite that way though. The first week of school he walked past the football field and stood watching the high school team practice. The coach ambled over to the big 13-year-old and asked if he'd like to try out for the team. Paul mumbled that he didn't know the rules or anything about playing. The coach said he'd acquaint him with the rules; all the boys had to do was knock down some of the other guys, and particularly the one with the ball. Or words to that effect.

Getting a change to do that was not easy. His parents were devoutly religious and looked on sports as a creation of Satan. None of his older brothers had ever dared to participate but there was something in young Paul's pleading eyes that resulted in an exception.

Football had indeed began to change young Paul Bryant's way of life, but there were some strange and even quixotic adventures along the route. At age fifteen, he talked his parents into letting him go to Cleveland, Ohio to visit a married sister and maybe get a summer job there. He said he and a pal were going to hitchhike. He lied. Hitchhiking would have been acceptable to his parents; they didn't know Paul and his buddy had planned to ride freight trains headed northeast, running the risk of getting beat up—or worse—by railroad dicks who were the traditional enemy on a hobo's wanderings.

They made Cleveland with close scares but no scars. Paul got a job at an auto parts factory and near summer's end was almost talked into staying in Cleveland and playing football at a local high school. A fist fight with an older worker (which Paul won with a first-punch kayo) over who should, or shouldn't, be dating a certain blonde, convinced young Bryant that life in Ohio might be complicated. He hit the freight yards again, southwest bound, was arrested only once, and got back to Fordyce just in time for the football season.

It was that summer, just before school began, that he acquired the nickname that would stick for life. A carnival was in town and one of the acts was billed into the movie theater. There as this carny who had a big, scruffy, muzzled bear, and he was offering anybody a buck for every minute he could wrestle the bear. Paul Bryant and some of his buddies were in the audience and his buddies finally goaded Paul up to the stage to take on the sullen-looking beast.

"It wasn't that I'd come loose of my senses," Bryant recalled later, "but a buck was big money in those days and a little ol' minute was only sixty seconds. So, suddenly, there I was being shoved at the bear, who was rearin' up on his hind legs lookin' seven feet high and mean as all hell. I grapped onto that scruffy fur and just tried to hug him tight, thinking maybe he wouldn't believe I was really menacing him. But he'd been trained pretty good and knew what he was supposed to do, which was pick me up and shuck me off.

"Suddenly the ratty ol' muzzle on his jaws broke apart and next thing I knew he had those big yeller teeth in my skull, just behind my ear and I could feel the blood comin' out. There'd been maybe only 30 seconds elapsed but I tore loose from that bear's embrace and flung myself off the stage and up the aisle and out the door. Hell, for all I knew, that bear might have been after me and they can move pretty good. Never got a cent from that carny for tryin', but it got me that nickname, 'Bear,' which stuck right with me all through high school and college."

He has never said so publicly, but Bryant has never liked anyone to call him "Bear" to his face. His intimates call him "Paul," and all others refer to him as "Coach Bryant." With the same kind of respect one uses in "Doctor" or "Professor."

In his senior year Fordyce came up with one of the best teams in the state and an Alabama coach, sniffing out raw talent across the Mississippi River, snared two recruits: young Paul Bryant, a Fordyce tackle, and a rangy, antelope-type end from Pine Bluff named Don Hutson.

Bryant's parents were a bit mystified at the prospect. Ten of their eleven kids had gotten by without going beyond high school. College? To play football? "I'm gonna learn something useful," Paul pleaded. "I'll never have to chop cotton again."

He didn't know exactly how the word *useful* would translate at Tuscaloosa but he was willing to try it all on for size and for some good ol' head-banging. His folks let him go and even packed him a lunch, convinced it might have to last a long time. Paul had dutifully explained what a "scholarship" was. Not a city-folks trick, Daddy. The food would be free and three times a day. Ida Kilgore Bryant still packed the lunch.

Bryant and Don Hutson made some electrifying history at Alabama. Coach Frank Thomas re-styled Bryant as an end. On offense he could block a Buick off the road. On defense he slammed the door on the best running backs in the Southeastern Conference. He rarely caught a pass. He didn't have to, nor was supposed to. Brilliant tailback Dixie Howell flung virtually all of the Alabama aerials to Hutson, maybe the greatest pass receiver in the game's history.

Howell-to-Hutson. A headline writer's delight. No twosome had ever put it all together the way they did. Inevitably, Bryant was dubbed "The Other End." The great song hit of the year was a haunting ballad entitled, "Stars Fell On Alabama." "The Other End," nevertheless, was one of the bright stars of that do-it-all club of Bryant's junior year, a club which, in addition to All Americas Howell and Hutson, included All America tackle Bill Lee.

The Crimson Tide engulfed Stanford in the 1935 Rose Bowl and the song became a companion piece to the national anthem in the state of Alabama.

Near the end of Bryant's senior year Thomas asked if he'd like to sign on as a graduate assistant coach. He still had a few credit hours to finish off his degree following the fall of 1935. Hutson was playing in the fledgling pros with the Green Bay Packers. Suddenly, Bryant knew the real reason he'd came to college. This was it. This, then, was the translation of *something useful*. The desire he had locked up in him for years, merely waiting for the genie to pop out of the bottle and show him the way.

He should have sensed it was coming. Shortly after the 1935 season, the coach of Union College, a small school in Tennessee, asked Frank Thomas to send someone to help install the Alabama offense. Thomas dispatched young Bryant, not yet graduated.

Bryant got less than $200 for the assignment. A fortune for such teensy-weensie part-time work. Hey, maybe there was more where that came from! He could have signed to play with the pro football team in Brooklyn, with some of his college buddies, but Thomas talked him out of it. "Your future is coaching," he said flat-out. Thomas put the lid on it by telling Bryant he'd be paid $1250 for the 1936 season at Alabama while still working toward his degree. Bryant's fingers trembled when he signed the contract, it was that scary and exciting.

Four years of assistant coaching at Alabama, followed by two years at Vanderbilt, convinced the career-hungry Bryant that he was ready to step up. He applied for the head job at Arkansas, then open, eagerly looking forward to going home.

He just knew he'd be a success. He'd fully demonstrated his technical skills and knowledge of the game. And he'd quickly discovered that college football, by the late 1930s, had evolved into a recruiting rat race. And as he put it to some sports writers one day: "They say you have to have the horses. Shoot, that ain't quite right. I've seen some sorry lookin' nags back in Moro Bottom. What you need is *winning* horses and how to spot 'em."

His recruiting technique was already becoming notorious in the Southlands. "First he hooks the Mamas and Daddys." said a coach at rival Auburn, "Then when he gets them on his side he looks the boy smack in the eye and asks him does he think he wants to be a winner or whether he thinks he's a winner already. Bryant has a way of spotting that subtle difference."

But the first week in December 1941, Paul Bryant had his final interview at Arkansas. At age 28, he'd be the youngest big-time coach in America. He'd had a verbal commitment from Arkansas, and everyone was pledging full cooperation. Everyone but the Japanese.

The day after Pearl Harbor, Bryant was on a train to Washington, D.C. and a commission in the Navy. A few months later he was on a troopship rolling and pitching toward North Africa. Four days out, they were rammed by another ship in the convoy. With a huge hole in its hull the ship listed dead in the water for three days.

Bryant was sure there were a dozen German U-Boat captains out there pulling straws to see who'd take the easy pot-shot at them. "I knew then and there," he recalled, "that if ever I got outa that one I'd know how to survive a goal line stand when all else seems to fail. Pray."

Eventually, after repairs in Bermuda, the ship made it to North Africa shortly after the American invasion, and Bryant was assigned to a physical training program. Subsequently he was reassigned back to the U.S. to coach the football team at the Navy pre-flight school at North Carolina.

He had met George Preston Marshall, owner of the Washington Redskins, a couple of years earlier and as the war was nearing an end, Marshall, who was quite taken with the gangling Southerner, offered him a job as an assistant Redskins coach. Bryant turned him down. He got offers for assistantships at several colleges and he spurned them, too. Then at the College All-Star game in Chicago in 1945, Marshall impulsively grabbed Bryant by the shoulders. "Why're you turning everyone down?" he growled. "What do you want out of life?"

"I want to be a head coach," Bryant said simply.

"Well, Jeeze, why didn't you say so!" Marshall, on the spot, told Bryant to go to his hotel room and wait for a phone call. Ten minutes later Bryant picked up the ringing telephone and heard a man introduce himself as Curly Byrd, president of the University of Maryland. Everyone in the South knew of the famed Byrds of Maryland, including the feisty, assertive Curly, who had once coached the Maryland football team himself. "You want to be my head coach?" Byrd bellowed.

"I sure do," Bryant stammered.

"See me in the morning in my office at College Park, Maryland," Byrd said, and hung up abruptly.

Flying all night for over seven hundred miles, Bryant arrived there at 8 A.M. In five minutes he had the job. Curly Byrd never bothered with details, or boards of regents, athletic directors, types like that. Curly Byrd ran his own show—classroom and playing field. So, when Bryant brought a dozen of his North Carolina Pre-Flight stars with him, wondering about their eligibility on such short notice, Byrd simply snapped: "Forget it. I make the eligibility rules. They're eligible."

Bryant knew he was taking on a flat and failed program that had been going nowhere for years and had shown exactly one victory the previous season. In the cliche-ridden jargon of football, the press referred to it as a "challenge" for Bryant. Bryant never used the word himself. "The only new thing we can do here is win," he said to his assembled squad of 1945, a week after his discharge from the Navy. "And only winners will play for me," he continued. "All you have to do is show me what you've got in you and I'll make the judgements."

With a minimum of pre-season work, his jerry-built team of flight school transfers and some fresh-spirited hold-overs posted a 6-2-1 campaign, including stunning upsets of Virginia and South Carolina in the last two games. Virginia, a certified toughie at the time, had won sixteen straight.

With a delicious wind-up like that it looked like gourmet fare for Maryland in the future under the budding genius of Paul Bryant. From the governor and Curly Byrd on down to alumni and the press, everyone was convinced that Paul William Bryant was going to lead the Terrapins to dizzying heights.

And he surely would have, had he not held the quaintly stubborn notion that, above all, he as to be The Man as far as his team was concerned. But not too long after that sweet enjoyment of instant success, Curly Byrd, for reasons of his own, fired one of Bryant's assistants without bothering to even consult Bryant. Hard on that no-no, Bryant, who had bounced a player off the team for breaking some hard-case Bryant rules, was stunned to hear Curly Byrd had summarily reinstated the boy to the team and his scholarship. Again without notifying Bryant. "The Kid's father is a big-shot politician," one of his assistants explained to him.

Enough! Too much, in fact! Bryant knew that Curly Bryd, the ex-coach, now president, would never cease thinking he was the supreme authority in Maryland football. For Bryant the idea was intolerable and unworkable. He went home and re-read a telegram that had arrived a couple of days earlier.

IF YOU WANT TO BE HEAD COACH AT KENTUCKY PHONE ME COLLECT. DR. HERMAN DONOVAN, PRESIDENT.

Kentucky? Over there, across the Blue Ridge Mountains? Kentucky? Race horses and basketball country? Where football ran a dismal third in the state's affections?

Bryant checked the record book. He had a hunch it would convince him he'd have to be crazy to place that call. Sure enough. Under K for Kentucky. Its last undefeated season was . . . Oh, my God! During the Spanish-American War, in 1898? Never had it won a Southeastern Conference title. Only ten times in the 20th Century had it won six or more games in a season. There hadn't been a winning season in the last five. The previous year they had gone 2–8.

Kentucky . . .? He'd have to be crazy.

Bryant placed the phone call. Sight unseen, President Herman Donovan offered him a job.

Bryant accepted but underestimated the impact he'd made on the Maryland students in just the few months he'd been there. Thousands went on strike, boycotting classes and screaming for Bryant's retention. Curly Byrd tried to backtrack but Bryant's mind was set. He'd face the unknown at Kentucky rather than Byrd's known pattern of meddling.

Arriving at Kentucky a few days later, Bryant found another student mob gathered to await him. He figured they were in a semi-lynch mood because they'd been insisting on getting a big-time name coach. "I hardly fit the description," he later recalled. "The only thing I was noted for was being the cause of a student strike. Then I saw this big sign one kid was holding. *WELCOME BEAR*. I thought, Lordy, if the students were friendly could the Kentucky players be far behind?"

What he soon found out about the football players he didn't generally cotton to. Kentucky, in Bryant's lightning calculation, was a party school with a notable lack of academic discipline. Its football players didn't seem immune to the syndrome.

In his first week of spring drills, Bryant saw some pretty good talent but little motivation and desire to work hard. He put his principles on the line. By the time Spring practice was finished a month later there were a dozen or more players who couldn't pack their bags fast enough to get clear of this lunatic workaholic.

He started his day at 5 A.M. and his first order of business, they assumed, was to sit down and invent some new maniacal demands on their bodies. They didn't know he was so emotionally involved that he would have to pull off to the side of the road and vomit virtually every morning before he got to his office.

George Blanda, the future Ageless Wonder of the pro's, later described it thusly: "Playing for Bear Bryant was like going to war. You may come out of it intact, but you'll never forget the experience. We were usually so tired after practice we would barely move but he'd make us run to the locker room. When you played for Bryant you ran everywhere. If he caught you walking he'd tell you to turn in your uniform."

That was the pattern set for Bryant's first year at Kentucky. Those who survived his first pre-season program felt a new element in their psyche: the desire to *win*. The same guys who's finished 2–8 a year earlier wound up 7–3 in 1946. A local minister started a sermon with: "What Hath Bear Wrought?" And then went on from there, telling the good folk what could be done with a positive approach to life. He said nothing about some soul-searing head-knocking that attended one positive approach.

So, Paul Bryant settled in. He averaged five hours sleep a night the first three years, brought bus loads of kids in for tryouts before signing them (slightly south of the rules) and told President Donovan he was on a five-year plan to get Kentucky into a bowl. His intent was made highly visible by such ploys as leaving his starting backfield at home for a big road game because they hadn't put out one hundred percent in practice. He won without them and it became part of the Wildcats' new religion.

On the way to the New Era, Bryant developed guys like Blanda and Babe Parilli, both All America and pro greats; and Bob Gain and Steve Meilinger, All America linemen and future pro standouts.

He made good his promise. His 1949 club met Santa Clara in the Orange Bowl and lost, 21–13, but Bryant was off and stomping. In 1950, the Wildcats won their first Southeastern Conference title, ever, and was picked to play Oklahoma in the 1951 Sugar Bowl, and the state of Kentucky went into a collective fit.

Bud Wilkinson's Sooners had a ton of All America that year: Billy Vessels, Buck McPhail, Eddie Crowder and Leon Heath. When the Wildcats won 13–7, ending Oklahoma's 31-straight victory streak, the local preacher called Bryant the new Moses who had led his people out of the wilderness of mediocrity and despair.

Bryant was embarrassed by the burgeoning idolatry, but, meanwhile, he was being flattered by coaching offers from a dozen other big-time colleges clamoring for salvation and sold-out stadiums. He turned them all down, each for a good reason. And he hadn't yet won enough at Kentucky. He had this fixation about posting a record that was not merely successful but glitteringly imposing.

He took the Wildcats to a third straight major bowl the next season, beating Texas Christian, 20–7. But something had begun to eat at him and he couldn't live with it. *Kentucky basketball and Adolph Rupp,* Kentucky's monumentally famed coach. Bryant was flat-out jealous of the statewide acclaim of Rupp and his program.

No matter how elated the Kentucky fans could get about their revived grid program, Bryant knew football would always be second banana. It was so obvious that Bryant could taste it, and it was all wormwood and gall for a man dedicated to football primacy. His blue eyes would always narrow and the mouthline harden whenever he recalled it, and the allusion he made wasn't meant to be funny. "I remember when Rupp won a Southeastern Conference basketball title and they gave him a big, shiny new Cadillac. I win their first and only football title and they handed me a little gold cigarette lighter."

In 1952, Kentucky basketball players were involved in a point-fixing scandal and the black ink was splashed all over the nation's press. Bryant felt splattered in the process. It would probably hurt his football recruiting but, essentially, he just felt pain, personally tarnished by association. He had to get out.

Twice, his alma mater, Alabama, had tempted him to take over. Louisiana State, Indiana and others wooed him. The university reluctantly gave Bryant his freedom. But by then there was only one major job still open. Texas A&M. In the winter of 1954, he signed with the Aggies. There were people—especially and including his wife—who thought he'd come unhinged from all reason.

Once again he was faced with rescuing a floundering program. The Aggies' bowl glory days of the late 1930s and early 1940s were long gone. In their place, year after year, grim mediocrity. Time for a change. Let's get us somebody with a Shake-Well.

The man they got had known the geography and had heard all the jokes and miseries of Aggieland in College Station, Texas. Farmland on all sides and in the middle of nowhere, ninety miles up the road from Houston. No women on campus. Actually an agriculture and engineering college but also a military school with compulsory enrollment for all, with a military mind and tradition which had supplied more officers for World War II than West Point. A&M was fetchingly referred to by the sophisticates at SMU or Texas as "Sing Sing on the Brazos."

So, how in the hell do you recruit for a place with no glamour and is the butt of jokes that go like this: "How does an Aggie break an arm and leg while raking leaves?" The answer: "By falling out of the tree."

"My first job," he recalled, "was to convince those students we could turn 'em into winners by working hard and making them believe in us and themselves." His first move was spontaneous and pure inspiration.

The first night on campus he was introduced to the student body. He faced 5,000 uniformed students and gulped.

Then, suddenly, Bryant yanked off his suit jacket, flung it to the floor and stomped it.

Next he took off his tie and stomped on it. As he rolled up his sleeves in front of the mike, the place went bonkers. A message had been sent and well received.

After a frenzied recruiting crusade to acquaint the state with what he planned as a new Aggie *attitude,* Bryant went into spring practice to find out what kind of players he had. He wasn't too interested in skills or techniques. He had to see if he had any *winners.* He had the hold-over bodies from the previous year but he sensed they held a negative spirit. He wasn't sure of his judgement. Something had to be done.

He finally got a handle on it when an assistant mentioned Junction, a mean, desiccated Quonset-hut camp 240 miles away in the hills of West Texas, used for a summer program for geology students. To say it was spartan was to suggest it was designed by Hilton. One observer, who knew, said the Japanese had better appointments in their prisoner-of-war camps.

Weather reports from Junction knew no variety. One report would do for a month: hot, followed by hotter; dusty, followed by dustier. The only breeze at night was made by the beating of mosquito wings. Would enough players take what he had in mind, to field a team? Whatever the result of his first year, could he establish a basis for Aggie football of the future? A desire to pay a price for winning? Maybe this was the spot, far enough away from prying eyes and hangers-on, to find out who the *winners* were . . .

Bryant's way of finding out became a *cause celebre* in the state of Texas because word leaked out and some of Bryant's boot camp details got into the papers. About sixty players rode two buses to Junction. Ten days later 27 survivors made it back to College Station. The rest had searched their souls, decided they weren't potential winners, packed their bags and went into oblivion. Suffice it that the next year the Southwest Conference banned off-campus training camps.

Those 27 won only one game, losing nine, in Bryant's first season. But he'd done the impossible the previous winter after his arrival. No blue-chipper in the state had wanted to be an Aggie for years. Bryant mesmerized a dozen of them, plus a few more whom he thought would at least give it a Bryant-type effort.

Those who stayed, or who came later, were at least in awe of him if not flat-out reverential. Bum Phillips, now head coach of the New Orleans Saints, who was an Aggie assistant under Bryant, vividly recalls one incident. "I came out of Coach Bryant's office and John David Crow was standing patiently outside. 'What do you want, John?' I asked.

" 'Oh, I just wanted to see The Man,' he said. Everyone at A&M called Bryant that. So I said: 'Nobody's with him. Go on in.'

"He said, 'Oh, I'll just wait.'

"Now, you've got to realize John David Crow was a senior, his career over, a two-time All America and a genuine Heisman Trophy winner, but I couldn't talk him into just goin' in. He just leaned against the wall and waited for Coach Bryant to come out.

"Which Coach finally did, 20 minutes later. 'What the hell you doin' out here, John?' Bryant said.

" 'Just wanted to talk to you.'

" 'Then whyn't you just come in?'

"John David just shifted his feet. 'Well, I thought you were busy or you wouldn't have the door closed.'

" 'Don't you ever again just stand around waiting for my door to open, you hear?' Bryant shouted.

" 'Yes, sir,' John David said, as Bryant/grabbed him and pulled him inside."

In the sophomore season of that first recruiting class of Bryant's, along with the Junction survivors, they went 7–2–1. In 1956 A&M minted an undefeated season and a conference championship. Players like Bebe Stallings and All Americas such as Charlie Krueger, Jack Pardee, and Heisman Trophy winner John David Crow had made them the talk of the nation. But there had been too much talk elsewhere down in Texas. Especially by over-zealous alumni with ready checkbooks, and next thing Bryant knew his team was on NCAA probation. He was sick about it. The cure came near the end of the 1957 season with a call from Alabama.

This time they wouldn't take "no" for an answer, even if they had to drag him back in chains. Alabama, the last few years, had wallowed in unaccustomed defeat. In 1955—may Walter Camp forgive us!—the Tide had lost all ten games, scoring only 48 points in the agonizing process.

Bryant had had the Aggies number-one in the polls in 1957 with two games to play, when he accepted Alabama's offer. Nothing was to be said until the season's end, but someone talked and the Aggies were so dispirited they lost their last two. It was tough leaving some great kids but Bryant's blood needed a transfusion of alma mater plasma.

It was at Alabama, of course, that Paul Bryant established

himself as the most successful and dynamic football coach in the game. Much has been made of Vince Lombardi's cogent comment that, "Winning isn't everything—it's the only thing." Actually, Bryant had beaten Lombardi to it with that theme. His first week at Alabama in 1958 he posted this notice: "WINNING ISN'T EVERYTHING—BUT IT SURE BEATS ANYTHING THAT COMES IN SECOND."

But then his first tactical observation became the touchstone of his future Tide teams. He would not recruit beef. Quickness and speed would be his priorities. Quickness, execution and just plain physical toughness and mental attitude. Over the years Alabama has had very few of the 250-pound linemen so visible on other clubs. Any fat on a recruit was soon run off in Bryant's boot-camp atmosphere.

"And okay, you guys, there's this six-minute demand I'm gonna make on you," Bryant rumbled. "If you tote up the time the ball is actually in play, there's only about thirteen minutes of action in a ball game. From the time the ball is snapped until the official blows it dead it's slightly more than five seconds on an average play. Whether you're offense or defense, you're puttin' out only half the total time in a game that has maybe 150 plays in it. You add up all the action you're gonna be involved in and it comes up to maybe six, seven minutes of the demands I'm making on you." Trenchant pause: "You'd better give me the kind of six minutes I want at Alabama, too."

At Alabama, Bryant never had a long list of the athletes he wanted each year. Most schools start with about 100, hoping to get thirty great ones. Bryant never started with more than fifty but all had been prescreened—the kind who meets his qualifications as *winners*.

Even so he stoutly insists he never has had many all-worlds on his teams. "Many of my clubs," he insists, "have had only three, four or five great players. I had some with only one or two," he adds, before breaking into a craggy smile. "But we usually had a dozen or so guys in the fourth quarter who got to *thinking* they were great." A pause. "Lordy, the mileage you can get out of winners like that . . ."

A visitor to his impressive office once asked if perhaps he didn't put too much emphasis on football. Bryant didn't reply immediately. He just looked around the room. Football pictures of Bryant's national championship teams lined two walls. Blackboards at opposite ends of the room were covered with a maze of the ubiquitous X's and O's. *Two* projectors squatted on a long conference table heaped with cans of football *film*. Bryant's desk was heaped high with mail, brochures and magazines in a state of organized confusion and chaos. If he had to sign or write something he'd have to shovel away a clear path to do it.

Bryant cocked his head at the question and a growl preceded his answer. "There can never be too much emphasis on football. Maybe some alumni and students do seem to put a lot of emphasis on winning but that suits me fine because I don't want to have anything to do with anybody who isn't a winner."

He backed up his beliefs in dramatic ways. It was reliably reported to him, once, that one of his players no longer felt like paying the price and had decided to quit the squad. Bryant didn't wait for the boy to inform the coaching staff. Bryant strode to the boy's locker and flung the player's equipment on the floor. "I didn't want to make quitting an easy or honorable thing," he recalled.

For those players desirous and capable of paying the price Paul Bryant exacts, he makes life clearly sybaritic off the field. Take the Bryant Hilton, for instance, which is what the rest of the Tuscaloosa community calls the football players dorm. Sometimes it's called The House of Lords. It's like nothing like an Alabama football player left home for. A huge fountain on the front lawn. Raised terrace in the rear. Air conditioned rooms carpeted ankle deep and fully draped. Beds seven feet long. Custodial service just short of personal maids. The boys merely have to make their own beds and empty the wastebaskets.

There are twin dining rooms, one of them for the traveling squad only, for a bit of caste system. High-backed, baronial, leather cushioned chairs. Steak or roast beef every night. A 20-member kitchen staff, and three professional dieticians. All the food they can eat, plus little red paper cups that hold their vitamins and salt tablets.

Italian provincial decor and classical art on the walls. An eye-filling 150-foot circular main lounge room with an enormous open fireplace, soft lighting and elegant, squashy leather furniture. Piped-in music throughout the building. Bryant himself had a personal "master bedroom," which he occasionally occupied. Three VIP rooms for guests. They've been used by Bobby and Ethel Kennedy, Gerald Ford, Al Hirt, Billy Graham, Red Grange, and a whole clutch of senators or congressmen. Two boys to a room, with personal wake-up service by the team's student managers. Oh, yes—a library and special study rooms for sessions with the Alabama "brain coach" in charge of tutoring. A couple of large TV rooms, of course. Anything missing from this list? It'll be tended to in the morning . . .

"Truth is," Bryant once stated, "I don't want 'em to be like other students. They can't be, and be winning football players. They have to make sacrifices and do without things others have. To win they have to have a togetherness and a pride in *belonging* to a small, special group.

"Some players came to me during our lousy seasons of 1969 and 1970 and told me they thought they should live like other students. Well, you know what I told em?" He nodded to himself. "I told 'em if they wanted to be like other students to get the hell over to the other dorms and be another student. You can't live like other students and have that sort of freedom of time and movement and keep up with schoolwork *and* football—and still *win*. So we have our dorm.

"We ask only one thing in return for our special dorm," said Bryant. "A deep respect for the place. No shirt tails hanging out and everybody wears socks . . ."

By the time Bryant was zeroing in on Stagg's all-time victory mark he was an institution in Alabama. He is said to have been a millionaire and was, many times over. He was on the boards of several banks, owned the Bear Bryant Hat Company (which supplied his famed checked numbers), was a partner in a meat company and a window company, owned a box factory and had a bulging portfolio of stocks, including oil.

At any department store in the state you can still buy Bear Bryant shirts, ties, chairs, watches and lamps. From novelty shops you can fetch home Bear Bryant bumper stickers, drinking mugs and pennants. At supermarkets there are Bear Bryant hot dogs, soft drinks and potato chips. Bill Battle, one of Bryant's pupils on the 1961 national championship team and former head coach at Tennessee, handled his business affairs and received at least two new proposals a day. There once was even a Bear Bryant automobile dealership. His lovely wife, Mary Harmon (always Mary Harmon, *never* just Mary) who was his college sweetheart, and his married children, Paul Jr. and Mae Martin, are low-key but intense family cheerleaders.

The winning patina shined with a year-round glow at Alabama. After four straight losing seasons prior to Bryant's arrival, the Second Coming by 1961 had produced a national championship and had launched the Tide on a gaudy, unbroken succession of twenty-four bowl games. Names with an all-time luster had pulled on cleats for him: Joe Namath, Kenny Stabler, Steve Sloan, Lee Roy Jordan, Ozzie Newsome, Johnny Musso, John Hannah. Today, former players and assistant coaches are spread all over the college and professional gridiron map including: Jerry Claiborne at Kentucky, Danny Ford at Clemson; Leon Fuller at Colorado State; Al Kincaid at Wyoming; Charley Pell at Florida; Jackie Sherrill at Texas A&M; Steve Sloan at Duke; Ray Perkins at Alabama, and among the pro's: Bum Phillips of the New Orleans Saints and Jack Pardee of the Houston Gamblers. Dozens of others occupy spots at fine schools with only slightly less luster as football powers, or as top-ranked assistants in pro ball.

In recent years Bryant claimed that his assistants at Alabama had been doing most of the work, and viewed himself more as a chairman of the board. He stationed himself high on a platform overlooking the practice field, with a bullhorn for an occasional comment as assistants separate the practice day into tightly routined segments.

Nobody ever believed Bryant was really that remote. However, it was uncanny how he could suddenly materialize behind a huddle or a blocking drill on the field, a deep, rolling rumble exposing a false step, a miscue of execution, an assistant's miniscule negligence in drill-time.

Despite his willingness to delegate responsibilities, Bryant was on the sidelines at every game, okayed every substitution and

every play that was sent in. His eyes under the brim of the checkered hat would seem to keynote pure calm under any circumstance,
but look again and you'd have seen the gunslinger glitter that
betrayed that apparent calm. The-Man-Was-In-Charge.

There was no arm-waving, no fist-shaking, no frenzied pacing
up and down the field, no screaming or shacking players. He
just stood there, usually with arms folded, hat brim shading his
squinting, cold eyes. When once asked to describe his coaching
routine, he stated, "I learned early in my career that all that
flappin' and stompin' around just saps your energy. I also found
out pretty quick that *anything* can happen in a game. The football's
not round, you know."

He would write down on a clipboard everything he wanted
to do each day because . . . "I really don't trust my memory
during a game and this system works for me—if I can remember
to glance at my notes."

He seldom gave pep talks between the halves. "I feel my players
are smarter than I am," he would add dryly, "so I just remind
them what they have to do to win." If the Tide should be trailing
late in the game, he could always fall back on the comfort of
what he had put into a pre-season letter to all players: "Winning
isn't imperative, but coming from behind and getting tougher in
the 4th quarter *is.*"

Only once, by the way, did he fail to wear The Hat. The year
after a heated controversey over alleged dirty football against
Georgia Tech, Tech fans in Atlanta were prepared to vent their
wrath, physically, on Bryant. He stalked onto the field wearing
a spare football helmet and never took it off during the
game.

The famed Bryant checkered hat, incidentally, was often the
target of juiced-up fans who always tried to snatch it off his head
as a souvenir and then run off with it. Consequently, in recent
years, Bryant was escorted off the field after a game by two beefy
Alabama state troopers. In fact, these same troopers received special dispensation from governors of other states to accompany
Bryant on road games to perform the same mission.

If Bryant felt beholden to the kids who played for him, he

felt no less obligated to the university which employed him. Over the years he had been the lowest-paid coach in the Southeastern Conference—which didn't bother him in the slightest—but had twice turned down raises so his assistants could be paid more. Eventually, the university twisted his arm and made him accept a big raise. He wouldn't reveal what it was but did say: "All I'll tell you is that my salary used to be more than I was worth, and now it's a lot *more* than I'm worth." Oh, sure . . . !

In the early 1960s when money was tight and the university needed to build an engineering building, Bryant, in charge as athletic director, simply donated $500,000 from bowl game.funds to the cause. "We made the money," he growled, "and we'll spend it as we see fit." And who was tough enough down at the state capital to say to him nay?

Paul Bryant was a low-key philanthropist. In the early 1960s the *Saturday Evening Post* magazine printed a story that said Bryant and Wally Butts, the Georgia coach, had conspired to fix their game to make a gambling killing. Both Bryant and Butts sued for libel on the preposterous charges. Before Bryant's case could come to court, the magazine offered him an out-of-court settlement and a retraction of the story. Bryant accepted the offer of $300,000 but said he wouldn't take their check. On principle, he insisted they personally bring him a bank cashier's check. They did. Butts, however, insisted on a trial and, declared innocent of the charges, and was given a $3,000,000 settlement, which the judge subsequently cut back to $460,000.

Later, Bryant made a gift of $100,000 to the University, to be used for academic scholarships for non-athlete students. A gift like that from a football coach was unprecedented in academia. Friends say he'd have made the grant even if he hadn't benefitted by the libel settlement. "Bear had money he couldn't even spend," they'd say, "and the scholarship gesture was made out of sheer love and devotion to Alabama."

Not that it was a *quid pro quo*, but shortly afterward, the legislature renamed Alabama's football stadium Bryant-Denny Stadium, also honoring a former university president. At the time, it was the only stadium in America named for a living active coach.

There had been serious efforts in the past to get him to run for governor or senator but he rebuffed them all. "What would I have done on Saturdays in the fall?" he demanded. They knew what he meant.

But Paul Bryant in mandatory retirement at age seventy would have been—what?—just hibernating, right? Pretty soon he'd rouse himself, stretch, leave the cave and mumble: "Now lessee—there must be something to be done *somewhere* where we can do some winning." And lumber off toward it.

Unfortunately, he never had such an opportunity. Fate took care of that.

# 4

# *Ermal Allen*

*"In the locker room at halftime, Bryant reached down and picked up that pooped 235-pounder, held him in his arms like a baby and said: 'Well, son, you gonna suck it up out there in the second half or ain't you?' Like, otherwise Bryant would drop him right on the floor."*

—Ermal Allen

Normally, the setting sun on the horizon to my left should have had a priority on my consciousness as the blues, purples and dark golds filled the skies to the west in an eye-filling pattern. But my mind was elsewhere as the sleek *Delta* 727 jet started to ease down toward the Dallas-Fort Worth airport.

This was the first leg of a mission which, I estimated, would take me perhaps 125,000 miles and fifteen months of my life to meet and sit down and talk with the men who had played for, or coached under Paul "Bear" Bryant. I had phoned them all to acquaint them with my purpose, and without hesitation—in fact, with unstinting enthusiasm—they'd all said sure, come on over . . . at your service . . . looking forward to it.

It was the kind of promissory cooperation which essentially should have made things easy for a writer exploring the recall of men who realize their lives have been touched by a legend.

It would be my job to dig the ore of their reminiscence—high grade assay, I was sure—but small doubts gnawed at me as the big jet bored through the sky toward the western horizon and Texas. Perhaps their original enthusiasm was only reflexive politeness. But what happens to the purest of motives when a stranger asks them to lay it on the line, to expose feelings long locked away—some of which might better remain so. Or, maybe, when it got right down to it, they wouldn't trust their memories or judgments that might be mitigated by passing years.

I had been told—even warned—that the best of intentions dissolve quickly on confrontation . . . That the moment I settled in a seat across from the man to be interviewed—the moment I snapped on a tape recorder—he might lose his enthusiasm for the project, or, just as importantly to me, find the juices of his memory suddenly dried up. And, just as suddenly, I would be an intruder not to be indulged, or even trusted.

So, there I was—dealing with an emotional spectrum that might range from real eagerness to open up to me, to a self-consciousness that would make it a painful effort for me to get inside them. Well, I'd know soon enough, at least for number-one on my list.

Moments after the jet touched down, I was behind the wheel of a rented car, slipping along the eight-lane interstate toward the hotel complex that I knew to be nestled near the Dallas Cowboys football office. I checked in and was too nervous to go down to the dining room for dinner. For all I knew I might bump into some of the Cowboys personnel and, somehow, they might be aware of who I was and why I'd come here. I didn't want any false starts on this project, no critical judgments of who I was and what right I had to be doing this in the first place. Not even if they knew of the four years of close association I had with Coach Bryant at Alabama. No, I wanted to walk into that office the next morning and take off on my own terms, eager but crisp.

So I stopped wondering what my interviewees would be like, and whether they'd accept me, and ordered dinner sent to my room. After I'd put away only half of a terrific steak (whatever happened to my usually robust appetite?) I plunged into the checklist of notes and observations I'd compiled on the man I'd be talking to. Call it my game plan for the following day . . .

Ermal Allen, an administrative aide with the Cowboys, goes 'way back in his close association with Paul Bryant. He'd been a tough, hard-nosed tailback for four years at Kentucky before Bryant took over the Wildcats. After service in World War II, Allen returned to finish work on his degree and, at 26, for what he thought would be one more year of football eligibility. He'd walked into the office of the new young coach, looked Bryant in the eye and said he wanted to play tailback for him. Bryant said he didn't think 26-year-old tailbacks could cut it again in college ball but gave him a chance. Allen played just one game before a belated eligibility rule axed his hopes for a final year. But Bryant liked the intelligence and drive of the rawboned retread and gave him a job as an assistant coach which he held for eight years until Bryant left for A&M.

Today, his eyes framed studiously by tortoise shell glasses, his iron-gray hair neatly combed, wearing a light blue shirt and dark gray trousers, Allen might resemble a well-turned out construction engineer relaxing in an office chair.

For it was the Friday morning before a Dallas-Philadelphia Eagles game and he could easily have pleaded concern with more pertinent demands on his time. But Ermal Allen knew he'd be talking about his good friend, Paul Bryant, and his eyes mirrored his desire to make the most of these moments.

\*       \*       \*

"I learned one important thing early in my relationship with Paul Bryant," he began. "When he gives you some advice you should accept it almost instinctively. Don't worry about how it'll work out. Don't even think about it. It's kind of like when he says 'frog' you jump. But in a nice way, of course.

"Paul had recommended me for an assistant's job at the University of Cincinnati, and his recommendation was all that was needed, so I got the job. But a couple of days later he drops by in his car and starts taking me for a ride, and if that's what he wants, I say *nothing*. I just go with him.

" 'Ermal,' he suddenly says, 'I want you to get into your car and drive up to Cincinnati and tell the athletic director in person that you can't take the job. That situation ain't for you. In *person,* understand? Not by letter or phone call . . . '

"I started to question him but he cuts me off sharply as only he can do. 'The people at Texas A&M called me last night and they've offered me more money than I have a right to take if I come down there as head coach—and with the situation here at Kentucky, now's the time for me to move on. I'd like to see you move with me, either as an assistant coach or assistant athletic director . . . Or you can stay here at Kentucky and gamble that the new coach will keep you on.' "

Ermal Allen's face, years later, was reflecting the deep indecision he must have felt at the time. "Finally, I got up the nerve to tell him I'd gamble. That I had my home paid for, that we also had a nice, small farm, that we'd made some strong ties in Lexington and didn't want to yank my kids away at this time. I said I'd stay at Kentucky if he'd recommend me for a job with the new coach.

"Bryant laughed sourly. 'That'd be the kiss of death for you, me recomendin' you. I'll be leavin' and a lot of folks will be awful mad at me.' I said I'd still gamble. Well, they brought in Blanton Collier as head coach and mad as some Kentucky folks were at him (Bryant) Collier still kept me on. I stayed eight years before coming out to Dallas.

"One of the last things Bryant told me before he left was that I should always remember there'll be people who'll outsmart me and outcoach me but it'd be a sin to let anybody *outwork* me. To Paul Bryant *working* meant leadership, and I soon found that the Cowboys' staff outworks a lot of other pro staffs. Heck, yesterday morning, for instance, I came over here at 3:30 in the morning because there were some things I wanted to iron out right *then,* and I didn't quit until 6:30 the next night. Paul Bryant would've approved of that," he grinned.

Ermal Allen shook his head silently, as if expecting the motion to help him conjure up other memories befrogged by time. In this case it helped. The chuckle started silently, then built up into real mirth.

"Football clinics," he began. "Yeah, the clinics. They were beginning to become very popular in the late 1940s and early 1950s as those thousands of high school coaches out there began to realize they could learn at the feet of the college masters. I mean, there'd been clinics for years, even back to Rockne's time, but now they were beginning to be big business. Not that a college coach could get rich, but he'd get a few hundred bucks for himself and if he took a couple of his assistants with him he could get them maybe a hundred each, plus expenses.

"Well, Paul was beginning to be invited to a lot of these. One year he came to a couple of us—ol' Buckshot Underwood and me—and said he'd take us to Long Beach, California to put on a clinic for high school coaches and a lot of service team coaches. Well, he could easily have said we'd fly out there—it was a long trip—but that'd mean we couldn't get to keep the total expense money we were being offered.

"So, Paul said: 'Hey, I've got a new car. We can keep the air fare and drive out there and save the extra dough. The three of us can drive to California without stopping. We can alternate, two hours on and four hours off, driving and we'll go all the way without sleeping and spending hotel money.'

"See? He was thinking of us, not him. In those days we sure could use every extra buck. So we each put $25 in the glove compartment for gas and away we go. Sure enough, we start alternating driving, just as he suggested, and those wheels never stopped spinning except for pit stops, day and night. Of course we're getting pooped and Paul must have realized we'd be dead for the clinic when we got there. So when we got to Yuma, Arizona, which is just on the California line, he said, 'there's a cheap-looking motel, let's stop here just for this one night.'

"But I reminded him we'd agreed not to stop until we got to California and he grumbled and said, 'Okay, an agreement's an agreement.' He was at the wheel, then, so he drove across the California line, a little way out of town. Suddenly he stopped, turned around on the road and drove back to Yuma. 'Okay,' he said, 'we drove to California without stopping. Now we'll get some sleep here in Arizona.'

"We drove in to Long Beach the next day, put on the clinic

for two days and drove back to Kentucky the same way we got there. Underwood and I made a few extra bucks but Paul had to get rid of his car. It was done for. Buckshot and I felt awful about it. Y'know, it cost him for us to make some extra money."

Allen allowed himself the luxury of a small, appreciative sigh. "The guy was so warm and natural—still is, of course, but it's always been part of his make-up. The strict, growling, physical disciplinarian on one hand and the very human being on the other. I think it was that combination that got more results out of his players and coaches than all his technical skills.

"Incidentally, a lot of people don't know that Bryant has always been a big party guy, a live-it up guy in many ways. He always was picking up the tab for parties for his players or assistant coaches so they could relax. He'd arrange a get-together in a hotel and even pay for the rooms for us. He was nuts about golf—still is, of course—and wherever we'd go, when it wasn't football season, he'd drag us to the golf course and pick up the bills.

"I turned out to be a good golfer—probably could have made the pro tour if I'd worked with it, and at one time in Kentucky I was playing par golf and even below par. One day he came to me and said: 'Ermal, I've got a couple of old coaching friends coming in from Arkansas and Texas and we're gonna play golf. You're gonna be my partner but they don't know what kind of golf you shoot.'

"I recall the look of anticipation on Paul's face as he continued. 'Last year when I played with them down in Arkansas I caught one of them teeing up the ball in the rough and he beat me outta ten bucks. It wasn't the ten, but I got to get even.'

"So, those guys come in and we're on the practice putting green and one of 'em asks me what kind of golf I play, and I tell him I had an 81 a few days ago, which was true because I had a sore hand and it was the worst round I'd played all year. Told 'em I three-putted three greens.

"They looked pretty smug and Paul got his bets down with them—'nothing serious, but maybe twenty bucks, just for fun,' he said. Well, I birdied three out of the first four holes and one of Paul's visitors says he's willing to pay off all bets then, but he wants to rearrange the game and take me for his partner. Bryant said nothing doing. I wound up with a 66 and Paul tells his old buddy from Texas that maybe nobody will ever tee up the ball on him in the rough again. His buddy grinned sheepishly and Paul just roared with laughter. They couldn't believe an assistant football coach could play golf like that—meaning me. Paul later said it was the most enjoyable round of golf he'd ever played."

Allen grinned conspiratorially. "That Bryant—he enjoys a game of chance. He and I have visited a few horse tracks in our time, too. I don't know which he enjoyed most, though—betting at out-of-town tracks where he was just a stranger or betting at Lexington, where everyone would know him and he'd have to play it cool. Often he'd have me go up to the windows to buy tickets and cash in his winners. He's actually a very moral guy, you know, and he sort of sensed that maybe the University of Kentucky football coach shouldn't be seen at a race track betting window. He eventually got over that slight embarassment, though, and now I understand he even sits at a table very visibly at the dog track in Tuscaloosa. I don't know if other people still make and cash his bets for him.

"Y'know," Allen continued, "I've never known anyone who combined strict discipline with a sense of humor the way Bryant does. I remember one year at Kentucky when Paul knew we were going to have a damn good club and he wanted to have as much going for us as possible. The rules prevented us from having a pre-season football camp before official practice started, but Bryant called all us assistants in and told us we were going to have a *retreat* at a boys' summer camp down at Millersburg, not too far from Lexington. We'd just run, get in shape and *preach* togetherness. That's what would make it a retreat and not the marine boot camp he'd probably turn it into.

"Oh boy, some *retreat.* The conference commissioner said we couldn't take a football along, so we didn't. So we take the whole team down there and we'd get up at 6 A.M. and walk and trot through plays and work our tails off for two hours. Then the kids would have five hours off for swimming, fishing and anything else they wanted to do. Then, after lunch, we'd have another hour or two of drills.

"Well, on the very first day, Pat James reported five minutes late to practice. Bryant doesn't say anything to him but two hours later when he ends the session, and before he sends everyone to the showers, he calls the squad together. 'Now, fellas,' he says, 'we had a player here who was five minutes late to practice. You never know when one man reporting late can cost us a ball game so I want to see what you think about this idea I have for punishment . . .'

"Bryant pauses and waves an arm out toward the scrubby practice field which was right adjacent to a cow pasture. And a lot of these cows had a habit of straying once in a while onto our practice field. 'I think we should give Pat James a shovel so he can clean up those cow piles that dot the field. I'm sure you'd all agree that it's no more'n right.' Well, nobody dared cast a dissenting vote, so Pat James was given a shovel and he cleaned up the field pretty good.

"Now, then," An expression of smug delight crept over Ermal Allen's face. "Some of the assistant coaches would be out recruiting and would report in to Bryant at night. Sometimes they'd be talking until two or three in the morning. Well, one time, Paul was pooped and slept in the following morning and got to practice a little late—maybe by fifteen minutes.

"At the end of the practice Paul dismissed the squad and Pat James puts up his hand. 'Hold on here,' he says. 'We have a discipline problem we have to straighten out. So let's take a vote on whether Coach Bryant cleans up the cow piles over in the pasture for bein' late for practice.'

"It was a unanimous vote for him taking up that shovel. He didn't say a word. Just stalked off with the shovel and cleaned up the entire area.

"Talking about recruiting," Allen went on, "Paul Bryant was almost a fanatic when he wanted a kid. Like Bob Gain, who turned out to be probably the greatest lineman Paul ever coached. In our conference we could start signing kids on December 2, but the real blue-chippers would hold off so they could visit six, seven or more schools.

"They'd keep you on the hook, bitin' your nails. Paul had Carney Laslie and a couple others visiting Gain every other day up there in Pennsylvania, or Ohio, or wherever it was. At eighteen, he was a grown man, a young monster with maturity. He wouldn't sign on December 2, and Bryant was really growling. We'd come back home on a Tuesday or Wednesday morning and he'd yell, 'Get back up there—we're gonna lose him!"

"So we'd go back up. And finally we signed him but Gain wouldn't give us the form back. He still wanted to visit a few more schools. Paul was having a fit. He had the greatest prospect in America all signed but the kid wouldn't let go of the papers. Paul was afraid he'd be trottin' around to other places—Notre Dame, Ohio State, Alabama, wherever—and change his mind, sign their paper and tear up ours. Finally Paul got hold of Jimmy the Greek, the famous oddsmaker, who was from Steubenville, Ohio, not far from Gain's home. Jimmy was a friend of Bryant's and I think it was Jimmy who finally put the collar on Gain and talked him into sending his signed scholarship.

"I think if we'd lost him, Paul would have come for us with a willow switch, and I mean he'd have *come* for us. Hell, the kid started as a freshman and in those days we elected captains for each game, on merit alone, and as a freshman he was captain as often as anyone else. When Bryant saw that, he said he'd get the shakes at night, just thinking of how we could have lost him."

Allen paused, "It's funny, the way things pop back into your mind when you think of your association with Paul Bryant. We were playing Florida down there, once, and it was hot as Hades. We had a better team than they did and were leading at the half, but Paul could tell that the second half would be murder for us because it was hotter'n anything we'd ever played in and Florida was more used to that humidity than we were. The mood among the assistants was pessimistic as we went into the dressing room. Paul was just as low as we were and he came to me and said, 'Ermal, I've got to shake 'em up some way but I don't know how.'

"I told him I didn't know, either, but he might start with one of our guards, Gene Donaldson, who hadn't had a good first half. I offered no hint as to *how* he'd start with Gene, who seemed to be lying down on the floor, practically dead.

"Well, Paul stalked over to him, reached down and picked

up that 235-pounder in his arms, held him there like a baby, and said to him, 'Well, son, you gonna suck it up out there in the second half or ain't you?" Like otherwise he'd drop him right to the floor. Or like it was a method to publicly expose a boy's weakness, holding him like that. I tell you, it scared the hell out of me, and shook up the whole squad. They didn't quite know what to make of it; it was such a strange and dramatic thing. But they all sucked it up in that terrible heat and we went back out there and held the lead.

"Actually, Bryant had a million ways he could revitalize a team between halves. I've been there when he didn't even show up in the dressing room and leave everyone just sitting there nervously, alone with their thoughts, maybe thinking of sins they'd commited against him in the first thirty minutes. Then, just a few seconds before an official came in to say we were due back on the field, Paul would walk in, stand there with his hands on his hips, and glance at 'em without a word. There was no other message he had to send 'em. They'd get the idea, go out there and knock the other team's heads off.

"I've never seen anyone in football who could work harder. And he was so visible doing it that players and assistant coaches couldn't help but respect him for it and just *feel* his leadership. He'd get out there on the practice field, just in his work clothes, y'know, no pads or anything like that, and he'd take a defensive stance and tell a lineman to try to block him. And I mean that player had to give it everything he had. He didn't dare pull the string on his effort, so he'd hit in there and try to crack Paul with everything he had.

"Sometimes Paul'd just shuck him aside, and sometimes the boy would hit him a fierce one and knock him off the mark. And Paul would say, 'Okay, let's see you block your man like that!' So, having demonstrated he could block to Bryant's satisfaction a boy didn't dare not perform 110 percent. Football is a tough, hard game. It's not an easy game, ever. Players who will do just about what you let them do. And if they do less than their best and you let 'em, you're not gonna be a winner. So they've always accepted Bryant's leadership, and he's always built confidence in them, and you know what *that* can do for your team."

Ermal Allen cocked his head and smiled. "But his leadership has never been arrogant. In fact, it is often touched with humility. Like the time Kentucky should have beaten somebody by twenty-five points in one of our games, and we were lucky to win by a touchdown or so. In the paper next day there was a quote from Paul which said, 'The alumni should be out looking for a new coach. I ought to be fired for the game plan I had this week.'

"Well, sir, Paul Bryant brought nothing but great success for four different major schools where he coached, and never once was in danger of being fired. You can't even *begin* to get down on a man who walks off the field saying, 'I was wrong. I made a mistake.' You just believe in him more than ever."

Ermal Allen suddenly leaned forward in his chair galvanically, his elbows barely coming to rest on the table without making a noise. Something had popped into mind that needed immediate disclosure and he cranked up with a grin. "I'll tell you something about Paul Bryant that could never be applied to another coach in the whole history of football . . ."

With that as a gambit, his grin broadened. "After World War II hardly anybody used the single wing except Tennessee, who was practically wedded to it under the influence of General Bob Neyland, who'd coached them to many successful seasons.

"Well, Tennessee was always the last game on our schedule at Kentucky so Paul always scratched desperately to schedule some college that still used the single wing so we could get in some defensive licks against it just before we met Tennessee. Well, the only one he could dig up that year was North Dakota. I think it was 1950. So North Dakota came down to Lexington and we didn't even work up a sweat, and we're beating them 70–0 at the half. Yeah, that's right, 70–0.

"So, in the dressing room Paul comes up to me and says he's going to take the first two teams, maybe it was the first three, outside to a practice field near the stadium and work them out because they really needed it. He said I should take what's rest of the varsity squad and finish up with North Dakota, but don't run up the score, and that's exactly how we started the second half.

"By that time people had started piling out of the stadium because it's strictly no contest. Suddenly they discover Paul scrimmaging his real varsity like crazy, right nearby. Just about all the fans go over to watch Kentucky's first two teams knock heads.

"Paul Bryant never had any thought about embarrassing North Dakota. He didn't have that in mind at all. He just figured his team needed another good workout before the Tennessee game next Saturday. My scrubs scored two more touchdowns in the second half and we won, 83–0. That was the game where Bob Gain, our All America tackle, set a college record by kicking ten straight extra points in a single half."

# 5

# *The Pupil*

*"Just after lunch we could tell who was gonna quit and leave that day because they'd be fully dressed and would go up to the water fountain between the huts, take a few sips to help gather their courage and then go see Coach Bryant in his cabin."*

—Bebe Stallings

People who write books don't normally get up at 5 A.M. to start work, but I had no choice. Bebe Stallings, the Dallas Cowboys defensive secondary coach, couldn't meet with me the same day I'd seen Ermal Allen in the Cowboys offices, but Stallings had left a brief message saying he'd be glad to see me at 6:30 the next morning. Yeah, he was a football coach, all right. Only peasants go to work at that hour but I'd already known, from Coach Bryant that football people also fall into that category.

So, who was Gene "Bebe" Stallings? My notes told me he'd been a sophomore survivor of Bryant's infamous Junction gig in Bryant's first year at Texas A&M. Later he'd served seven years as one of Bryant's assistant coaches at A&M and Alabama before returning as the Aggies' head coach and leading them to a Southwest Conference title in 1967. And, as destiny (fate?) would have it, Bebe Stallings became the first Bryant pupil to defeat The Master, beating him in the Cotton Bowl that following year, 20–

16. Oh, yes—there was another note. Stallings was often referred to as "Baby Bear" in his Aggie years . . .

I walked across the Cowboys' parking lot, and dawn was just beginning to break. I couldn't help but notice a single light glimmering on the ninth floor of the building that housed the Cowboys offices. Finally, the elevator opened to the ninth floor, and when it did, I was welcomed to a world of navy blue and silver that carried a 5-letter message from the gridiron to the front office—*class.*

*     *     *

Bebe Stallings shook my hand in a firm, friendly grip, a slight smile on his face. He was tall, lanky, with short black hair and a Texas drawl. No doubt, he was a physical copy of a younger Paul Bryant. He relaxed easily in his big leather chair, frequently tilting back in it and glancing out the window at the breaking day. There were frequent and long pauses in his speech, and what seemed like a slight stutter. He had played end for Bryant at A&M, and time had not dimmed the reflections of Bebe Stallings and his world of 1954 . . .

"There are a couple of things that will always be stamped on my mind, over all others," he was saying now. "It happened the first season Coach Bryant was at Texas A&M, and I was playing for him. Oh, Lordy was it ever going to be a tough, long year. We were losing every game, but every game was close. We'd almost make it, and then we'd just fall short, or would get beat by an opponent's big play, and it would sap our spirits every Saturday.

"The team had been working extra hard in practice to get ready for Southern Methodist, which was one of the nation's best teams at the time. Anyway, at 12:45 A.M., on Thursday, the coaches and managers came around and woke up all the players. Eventually, everyone was assembled in the lobby of the dorm in their pajamas or shorts, mystified as to what was going on. We'd been told nothing and it was a strange experience for us, this midnight muster.

"Finally, Coach Bryant came in and glanced over to one of

the players and said, 'Didn't I see you across the street at the Twelfth Man Inn getting some chili about 10:30 tonight?'

"The kid said, 'yes,' and Coach replied, 'Well, you're excused.'

"That shocked us—every guy sitting there. Then we got to thinking—where were we earlier in the evening? You could have cut the curiosity in the air with the knife. What was going to happen next?

"Well, what happened changed the rest of my life, because Coach Bryant pulled out a Bible and quoted some scripture about moving a mountain through faith: St. Matthew, 17th chapter, 20th verse.

". . .'It was because you do not have enough faith,' answered Jesus. 'Remember this! If you have faith as big as a mustard seed, you will be able to say to a hill, 'Go from here to there!' and it will go. You can do anything!'

" 'Now, I know if you'll just hang in there, then eventually you'll win a championship,' Bryant was saying. 'Maybe not this year, maybe not even next year but you'll win at A&M before each one of you walks off this campus for good. I believe that— and I want you to believe that . . .'

"And then he passed out, to each one of us, a little capsule. Inside each was a tiny mustard seed. He told us to put our capsules away in a place where they could never be lost, and that we'd feel an urge to look at them once in a while. Then, abruptly, without another word, he said, 'good night,' and walked out.

"And there we were, in our pajamas or skivvies, rooted in the lobby of our dorm all wide-eyed and almost afraid to look at each other, but each of us"—Bebe Stallings paused here—"each of us feeling something different, but really all the same, if you know what I mean, and all of us, I swear, believing we could give SMU a helluva game on Saturday if not flat-out beat 'em. It was a long night for most of us because we were too excited to sleep, and God knows how many of us picked up his mustard seed capsule and studied it.

"On Saturday, SMU came in there runner-up to Arkansas for the league title, and had to fight for their lives to beat us, 6–3. They were favored by four or five touchdowns. We only won one game that year but all of us knew it was just a matter of time—just a matter of time. There's not one of us today who can spread mustard on a sandwich and not visualize Coach Bryant standing up there quoting the scriptures."

And was that the beginning of it, Bebe Stallings was asked? The laying of the foundation stone for the Aggies' coming success?

"That and one other thing," Stallings said. Another pause as a faint, crooked smile tugged at the corners of his mouth, as though what was to follow was something he wanted to share but maybe just a bit grudgingly.

He cocked his head. "You ever heard of a place called Junction?" he stated softly.

Well, yes, I guessed I'd heard something about it. And ironically, the word junction means "a point, or place of crossing or joining." Significantly, a lot of Aggie young men, at a place three miles outside of Junction, Texas, came to a significant crossroads in their own lives.

"Well, maybe you've *heard* of it," Bebe Stallings was saying, staring out the window again. The sun was up, now, gathering its promise of mixed glare and cheerfulness. "But you really haven't, not the way I mean." His eyes squinted slightly. "When we got back to school that summer of 1954, Coach Bryant told us to pack a couple changes of clothes, a towel or two and a pillow because we were gonna take a little trip. He said we should be packed in ten minutes. We were packed in five and gathered in front of our dorm as two big buses rolled up. We climbed aboard and moved off toward an unknown destination. And nobody *asked* where. It was that kind of feeling.

"Well, the buses journeyed forward from one side of Texas to another and, finally, we pulled off onto a side road near Junction and we piled off, with the coaches, in a camp area with some old tin-roofed Quonset huts like those used by the army in World War II. Coach Bryant said we were here to learn football—*his* way. He let us just frolic in a nearby river for a whole day, and then we started *learning* football.

"Each morning, by sun-up, we were on the practice field. Then we had breakfast, followed by a brief nap. You'd just start forgetting your aching bones when a student manager would be shaking you for lunch and another practice session following it. Those afternoon sessions were something to regret. Heat, dust, no grass and a lot of cactus. Any time you got knocked down you had to avoid the prickly sandspurs.

"After dinner we had a squad meeting with the coaches, with all the guys doing their best to keep their eyes open. When we were dismissed we just made it to our bunks before falling down. Then at six o'clock the next morning there'd be those managers tapping us on the shoulder again, like it was just an hour ago we fell off to sleep."

Bebe Stallings chuckled grimly, but with a hint of real satisfaction. "Around 1:30 each afternoon, just after lunch, we could tell who was gonna quit and leave that day because they'd be fully dressed and would go up to a water fountain centrally located between the huts, take a few sips to allow their courage time to gather, and then go see Coach Bryant in his cabin.

"Knowing what was about to happen, a lot of us other guys would crowd around the hut, but out of sight, to watch the action, like frontier folks witnessing a public hangin'. A guy, maybe two, would come out of Bryant's place, all limp but sort of relieved, and another or two more would go in. After maybe a half dozen had been inside, a student manager would pile 'em in an old black sedan, drive 'em into town and put 'em on a bus bound for College Station."

Stallings plucked at his ear, as though trying to pull forth a nugget of something that had escaped him momentarily. When it surfaced, he grinned. "Of course there was the occasional bit of humor to lighten our load. Not many, but one in particular." He shook his head. "It was a Saturday night in a team meeting after a particularly rough two-hour scrimmage. Yeah, that's right, a two-hour scrimmage, and I don't recall any time-outs for strategy or other extraneous stuff. You can figure out how we were feeling. Bryant seemed to even take notice as he looked us over that night.

" 'Tomorrow being Sunday,' he began, 'I'd like to see a show of hands of those desiring to attend church in Junction.'

" 'Well, okay, keep your hands up,' he went on, and sent a manager around to list each player's intention, by name. You could hear guys around the room shoutin,' 'hey, don't forget me, don't forget me!'

"Then Bryant looked at the list and said, 'Now then, this is everyone who wants to go to church tomorrow?'

"And everyone shouted, 'Yes, sir,' and Coach Bryant said, 'Fine. You'll all go to church in the morning right after practice.'

"He'd out-smarted us, but we had to admit he'd been pretty slick. Anyway, after a head-knockin' practice we loaded up one of our buses and drove to church. The preacher was great and he had some fine and lively things to say but there were about twelve rows of football players who never heard a word because they were sleepin' the sleep of the exhausted and the damned."

Now, an immensely successful assistant coach on the Cowboys staff, Stallings still finds his experiences with Bryant to be touched with the most memorable accents of grace and humility of his football career. "One of the greatest lessons I learned from Coach Bryant," he continued "came when I was his assistant at Alabama. It was a fine example of the way Bryant handled a sticky situation—or the way he handled people and that's probably his greatest attibute.

"I had been assigned a particular recruiting area in west Alabama and the local blue-chip 'stud' was a youngster from Gordo, Alabama, a small town between Tuscaloosa and the Mississippi state line. During the spring of this youngster's junior year, his football coach persuaded me to help with the coaching for a day because his assistant was sick.

"So I drove over there but suddenly while we were walking to the practice field I stopped and said, 'I can't do this.'

"But he calmly assured me that all of the Alabama assistant coaches used to do this to help the high schools. 'Besides, you want this young man,' he said significantly, 'and now you'll have a chance to see how he works.'

"Well, we had a heck of a practice. And the kid was one helluva prospect. I felt great about it. I drove home and nothing was ever said until Carney Laslie, Bryant's top assistant, brought back a bit of conversation he'd heard at a conference coaches meeting the previous week in Florida. It started when Shug Jordan, then head coach at Auburn, asked Bryant if he thought the league would allow assistant coaches to evaluate prospect high school recruits by helping coach them in the spring at their schools."

Stallings chuckled as he recalled Bryant's reply. " 'Hell, Shug,' he said, 'we can't do that. It's against the rules.'

"And then Shug gives Coach this sidelong look and says slyly: 'Oh, it is, hey? Well, one of your coaches has done it.'

"Well, Coach Bryant gets all lathered up by that suggestion and says: 'That's horsefeathers, Shug. I ain't got anyone on my staff stupid enough to pull something like that, and I'll prove it.' With that he grabs a phone and puts through a call to Tuscaloosa and gets hold of Sam Bailey, an assistant who just happened to know I'd been guilty of doing that. Sam started to explain why it was true but Coach just cut him off, banged the phone down, and began to turn red with embarrassment. The other head coaches with him caught on immediately and cracked up laughing, knowing that Coach himself hadn't been involved.

"Anyway, when Bryant got back to the campus he called a staff meeting for 7 o'clock the next morning. Sam Bailey leaked to me what it was all about and believe me, I began working up one heckuva sweat because I knew Bryant would really unload on me. And when we were all gathered around the conference table I knew he'd embarrass me in front of the whole staff.

"But Bryant never glanced at me. Instead, we talked about football, turkey hunting, golf, the high price of shrimp, the new university budget, recruiting and about everything else under the sun—but nothing about illegal coaching. Whenever there'd be a pause in the conversation Coach would pick it up with something new to discuss and he didn't seem to run out of things. And in the meantime my heart was pounding and my palms were wet.

"Finally, maybe three hours later he said, 'that's all.' I grabbed my books and started to hustle toward the door when he said, 'Wait a minute, Bebe, I want to see you.'

"He motioned for me to sit down again and gave me a long, silent look while all of the others moved at a brisk pace to avoid the onslaught. Finally he tilted back in his chair and started to tell the story from the coaches' meeting. Looking up at me he asked, quietly: 'Did you do it, Bebe?'

"I said, 'Yes, sir,' and then he asked, 'Why?'

"Speaking honestly, I told him how badly I wanted the youngster and how we had actually gotten him, too.

"Then Paul Bryant, the coach, became Paul Bryant, the man, once more. He leaned forward, his gaze boring into mine. 'It wasn't very smart, was it?' he demanded softly.

"I said, 'No, sir, it wasn't—and I feel awful about it.'

"Then he said just five words. 'DON'T EVER DO IT AGAIN.'

"I'll never forget how he said them. They were planted in me forever. Not just for the circumstance that had brought it all on, but as a key to Coach Bryant's true moral values in coaching. The point is that he had bled me for several hours—not for doing my job wrong—but the way I had approached the situation, and violated a rule, didn't justify the end product. Coach got his point across and I learned an invaluable lesson. You agree?"

How could anyone possibly not agree? Certainly not someone who had been exposed to Bryant for any length of time as I had been.

"A lot of people play football for different reasons," Stallings was saying now, caught up by another strong recollection. "Just as a lot of people are successful in life for many different reasons. But the main reason that guys at Alabama or A&M, or wherever else, were successful was because of a certain element of fear. Not that you were necessarily afraid of Coach Bryant, but there was always the emotional doubt that you might not play up to the potential that he expected of you and that's the fine line in coaching you want to achieve. If the player is gonna go out on that field and do everything to please you as an assistant coach you're gonna do everything in the world to please your head coach. Then, in turn, the head coach will do everything possible to please the athletic director and the school president. And before long, the much desired chain of command is established.

"From my own experience, both as a player and a coach, one of the greatest things Coach Bryant used to do was pass along the credit. For example, he liked to go into a squad meeting and tell the team that such-and-such was Coach Claiborne's idea, or Coach Stallings' idea.

"Then in a staff meeting he'd say, 'You know, I've been thinking about this particular problem for two days and just can't find the answer.' But the truth of the matter was that he already had the answer and would neatly maneuver the coaches all around it till somebody would say, 'Hey, coach, I've got an idea. Why don't we do it such-and-such way?'

"And he'd say, 'That's *it!* Why couldn't I think of that?'

"Even more impressively though, Coach would then go into a squad meeting and explain, 'We were in a staff session, and Coach Donahue came up with a great idea.' And he'd continue, 'I think we're gonna use it, too!'

"Now there's old Coach Donahue sittin' there beaming, and everyone knows that it's his idea—so what's he gonna do? He's gonna work twice as hard to make it work because everybody knows it's his idea. When we win on Saturday, Coach Bryant will get the credit—that's the way it's supposed to be. But within the inner circle of players and coaches, they know it was ole Ken Donahue's idea what won the game. That's handling people!"

*       *       *

Handling people apparently, was mostly what it was all about in Paul Bryant's scheme of things. It was a recollective element that surfaced so often whenever I talked to Bryant's boys . . .

**6**

# *Four from A&M*

> *"At halftime an enraged Coach Bryant grabbed a big tackle by the jersey collar, shook him fiercely and hollered: 'If you ever let them shoot the gap on me again, I'll kill you!' The kid turned white. Hell, he* should *have. He hadn't even been in the game!"*
>
> —Dennis Goehring

You've read earlier in this book how Paul Bryant arrived at Texas A&M, and brought about the remarkable transition from a wallow of defeat and despair to the brilliant heights of success and victory . . . How he used the infamous crucible of Junction to set his pattern for winning football . . . How he changed the one-dimension atmosphere of an all-male, military-type school . . . How he took advantage of its loyalty and dedication to duty and making it something lustrous and admirable to all the common folk in the state of Texas.

At Texas A&M, you find such enthusiasm and pride in its football team that all students—men and women, too, now that the Aggies are co-ed, stand throughout every football game. For a very special reason. It is a time-honored symbol of their willingness to volunteer for front line duty should their services be needed on the field below. It is a story unique in American collegiana, and, who knows, maybe it could have happened only at A&M,

given the Aggies' Twelfth Man theme. Yes, the Aggies always have a Twelfth Man at their games, and the Twelfth Man is the entire student body because of something which happened back in January 1922.

The 1921 football season had ended and the Aggies, as conference champions, had been invited to play Centre College in January, in what was then called the Dixie Classic in Dallas. Centre was the famous small college in Kentucky, featuring the legendary Bo McMillin, which had beaten then-mighty Harvard in one of football's all-time upsets.

E. King Gill, a player on that Aggie team, was also a basketball star and was needed on the A&M quintet. In Dallas to see the football game he was asked by grid coach Dana X. Bible to spot plays for a reporter in the pressbox.

Immediately, a rash of injuries beset the Aggies by the time the first quarter was over. Suddenly, Gill, in civilian clothes, was given a message that Dana X. Bible wanted him to come down to the bench. There, Bible told him to put on a football uniform and be ready to play if he was needed. Gill hadn't practiced football for more than six weeks. The team had changed clothes at their hotel. There were no dressing rooms at that stadium. Gill and an injured player went under the stands where Gill put on the player's uniform and the injured man donned Gill's civvies.

Gill went to the Aggie bench and was ready to go if needed. He never got into the game but the story swept the Aggie campus and was established as the finest of all Aggie legends. So, to this day, the entire Aggie student body—men and women and their dates—stand as the Twelfth Man throughout a game. Ready if called.

So, on a big football weekend in Aggieland—the Baylor game— I journeyed to College Station, Texas and met with four graduate examples of the "Twelfth Man" tradition, who as Aggie players were not only exposed to the tradition but to Paul "Bear" Bryant. They were Marvin Tate, the athletic director at A&M; Bobby Lockett, a successful engineer with Sun Oil Co.; Loyd Taylor, the dean of admissions at A&M; and Dennis Goehring, president of the Bank of A&M in College Station. Successful examples of the Bryant mold? Just take another look at those credits after their names. We sat around, the five of us, and I was overcome by their eagerness, their delight in sifting through their memories of Bryant.

Tate—a big man, with hints of power still present. His high-pitched voice easily excitable as he talked. Sharply-tailored, almost elegant clothes. Lockett—gray-haired, with lingering touches of black, the brilliant engineer now in cowboy boots and blue jeans, the "gosh-darns" permeating his quick, informal speech. Taylor—not much more now than his playing weight of 176, the animation in his face and speech a clue to why and how he has tripled A&M's enrollment in nine years from 10,000 to more than 30,000. Goehring—holder of two degrees, (engineering and business administration), and a pilot's license. Typical of a banker, he never says anything in a hurry, but as he talks of Coach Bryant every word and thought is cloaked in obvious affection and respect.

Let's talk about Coach Bryant, was what I told them I wanted, and now, as the five of us sat around, they almost verbally trampled on one another as they competed for equal time. It went something like this, their random recollections spilling across any time-frame or sense of organization.

\*       \*       \*

TATE: "The man had an amazing ability to come up with a spontaneous word or line that was just perfect for the situation, and because it was so spontaneous it had even more effect than a lecture. There was our opening game of 1954 against Texas Tech, and they just about tore us to pieces, 41–9. In the dressing room after the game Bryant just sauntered in, looked at us bleakly and said: 'I want y'all to just go back to the dorm and go to bed 'cause I'm gonna let the Texas Tech players have the girls tonight—they deserve 'em.'

"Well, believe me, we all went back to our dorms, and even those who had dates, every one of us, we just stayed put. We didn't *dare* leave the dorm.

"Then, on Monday, we went to practice and found our practice uniforms were gone. Hanging in our lockers were our game uniforms, still all muddy and clammy with sweat. Normally, they'd go to the cleaners right after a game. We didn't know what we were supposed to do. Finally, Coach Bryant came in, and glared around at each of us. 'Okay,' he said, 'we're gonna pick up where we left off Saturday afternoon,' and then marched us over to Kyle Field stadium, put the ball down on the 35-yard line where it had been spotted when the game ended and said we were gonna scrimmage.

"It lasted three hours and wasn't any less spirited than Waterloo or Gettysburg. A couple guys packed their bags that night and went home to some comfort and mama's cookin'. Coach Bryant then took the rest of that group on to a conference championship a couple years later."

GOEHRING: "We were playing Arkansas one year up there. Coach Bryant had decided we'd all spend the night in a small town outside Fayetteville and then ride by chartered bus into the stadium the next morning. It'd only be a twenty minute trip, or so. We started out and all the guys were joking it up, having a big time of it kidding each other about their home towns, many of them just tiny whistle stops or farm communities. Oh, so you're from so-and-so. Or hey, that isn't even on the map.

"Suddenly, Bryant jumped up from his seat in front and bellowed for the driver to pull over to the side of the road. He scared the hell out of us, and a quick calm settled over the entire bus, a lot of mouths froze in wonderment as we focused our eyes on The Bear, wondering what it was all about.

" 'All right you sonuvabitches!' he was hollerin'. 'Nobody is really interested in playing a football game with Arkansas so let's all just get out, go sit under a big shade tree and have a picnic. I'll send the driver into town for some hot-dogs, Cokes and marshmallows. I'll go cancel the game and we'll just spend the day tellin' stories!'

"We sat there holding our breath until he said, quietly: 'Okay, let's go and play the game.' And for the rest of the trip nobody said a word because we were concentrating on our assignments and those red jerseys we'd be lining up across from us. Which is what he had in mind all along.

"There wasn't a word said 'til we reached the stadium, where a beefy, red-faced man waving a big Arkansas banner stopped the bus and insisted on getting in. He was all juiced up and asked: 'Which one of you guys is The Bear?'

"Assistant coach Jerry Claiborne pointed. 'He is.'

"The drunk peered down at Bryant. 'I just wanna tell you, Coach, that you'n I are kinfolks from up near Fordyce, but today I'm pullin' for Arkansas.'

"Ol' Bear, he grabbed this guy and hollered for everyone to get out of his way and flung that kinfolk, whoever he was, right outa the bus. 'Ain't nobody pullin' for Arkansas aboard this bus, right?' he snarled.

TATE: "Yeah, that was some game. It was 0–0 at halftime, on one of the most humid days of the year. When Coach Bryant came into the dressing room he kicked a bag of balls and a dozen of them went flying every which way. Then he began shouting: 'I want all the riff-raff outa here.' He meant a few visitors, managers and others, but he'd just started. He lunged over to a big tackle, grabbed him by the jersey collar, shook him fiercely and hollered: 'If you ever let them shoot the gap on me again, I'll kill you!' The kid got instantly white as a sheet. Hell, he *should* have. He hadn't even been in the game!"

GOEHRING: (Beginning to laugh hilariously) "Then he shouted: 'I want everybody outa here!' Bobby Drake Keith got scared and headed for the door but Bryant waved him back to his seat. 'Not the players, you clunk-head. Just the coaches.' It didn't make much sense to us, but you don't ask for clarification outa Coach Bryant at halftime when he's got a mean streak going.

"Maybe he was feeling like a father who didn't want to larrup his kids in front of strangers. Who knows? Anyway, that's when he really started belting guys all over the place. Some of us had learned not to take seats in the front row when they thought Coach Bryant might have reason to be ticked off between halves. Jim Stanley, who'd missed a few key blocks, tried to hide his chair behind the biggest guy on the team but Bryant found him anyway. Got him up on his feet and used him as a blocking dummy to demonstrate technique. We went out and really put it to Arkansas in the second half."

TATE: "How that man could rev you up in the strangest way . . . (The others all eagerly nodding their heads in agreement) I'd been hurt and in the hospital for almost two weeks, my senior year. I got out of the hospital shortly before the Houston game and started bugging Bryant about playing, and he said: 'When you're ready to play, I'll know it, and I'll let you play.' So, against Houston we got a quick touchdown and he called me over on the sidelines and said: 'We're gonna pull off an onside kick and I want you to line up out there with our kicking team and recover that onside kick.'

"I didn't think he was crazy, or anything, but it did occur to me that there were ten other guys on our team who also had a chance to get that ball, as well as a whole bunch of Houston guys lined up right in front of us waiting for it. I started thinking of the odds against me, and what if Coach had meant it as a *command*, y'know? So, we dinked that little ol' onside kick and we all tore after it. It bounces off a Houston player and right into guess who's hands—mine.

"I thought I was a real hero and raced off to the sidelines wearin' a huge grin, waitin' for Bryant to pin a medal on me for following orders so faithfully. He just looks at me and growls: 'Hell, son, you should have lit out with the ball and scored.' "

GOEHRING: "Coach Bryant had that uncanny way of judging how much our bodies could take. A doctor or trainer might fault his methods but we came through, anyhow. There was the time before a game with a very good Baylor team and we had eight starters out with various hurts and injuries. All the walking wounded were lying around in the dressing room the Thursday before the game when Bryant came in with ol' Smokey Harper, the trainer. He stood there with hands on hips and said: 'Everybody that's going to play Saturday, I want to see scrimmage today.' Then he walked out.

"Ol' Smokey, he just shook his head and said: 'Fellas, I guess you better go put them on.' We looked at each other, put our pads on and went to scrimmage. We beat Baylor."

TATE: "Yeah, when ol' Bear calls on you, you don't refuse. Not in *any* situation. I only played one year, my senior season, under him, but he treated me like a son, and in one year I learned and felt more about loyalty than at any time of my life. I remember one day in 1967 I was working as a stockbroker in Houston. The night before, President Johnson had made his State-of-the-Union message and for various reasons the market was going bananas. Bryant was in town for the annual American Football Coaches Association convention, and he phoned me that morning and asked about some stocks he'd invested in. Then he said, 'Hey, Marvin, if you don't have other plans, why don't you join me for some lunch?'

"I started to decline because the phones and the whole office were going crazy. It would be the busiest market day of the year, but I couldn't get farther than two words when he said, 'I'll expect you at noon,' and he hung up.

"Just before noon I walked out of my office like I was powerless to do otherwise and soon found myself in his hotel room where he'd ordered up sandwiches and coffee, and in a couple of minutes in walk guys like John McKay of Southern Cal, Frank Howard of Clemson and a couple other big name coaches, and pretty soon they're talking up a storm about all kinds of things, particularly duck hunting, and very little about football. And the thing that impressed me most was that Coach Bryant was the dominant focus of attention in this group. A leader among leaders. A man of magic. Suddenly I realized why it was that when Coach Bryant summoned me there was no way I couldn't be there. Hell, it occurs to me, even today, that if he should phone me and say, 'meet me in New York because we're gonna make the Hudson river flow north instead of south and we'll whip the ass off anyone who says we can't do it,' I'd join him, know what I mean?"

TAYLOR: "Oh, we know, we know. Coach Bryant, he tells you, you listen and he makes you *believe*. Heck, never as long as I live will I forget a game against Rice. With three minutes to play they had just scored to go ahead 12–0, and a lot of the 70,000 people at Rice Stadium in Houston were beginning to leave the place. We tried to move the ball after Rice's second score and got nowhere. With 3:18 left in the game we got the ball back again and as Coach sent in the offense, he said: *'There's still time enough to win this game if it means anything to you.'* Regardless of the situation he made it sound absolutely believeable—and next thing I knew he had his hand on my shoulder, gripping hard, sending me in at halfback. In the huddle there wasn't a guy who didn't feel re-charged.

"On the first play I got the ball on a sweep around left end, veered to the sidelines, and behind two inspired blocks I raced fifty-five yards down to the three-yard line. Then on third-and-one, I sliced in for the score. After the conversion there was 2:08 left and Bryant ordered an onside kick.

"People starting for the aisles suddenly stopped and waited. Rice, of course, knew the onside kick was coming and had ten guys jammed up to the 40-yard line waiting for it. Jack Powell plinked the short kick. The ball took a crazy spin, and bounced around on the Rice 45. Two Rice guys were almost on it when Bebe Stallings, our end, dove through the air between them and smothered it on the Rice 49.

"On the first play from scrimmage, Jimmy Wright, our quarterback, faded back and rifled a 49-yard strike over my left shoulder which I grabbed for the touchdown just as I crossed the goal line. Again we converted and led 14–12.

"We kicked off to Rice and they were desparate. Down two points they had to go to the air. Their first pass was intercepted by Jack Pardee who returned to the Rice eight-yard line. Then, tough luck for Rice, who was penalized to the four, for delay-of-game. On the next play, Don Watson crashed over for the third touchdown for us.

"I remember I couldn't hardly figure out the score so I looked at the scoreboard: *A&M 20, Rice 12.* We'd got three touchdowns in two minutes eight seconds. There was 1:10 left but it was all over. It was probably the wildest finish in the league's history, and a lot of folks who left early, missed it.

"Later, in the locker room, a writer asked Coach Bryant: 'What in the world happened, Coach?'

"He shook his head and just mumbled: 'I don't know and I

might never know. I was too busy prayin'.' But, heck, he needn't have had to pray. He'd already told us we could win if it meant anything to us."

"Amen," said Bobby Lockett.

GOEHRING: "Do we all fully realize how many facets there were to Bryant's character, and how he revealed them to us? How about the fact that he always was so disgusted that we had so many engineering majors on the team. I think he was secretly proud of it, but a lot of them had class or labs until 5 o'clock and couldn't make the normal 3 P.M. practice time. There wasn't much he could do about it but he finally realized he'd rather have smart guys on his team than a mess of idiots or basket-weaving majors. He'd come from Kentucky where there were more coal miners than engineers and I think he made a remarkable adjustment in how to handle his players."

LOCKETT: "He established personal discipline pretty fast, too. As freshmen our chow hall was like an animal house. He changed all that his very first spring when he came. Several guys got into food fights in the dining hall and Coach Bryant kicked them off the training table. After three weeks, one guy came to Coach and begged to be taken back onto the training table because he was almost starving to death. 'Not a chance,' he told him, and made him stick it out, on his own, until the end of the semester. There wasn't another food fight during all of Bryant's years at A&M."

TAYLOR: "Remember his reaction to Reveille?" (I had to ask who "Reveille" was and learned it was the Aggies' big, shaggie dog mascot. Reveille always appeared on the field, in an A&M dog blanket, to perform with the band during halftime.)

LOCKETT: "Bear didn't know that it was a trained ritual for Reveille to crap right in the middle of the football field at every game and the fans would roar with delight. In the Arkansas game Charlie Krueger came into the huddle after one play and said: 'Either I found Reveille's spot or I knocked the crap out of somebody with my last block.' What he didn't know was the stuff was all over his back from where he'd landed.

"You could hardly get in the huddle with him. On the sidelines nobody would stand near him. Coach Bryant put a stop to that. 'Anybody who shies away from ol' Charlie,' he barked, 'doesn't get back in the ball game. He's the only one here with the evidence he's really been down there in the dirt and the trenches.' And you know something? He meant it just that way."

GOEHRING: "I think I'm the only guy Bryant ever coached who had his blessings for deliberately doing something mildly dirty and deliberately drawing a penalty for it."

LOCKETT: "Do I know that one?"

GOEHRING: "I was a sophomore guard weighing only 180 at best and I was in and out of the starting line-up and I really wanted to be the permanent starter. I couldn't ever take any chance of looking bad, but against SMU Bryant had me playing offensive guard and defensive tackle. Now, at that weight how the hell could I survive as a defensive tackle? Especially when I found myself facing a big 235-pound SMU offensive tackle.

"I didn't get into the game until the third quarter but the instant I lined up across from this guy I knew I had to do something smart or desperate—or both—in order to beat him and keep Bryant from yankin' me outa, the game. . . ."

LOCKETT: "Oh, yeah, I remember . . ."

GOEHRING: "Yup. I deliberately charged offside in the first play. With that ol' forearm cure. Took him by surprise, naturally, and hit him right in the chops, knocking him right into his own backfield. I knew Bryant would chew me out for bein' offside but it did the trick. I made that big, ol' tackle respect me right away and be a bit gun-shy. It was the only way I could beat him and when I explained it to Coach on the sidelines later, he stood there an instant, with a frozen face and a growl that didn't quite make it from his lips, and then he gave me a crooked smile. 'Son,' he said, 'I always did like a lineman who could think in an emergency.' "

All four of them cracked up in unison. It was the acknowledgement of deliciously shared moments that would never fade.

"Oh, that man," Marvin Tate murmured. The others merely nodded. Nothing needed to be added.

# 7

# *The Recruiter*

" *'Here are your recruiting areas.'* Coach Bryant said. *'East Texas, Eastern Oklahoma, Arkansas, Louisiana, and all states east of the Mississippi River and knee-deep in the Atlantic Ocean.'* "

—Elmer Smith

There I was, on the road again. Or rather in the air, taking off to milk the memories of still another of Bryant's boys, and by now I'd discovered that each would be a startingly new personality, each would have his own unique insights to The Master, and that each would be an almost unquenchable fountain of reminiscence.

This one would fit the pattern well, I was told, as the chilling temperature and swirling fog greeted me at the Tuscaloosa airport where I boarded a private jet to Little Rock, Arkansas. I was going, first of all, to the usual bloodbath that was the annual Texas A&M–Arkansas football game. It turned out to be exactly as advertised, and the famed Arkansas chants of "Sooie Pig" filled the night, long after the final gun signaled a Razorback victory. They were pretty crazy here, too, about football, and some of the folks I was with in a particular party saw to it that I had less than four hours sleep before I pointed my rented car northward the next morning toward Petit Jean Mountain. It was a mountain made famous years before by Winthrop Rockefeller, before he became governor of Arkansas, by carving away a major piece of it and establishing Winrock Farm, a spectacular experimental farm for Santa Gertrudis cattle. But the mountain was big enough for more than one, and a bit of its acreage had been taken over by Elmer Smith, an assistant under Coach Bryant at Texas A&M, who occupied a special spot in the state of Arkansas athletic lore.

It was a beautiful one-hour drive through mountains and valleys, with scenic vistas unfolding one after another. It was a special place, befitting the retirement plans of a very special guy.

Elmer Smith had grown up in western Arkansas when it was still close to being a frontier. He'd played football and baseball at Hendrix College and had re-established a successful football program as coach of Southern State University of Magnolia. For nineteen years he was an assistant football coach at Texas A&M under four different head coaches and battled cancer for a decade, and won, and generally was one of the most beloved and respected men in the Southwest Conference. He was the only assistant coach in Aggie history to whom the players had awarded a game ball. *That* kind of man . . .

I walked toward the screened porch of the sprawling house and it was opened even before I got up to it by a mountain of a man, 6–1, 250 pounds, who stuck out a huge, friendly hand and said "Howdy" like howdy is meant to sound when full of honest warmth and welcome. He was more than seventy, but his hair was still sandy, his eyes behind the spectacles still sparkling.

Before entering I turned around for a look at the splendor of the valley below, punctuated by two or three sparkling brooks, thousands of acres of pine and spruce, red-roofed barns and white painted fences.

"Yeah," he grinned, as if reading my thoughts. "One helluva place for a guy after he's hung up his cleats and whistle." We went inside for a few moments while he showed me around the main house. Then we left for his hut—his office—a separate building 75 yards away. The hut was an overflowing precious repository of athletic photos, plaques, cups, old game balls with precious legends printed on them, some still inflated, others collapsed; dusty, retired baseball caps, framed scrolls and letters; all the treasured memorabilia of a man who remembered and was remembered by many.

After a few moments for coffee and small talk, Elmer Smith settled back in a well-worn, favorite chair and laced his hands across his ample chest. He was wearing a green flannel shirt and old, but still serviceable, gray-green pants and venerable cowboy boots. Later he would point to two other pair of boots sitting on a stand in the corner, near a big open fireplace, which were given to him by Bryant.

"I can recall it so clearly," he said carefully. "My fixed relationship with Coach Bryant. It was exactly 9 P.M., February 25, 1954. I was in my office at Southern State College in Magnolia, Arkansas, where I was coaching. I'd known Bryant for years, and apparently he knew how I'd been doing at Southern State. He hadn't said much more than 'hello' when I was dumbfounded to hear him ask if I'd like to be one of his assistants at Texas A&M. He'd just accepted the job to rebuild the Aggies' football fortunes. Well, I was just flattered as hell and told him I'd be there to talk to him the next day.

" 'You know how low things have been here at A&M,' he told me as we took a walk around the stadium the following morning, 'and of course there's always the danger that things won't improve much, which means you'd risked a lot and would've lost a lot by leaving Southern State to come with me.'

"I looked at him and spit in the dust, and I knew just what I was sayin'. I said, 'Hell, Coach, comin' with you wouldn't be riskin' anything at all.'

"He said that was nice and flattering but I shouldn't just plunge into something and should take my time making up my mind. How much time would I need, he wanted to know. Not much, I told him. I took about two seconds. It wasn't difficult. I'd always been impressed by him. When he was a young assistant at Alabama he'd given me some good advice when I was a high school coach.

I'd also known what he'd done at Maryland and Kentucky. You talk with Paul Bryant just one minute and you know you're in the presence of a man you hitch your star to. I felt no hesitation in leaving a head coaching job at a smaller school to become an assistant under Bryant. Hell, when you go with Coach Bryant from *anywhere* to *anything,* that's a promotion.

"By that time we were up in the press box, and oh how that man is always prepared. He hauls some maps out of a desk. Maps of the South and the Southwest and starts drawing red crayon lines on them.

" 'I'm outlining your recruiting areas, Elmer,' he said. 'East Texas, eastern Oklahoma, Arkansas, Louisiana, all states east of the Mississippi River and knee deep in the Atlantic Ocean.' "

A deep, ironic chuckle surged up through Elmer Smith's massive chest. "Well, I didn't know how close to the truth he was talking about but I soon realized he was sending all his assistants on the damnest recruiting crusade the state of Texas ever saw. He had to because of the low esteem the Aggies had fallen into. Anyway, on March 6, I hit the trail through East Texas and returned a week later to report to Bryant on prospects I'd seen. I particularly stated that the Palestine, Texas area didn't have a kid suitable for Southwest Conference football. They were all too small.

"We'd just walked out of Coach's office when a man in a big, black Cadillac drove up with four boys in the car. He introduced himself as 'Mr. Gregg, from Palestine in East Texas.' He was an Aggie alumnus and had rounded up four fine football players for Coach Bryant, and Coach should count on his judgment and just sign the boys to a scholarship on the spot. Well, Coach looked those boys over like someone in the paddock preparing to bet on a race horse.

"Then he took Mr. Gregg and me aside and said to him, 'Well, if thin shoulders and a skinny ass will get the job done, you've got four All Americas but they're not for us, thank you.' Mr. Gregg turned purple as sage brush and packed his merchandise back in the car as Coach Bryant turned away from him. Three important things happened that day: (1) Mr. Gregg would never come back, (2) I knew never to recruit a skinny kid for A&M, and (3) I learned not to trust an alumnus with a big, black Cadillac who really didn't know a football from a chamber pot.

"Coach put his hand on my shoulder. 'Some of these old alums, they just want to look important in the coach's eyes and set themselves up for 50-yard line tickets, and you have to be careful about who you can trust.' His words of wisdom were to come back to haunt him a couple years later when the Aggies were hit with a recruiting scandal caused by some of those alums.

"My next recruiting trip was into northern Louisiana to visit future Heisman Trophy winner John David Crow and his parents at Springhill. This was a familiar football family visit, since John David's older brother, Raymond, had played for me at Southern State and was captain his senior year. John David himself was a frequent visitor on the bench during many games, and I had given him a pair of special light football shoes to wear during his outstanding high school career. You never know when a simple gift like that will pay big dividends.

"His dad, Harry Crow, remarked on my visit that John David definitely wanted to play football for Coach Bryant but would not make a commitment at that time. Other schools were in the picture. But, being encouraged, I continued to see him once a week. As a matter of fact, we were visiting so much that John David said: 'Coach, I don't think I'm going to graduate, because you are taking so much of my time.' But John David finally visited our campus at College Station and was greatly impressed with the school and Coach Bryant. Before leaving, he verbally committed to attend Texas A&M.

"On signing date in the Southwest Conference there was a standing rule that all 'letters-of-intent' could not be released from each school's athletic department until 8:01 A.M. on a set date. Signing the kids was always an iffy thing. You might think you had a boy all sewed up but the pressures on him, and the 'kidnapping' that went on, was unbelievable. You had to hustle to the boy's hometown and his house to be there on time and fend off the other recruiters trying to break him down. And with so many boys to sign, you could spread your staff pretty thin covering them all. Coach Bryant knew what a hot prospect John David Crow was and with one burst of imagination he not only solved the problem but set a pattern that most everyone in the Southwest Conference had to follow in the future.

"Bryant had me stationed at the airport in Shreveport, Louisiana while John David's letter-of-intent was flown out to me from the A&M campus in the plane of an oil company owned by an Aggie alum. I grabbed the papers and quickly drove to Springhill for the signing. I had a leisurely breakfast with the Crows, said our goodbyes and by 10 A.M. I was on my way to sign a couple other kids in the area.

"Several other coaches got to the Crow's house by noon and were stunned to find the boy signed. They couldn't believe I had picked up the papers at 8:01 A.M. in College Station, Texas and driven to Springhill, Louisiana in such a short time. John David's daddy simply reminded 'em there were such things as airplanes. Bill Henderson of Baylor, who couldn't believe it, and who thought he had a good crack at John David, later returned to the Crow house and asked Mrs. Crow what color the papers were that had been signed. Turned out to be the right color, of course. 'That damned Bryant!' he sputtered. After that, flying letters-of-intent became standard survival tactics in the Southwest Conference.

"Whipped on by Bryant, who knew what a long recruiting way he had to go, our new staff signed 104 prospects that first winter and spring. Bryant kept accenting 'quality' but secretly, down deep, he knew we had to have numbers, too, because he knew the casualty rate was gonna be high once spring drills started. How right he was . . .

"When that famous first spring practice did start, everything was contact drills, very little team drills. It was 'gut-check' session from start to finish. A large blackboard was placed in the coaches' dressing room and after practice each coach would add, on the right side of the board, the name of any player he had found that day who was a contact man—a hitter. Also, there was room to the left for those a bit anemic around the heart.

"As the work progressed and the drills became tougher, our

blackboard eventually began to tilt to the left. However, Bryant felt that it was the way the players had previously been permitted to practice, so he didn't dismiss anyone from the squad that spring. But it was this fact that brought about the need for the famous Junction episode." Elmer shucked off one boot and wiggled his toes a bit, then put the boot back on, talking all the while.

"After spring practice, we hit the recruiting trail again to try and bring in numbers to off-set what was about to happen at Junction. I was hopping all over my area and eventually found myself at a high school all-star game in Tuscaloosa sponsored by the University of Alabama. I found that every kid had signed somewhere, except one player—believe it or not, a one-armed fullback who weighed 175 pounds. I watched him in practice. The kid was tough and quicker'n a hiccup. Standing next to me was Hank Crisp, line coach at Alabama, who I should point out, had a stump for one arm. He didn't look at me when he just sort of murmured: 'Elmer, that boy would help beat a lot of people somewhere if only somebody had the heart and sense to sign him.'

"Later in the week I phoned Bryant and painted the general recruiting picture at Alabama, which was pretty dismal for us.

"I could just see those wrinkles in his forehead getting deeper and deeper as he listened. Finally, he said, 'Hell, Elmer, ain't there even *one* unsigned kid who can play?'

"I took a deep breath and told him there was one.

" 'Then sign him,' he commanded.

"I hesitated before saying, 'But Coach, there's something I oughta point out. He's only got one arm and a stump for the other, amputated just below the left elbow. Ol' Hank Crisp liked the boy but couldn't convince Alabama to sign him.' I started to say something else but Coach interrupted me excitedly. 'Hank Crisp liked him? Hell, ol' Hank only had a stump of an arm when he coached me at Alabama and used to knock my head off with it. If that sonuvagun says the boy's a player you sign that kid or it'll be your ass when you get back here!' "

Elmer Smith grinned with deep satisfaction. "Well, before that all-star game I got Murray Trimble—that's the boy—and his parents together and signed him to a four-year scholarship.

"Actually, I didn't think the boy would really show up in the fall. I figured he'd go to a smaller college in Alabama, if he hoped to play at all. He showed up, however, but in terms of hours spent in practice he may have been the most unproductive freshman in the history of college football. Bryant let him always wear a yellow sweat suit which indicated 'limited drill because of injury.' I didn't know what Coach had in mind. I should have known it was *somethin'*.

"Frequently, though, I would see Bryant with his arm draped over Murray's shoulder talking with him. This always pleased me, because I was so sure that everytime I saw the yellow sweat suit that I had signed a lemon, even though I'd done so at Coach's urging. But Bryant did the greatest coaching and motivation job on Murray Trimble that has ever been done in football. He transformed a shy, self-conscious boy into a holy terror on the football field.

"He could wrap that arm-and-a-half around the ball, blast through a hole or run wide, and cause an opponent to fumble. The way the good Lord works his compensation he'd given Murray greater power in his legs and more heart in his chest, and Coach Bryant arranged things so the boy could use it all. Bryant watched him very closely and every time Murray Trimble did something well, he'd call the boy over, and even if practice was only half done he'd drape an arm over Murray and tell him he'd had a terrific day—that he should go on in and take a shower and he'd see him tomorrow.

"Never have I seen a coach instill such confidence in a kid. That boy walked so tall and became so vicious with that stub arm that was amputated just below the left elbow, that it was more of a help than handicap, the way he could jab and hurt you with it. Charlie Krueger, our All America tackle, once got mad at Murray in practice for using his stub arm that way and snapped at him: 'Murray, if they let you get by with that, I'm going to have one of my damned arms cut off!' "

Elmer Smith's face echoed the sentiments he was feeling, now. "That *handicapped* boy piled up a lot of opposing running backs for A&M, and I like to believe it was due in great part in the way Coach Bryant handled him."

Elmer Smith held up an index finger like a heavy, gnarled pointer. "You see," he continued, "You have to understand that underneath one of the toughest physical exteriors that's ever been laid on a football coach, there was a sweet, sensitive side to Coach Bryant. Now, y'know that he always got to his office at A&M long before his assistants, and often, when I was next to show up, he'd take an early break by asking me to go on a short drive with him while he collected his thoughts or tried some of them out on me. We'd always take the same road, as part of his habit, but this particular morning I noticed we were on a road I'd never seen before.

"Soon he drove to a small, sort of run-down house where two little black boys were sitting out front. Coach stopped, got out, and without saying anything to me, he went up to those little kids, put his arms around them and said something to 'em. Then he patted them once or twice and came back to the car. I asked him what that'd been all about.

"He was silent for a moment, and then explained. 'I came by this morning, just to take a different route to the office, and I'd run over a dog near their house. I got to thinking about it after I got to the office and since theirs was the only house near here it might've been their dog. So I came back here and when I found out it was, I promised those kids they'd have another dog before the next night.'

"Well, Coach Bryant hardly did any work that day until he'd gone out and tracked down a kennel where he could buy a pup and had taken it back to those kids.

"My relationships with Coach Bryant were the kind that make everlastin' memories," Elmer Smith continued. "Like when he sent me to Little Rock in the Spring of 1955 to sort of scout Paul Dietzel, then head coach at Louisiana State, who was gonna be the head speaker at this high school football clinic. 'We play LSU the second game next fall,' Bryant said, 'and you just might pry a secret or two outa him.' So I went up there and listened to Dietzel boast about lovin' to play against stuntin' defenses. And then he outlines on the blackboard all his tricky offensive line splits, and the quick, brush-blocking options he likes to use, and I'm out there in the audience givin' birth to a radical idea.

"What it amounted to when I got back to College Station was a defensive alignment that did strange things with our 6–1 defense—things that no sane coach would do. It took guts for me to put my ideas up on that blackboard and when I was through there was this awful hush when I turned around. Bryant was staring at it and then he looked at me and finally said: 'Elmer, are you sure you went to Little Rock and listened to Paul Dietzel? 'Cause this is the damndest thing I've ever seen.' And then all the other assistant coaches burst into fits of laughing.

"Nothing more was said about it and we went on to other matters, but the next morning Coach Bryant walks into the conference room like he has a song in his heart and announces: 'Well boys, I've got our LSU defense all set and nobody's gonna change my mind.' And then he proceeds to draw the same 6–1 defense I'd put up the day before, except that he's refined it a bit with every imaginable stunt worked into it. Nobody said anything and nobody looked at me. We put it all in the week before we played LSU and by the second half our players on defense could hear guys fussing in the huddle, because they couldn't figure out proper blocking schemes for our defense and we beat 'em 9–7 in a big upset.

"What most impressed me about the game was the way Coach Bryant had taken an idea—no matter how wild—and molded it into reality. But I wasn't surprised. You see, in essence, Coach Bryant gets the job done by coaching his coaches—by delegating responsibilities and then inspecting the results."

Elmer Smith pulled over a small footstool nearby and placed it very precisely in front of him and then stretched out his legs on it. Settling back he glanced off obliquely. "But I think my most vivid recollection of Coach Bryant will always be the incident dealing with his return to Alabama to become their head coach.

"It was always the dream of his life, and when they finally

summoned him he accepted immediately, but found it heartbreaking to tell his Aggie players he was leaving. I think that was the closest Paul Bryant ever came to sheddin' tears in public, far as I could tell. And then he told me he wanted me to come with him. I was just filled up with pride and pleasure and jumped at the chance. He said he particularly wanted me to head up the Alabama recruitin' program.

"So, when we all go to Tuscaloosa my first bit of business was to contact all the prospects that had been signed by the former staff at Alabama. I bounced all over Louisiana, Florida, part of Mississippi and, of course, Alabama, lovin' every minute of it. I came back and started to give him a detailed report on each kid, but even as I talked—so excited, I thought—I somehow sensed that Coach had something on his mind, troublin' him, as I was talkin'.

"I finished and he nodded, almost as though he's suddenly stopped listenin', really, turnin' away a bit. Then he looked back at me and said, 'Elmer, I guess I have to say this straight out . . . Jim Myers called me from College Station, and he wants you back at A&M. He says he needs you desperately to help get his new program goin'.'

"Myers had replaced Bryant at A&M, and Coach Bryant had this warm feeling for the place and obviously thought he owed 'em all somethin' and as much as he wanted me to be with him he told me that all kinds of A&M alumni and school officials had been callin' him, beggin' him to release me so I could return.

"Coach then gripped my arm and said: 'Elmer, I think you oughta go back to A&M and give it a try. If things don't work out for you, just remember you'll always have a job here with me, or wherever I am.' "

There was a faint smile on his face as Elmer concluded: "I went back to A&M because I knew Coach Bryant was right. Fortunately, I never had to call on him for help. But there was never enough cotton in the South to make me believe that if I ever needed him he wouldn't be there for me."

# 8

# *The Heisman*

> "... *It was obvious that Coach Bryant was a defensive genius . . . Not that he wasn't sharp on offense but there was something in his grappling with life that made him believe: 'No—they can't do this to me. I won't let 'em.' That's a pure defensive attitude, know what I mean?*"
>
> —John David Crow

John David Crow, one of the greatest running backs in the history of college football, was seated comfortably in his office at Northeast Louisiana University, at Monroe, where he was head coach. A two-time All America and Heisman Trophy winner at Texas A&M, he had been one of Paul Bryant's early superstars. Later he was an All-Pro running back, then an assistant under Bryant and an assistant with several professional teams before becoming head coach and athletic director at Northeast Louisiana, where he had rebuilt that program into a winner.

His graying blond hair was a bit longer than the familiar brush cut of his college days, but the blue eyes in his handsome, strong, square face had lost none of their boyish brilliance. Especially so, since he was rolling back the years, embarked on a favorite subject.

John David Crow was sure he had the best, true clue to the particular genius that was Paul W. Bryant. "A lot of people, when they start remembering Coach Bryant and try to reveal their innermost thoughts about him, get it all wrong. Somehow they get stuck with that physical image—that big hulk of a guy-6–3, 225 pounds, which was big for a coach twenty-five years ago. Of course, today's players, like most of the pro linemen, are huge guys that would have scared most players to death twenty-five years ago. But in his early coaching days Coach Bryant was a big man who sort of superimposed a physical fear on his players, and backed it up with those awful tough practices of his.

"But, like I say, I think I have a different angle on what really got best results from Coach Bryant. Now, a lot of coaches motivate ball players with praise, a pat on the back, a lot of encouragement. Others use the kick in the butt, meanness, a snarl, a good chewing out, even scorn. Know what I mean? Well, at various times Coach Bryant used all of those things on us back at Texas A&M, but I really think his best tool was his ability to put mental strain on you. He was always maneuvering you into doing the best you could, letting you know you could do better. It seemed to be constantly on your mind: 'Coach thinks I'm letting him down and letting the team down . . . Coach doesn't believe this is the best I can do on that block, or adjusting on defense . . .'

"Sure, there was always the fear that he'd get mad enough to chop you one, or cuss you out something awful, but he had his way of putting pressure on you that was purely mental. Don't ask me to spell it out any better. Maybe somebody like a psychiatrist or psychologist could come up with some fancy phrases on it.

"I think part of it was when he'd walk into a room, or a squad meeting and everything would immediately get quiet just out of the sheer respect the guy got from everybody. It's even more noticeable today because of the fantastic record that he built up, but we sensed it back then when he was only 38 or so. I still think that was the biggest thing he had on kids. Some say it was the physical thing but I claim I know better.

"In fact, that intangible stuff was one of the things that kept a lot of guys from packing in and going home when Coach Bryant

The Bryant family of Moro Bottom, Arkansas in 1915. The barefoot boy on the far left is Paul.

The Fordyce High Red Bugs were Arkansas State Champions in 1930. *Below,* Bryant was a member of the 1934 Alabama squad that defeated Stanford in the Rose Bowl.

The surprise welcome Bryant got at Kentucky in 1946 was an indication of great things to come.

George Blanda of Kentucky was the first of Bryant's many great quarterbacks.

Bryant instructs Kentucky receiver Charlie McClendon on sidelines during 1951 Sugar Bowl win over Oklahoma.

Bryant, the great teacher, instructs his triple threat quarterback, Babe Parilli. *Below,* the Wildcats celebrate their 20–7 win over TCU in the 1952 Cotton Bowl.

*Above,* Bryant's "Junction Boys" returned to the Texas desert war camp twenty-five years after the fact. *Below,* the training camp as it appeared in 1954 and the eight Aggie sophmores that survived.

*At right,* All-SWC quarterback Elwood Kettler, Bryant and All America lineman Dennis Goehring recall a memorable story. *Below,* Aggie athletic director Marvin Tate introduces his former teammates at the Junction Reunion.

Wherever Bryant went he always attracted a crowd. *Above,* he addresses the Aggie Corps during welcome celebration at Grove Theatre. *Below,* Red Grange, Lindsey Nelson and Bryant discuss A&M strategy for 1957 Thanksgiving Day game against Texas.

*At right,* actor William Bendix gives Bryant a few sure fire plays. *Below,* Bryant relaxes with Aggie greats, Bobby Lockett, Lloyd Hale and Jack Pardee.

John David Crow (*right*) receives Walter Camp Memorial Trophy for outstanding college back of 1957, along with other honorees Lou Michaels and Lt. Huston Patton, USAF.

Texas A&M seniors, Bryant and Aggie coaches whoop it up after defeating Texas Longhorns in 1956 Thanksgiving Day game at Austin.

John David Crow receives 1957 Heisman Trophy from the New York Athletic Club.

*At left,* Steve Meilinger shows All America form as a Kentucky end. *Below,* Bryant on the sidelines of Texas A & M.

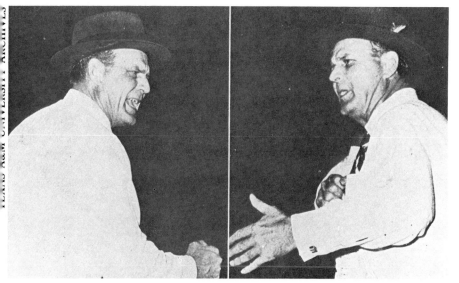

Bryant, the jittery genius, exhorts his young Alabama squad from sidelines of 1958 game vs. LSU.

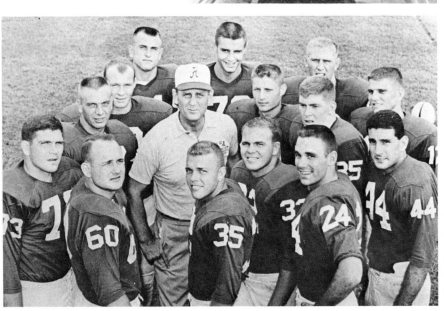

Bryant gathers with the leaders of his 1961 team prior to season opener against Georgia.

Bryant and quarterback Pat Trammell on the sidelines in 1961.

President John Kennedy visits with Bryant and members of the University of Alabama delegation prior to 1961 National Football Foundation and Hall of Fame banquet.

Alabama president Frank Rose and Bryant accept 1962 Sugar Bowl invitation to pla
Arkansas.

Bryant and USC Coach John McKay after 1971 contest in which Alabama unveile
the explosive wishbone offense and won, 17–10.

was working their tails off so unmercifully. Today, most kids have some place to go to if they don't cut it right away. Often they can transfer, because everyone is looking for football players in great numbers, with all those athletic scholarships available. And heck, in the American type of society and economy kids today can just go home, period, and get a job. No such thing in our day, so when Coach was putting the pressure on you, you did a lot of thinking before gettin' down your suitcase. Oh, sure, I know he ran a lot of 'em off purposely, but those were the guys who probably couldn't play *anywhere* because they weren't geared for the pressure or the physical demands on them.

"I saw a lot of that, personally. I was a freshman at Texas A&M, the year the varsity guys came back from that Junction ordeal. We were all in a dressing room about the size of a classroom, and with more than 100 players we had three or four guys to a locker. Pretty soon there were some empty lockers; guys would come at night and slip away with their personal belongings because they didn't want you to see them in their embarrassment. And some of those guys who left were so-called all state selections in high school.

"It was a lot easier getting into A&M, in those days than getting out. There was no entrance requirement of any kind—even for football players. You just had to be a graduate of high school. We took some kind of test when we came in, but it was more of a placement exam, to see what kind of courses we were best suited for. But Coach Bryant was always interested in the results.

"In those days freshmen weren't eligible for varsity but we played five frosh games and won four, so Coach knew he'd had some pretty good recruiting success. We lost only to Baylor. We rode over there on a bus on Thursday, played that same night and got beat. We came back to College Station on Friday morning and practiced against the varsity that same afternoon. None of us liked the way Coach Bryant looked at us during practice. We were his first recruiting group and it was as though he'd been insulted by our loss. We didn't plan on getting beat again as freshmen, and we didn't.

. . . *And after that freshman year? Did he have any idea what*

*was in store for him for the next three years under Bryant? Any*
*doubts or trepidation?*

Crow clasped his hands behind his head, then stared hard at
his interviewer. "Do you mean did I think of quitting?" he asked
brusquely. "If you're Coach Bryant's kind of ball player, if he
gives you the idea that he thinks you're a winner, then quitting
or transferring is the farthest thing from your mind. And if you
stay on with him, most guys have that attitude for life.

"I was real fortunate because I grew up in a hurry and became
a first-teamer in spring practice after my freshman year. So, I
was going to start as a soph, it seemed. But as I look back at it
now, I realize it was a constant fight to hold my job. That's
what I thought at the time, but it really wasn't. You see, Coach
Bryant had that uncanny ability to make me *think* my position
was in jeopardy, even though all along he had me pegged as a
starter.

"But many times on a Monday or a Tuesday he'd have me
running with the second or even third team. He found that could
get more out of me by hitting me in the face—no, not literally—
than by patting me on the back.

"The treatment was great for me but not for some others. But
he had a problem nursing that sophomore class that was a big
part of his second club. We'd never been anywhere. The first
game of the season was at UCLA, it was the first plane ride for
all of us. I started the game, and at kickoff I'm sure I was white
as a sheet. Butterflies the size of a bat were in my stomach.

"Coach Bryant knew he had a bunch of unworldly kids out
there for an opener and it could have been more disastrous than
it was—we lost 21-0, but he sure shaped us into one fine, 7-2-
1 season, and we were off to the races the next two years. But
I'll never forget our fear in that opener—scared of the possibility
of letting our teammates down and letting Coach down because
Texas A&M is the kind of secluded place where everybody has
to be close to one another, with Coach Bryant the central figure.
That's where I first learned humility, togetherness and loyalty
and it came right out of that big, growling, motivating force named
Paul Bryant."

John David Crow tilted back in his chair, an adjunctive thought bringing a spark to his blue eyes. "But it was Bryant's last year at Texas A&M which will always live longest in my memory. It not only made an all-time believer out of me as far as Coach Bryant is concerned, but it opened up a fresh window on life for me. It was his attitude that was put on display toward the end of the year. He'd taken us to the top the year before when we were unbeaten, except for a 7–7 tie with Arkansas that maybe never should have happened.

"But by now, everyone throughout the country was aware of how Bryant had lifted the Aggies out of despair and defeat. They were no longer the laughing stock of the Southwest Conference. In fact, it was generally felt that we'd be a perennial threat in the league—and for national honors—as long as Coach Bryant was around. And no one ever thought he wouldn't be there practically forever, the way he had things organized with players willing to pay the price he demanded of them.

"So the following year, 1957, we had a veteran team coming back and people were touting me as a strong Heisman contender, with the team making a real run for national honors. In fact, after we'd won eight straight we were number-one in the polls. Then the stories and rumors started cropping up in the papers about Paul Bryant leaving to go back home to take over at Alabama. We all figured they were just that—rumors. Look what he was doing here. Look how the guys were taking to him, and all. We believed *nothin'*. It's kind of like a husband who has a wife runnin' around and he's the last one to know. We had so much respect for Coach Bryant that we didn't believe anything in the papers. He always laid it on the line for us. He'd have told us.

"But by the time we played Rice in our next to the last game of the season it was pretty much an accepted fact, Coach was going back to Alabama. Telling his players was just about the most difficult thing he'd ever had to do in his life. It wasn't like his leaving Maryland after only five months, with all that interference from the university president. Nor was it as tough to leave Kentucky because of all that emphasis on Adolph Rupp and basketball.

"But he'd come to love A&M and what it stood for, and, after that first rough year when he was establishing his philosophies of football and sacrifice, he'd become very close to his players. I think for the first time in his life, Coach Bryant shed tears in public as he told us, yes, he was going back home. We knew he could never have left us for anyplace but *home.*

"But Bryant proved his dedication to us and to his profession. We were ranked number-one at the time and had two games to play. Rice and Texas. We figured to win both and be national champs. And Coach worked as though he was going to be at A&M forever. On Thursday we scrimmaged. Maybe the toughest scrimmage of the year. We played both ways, then. I was a running back on offense and a safety on defense. I never came off the field in that scrimmage. I don't think Coach would have worked us that way if he had it to do over. But because he knew he was leaving, he knew he couldn't leave any room for doubt in anyone's mind—particularly his—that he was still A&M's coach.

"We lost to Rice, 7–6, when we missed our point after. And the following Saturday we lost the finale to Texas, 9–7, on a field goal.

"But we still got invited to the Gator Bowl to play Tennessee. After the Texas game I was announced as the Heisman Trophy winner and shortly after I got back from New York I had enough confidence to go in and talk to Coach. We'd already been picked for the Gator Bowl and I went into his office and told him we, the players, just couldn't understand. Here we were, just like spring practice, holding blocking and tackling drills. I knew I was going to sign a pro contract that winter but I still wanted to beat Tennessee as much as any sophomore wanted to.

"He was silent for a long minute, staring out a window. Then he looked back at me and said: 'John, you have to understand something. I coach a certain way and have to do things a certain way. Bud Wilkinson does things his way. I coach mine. We both have the same goal, even though we reach it differently. I can't do anything to change my methods. They're part of me, for better or worse.'

"Well, we lost to Tennessee in the Gator Bowl on a last-minute field goal, 3–0. We'd missed an undefeated season and a national championship by a total of six points spread over three games. It hurt. However, it hurt Coach Bryant most. It made his leaving all the more painful.

"Now that I'm coaching at Northeast Louisiana University, I'm sometimes asked if I've adopted any of Coach Bryant's methods or attitudes. Well, I've always said I'd never try to copy anybody because then I wouldn't be *me*. But do we do it unconsciously? I don't know. We don't really know what makes certain people succeed. What are the intangibles that made Patton a great general? What were the intangibles that took Jimmy Carter from obscurity to the presidency his first time around? If you say their technical and intellectual gifts you could be wrong because millions of people have technical and intellectual gifts to match them. So, maybe it gets around to *believing* in somebody or something. The way we believed in Coach Bryant. Is it a two-way street? Does the *believing* on the part of the followers add to the leader's strength? I think maybe it does.

"A lot of people think Coach Bryant could have succeeded in so many other ways besides football. He could have gotten out of football any time in the last few years and it wouldn't have bothered him because he could have stayed busy with other ways of life, don't you agree?"

The phone rang and Crow picked it up a mite impatiently, and even before his secretary could say a word, John David told her, very quietly: "Not now. Not for anybody. I'll call back." If I wanted to, I could imagine John Crow being too wrapped up in his subject to be interrupted for anything less than national cataclysm. Soon, he hung up the phone and was at full go once again.

"I've often thought there wasn't anything I wouldn't accept from him, but there was one time when I had to go against him. I'd just finished my days as a pro player and had gone into the real estate development business in Pine Bluff, Arkansas. I was doing very well, too, and the future seemed unlimited. But there was something inside me that kept eating away at me, trying to get to the surface, and though I knew what it was I kept putting off the certain knowledge.

"Finally I had to face up to it and I talked it over with my wife. I was missing football more than I could bear, and maybe I belonged back in it as a coach. Well, she knew how to approach it. 'Go see Coach Bryant over at Alabama and talk it over with him.' So, early in the Spring of 1969 I went over to Tuscaloosa. For two solid hours Bryant did virtually all the talking—trying to talk me out of going into coaching. I almost couldn't believe his persuasiveness, his logic and sincerity. I had thought it would be just the opposite. I was just vain enough to think he'd consider me good coaching material, but here he was telling me how many pitfalls there were, what the unreasonable demands would be, how thankless it could be, how the pressures were so unfair, and what a lousy life it was, all around. 'Your wife will never forgive you for it,' he grumbled on. And in winding up he said the only way he wanted me in coaching was to be a successful coach, and since he knew I'd be just that, I'd have all those years of misery ahead, for a long time.

"I was stunned, but when he saw I was determined to give it a shot he suggested I do it on a trial basis. In fact, he'd take me on as an assistant during spring practice, for preparation and drills, two months altogether, and then we'd talk again. So I did—and we did. That was May. He said I should think it over for a couple of months and late in July I should let him know if I wanted to sign on as a full-time assistant. So, I went back to Pine Bluff and my real estate business, discussed it with my wife and thought about my decision.

"Lord knows that was the place to study football," Crow went on. "Even way back at A&M, it was obvious that Bryant was a defensive genius. Not that he didn't have a sharp mind for offense, because he did. But there was something in the man's personality, his grappling with life, that sort of made him believe, 'No—they can't do this to me. I won't let 'em.' That's a defensive attitude, know what I mean? And as a defensive coach he was way ahead of everyone, and every coach knows—or should know—that championships are won mostly by defense."

The smile broke widely on Crow's face as he returned to the main narrative thread. "Well, sir, I wasn't back in Arkansas one damn week when I get a phone call from Coach Bryant. He says he thinks I ought to sign on with him as a full-time assistant. I reminded him that he said I should take until July to make up my mind and he replied that he has to make up his budget right now, and that he thinks I would make one damn fine coach and should sign on right now." Crow flashed a wide grin. "So much for Coach Bryant thinking that football coaching wasn't the kind of work I should be getting into.

"So I spent three marvelous and instructive years at Alabama coaching offensive backs. Let me tell you, *that's* where I learned all about football, under Bryant, and soon I allowed the Cleveland Browns to steal me away from him, and two years later I became offensive coordinator for the San Diego Chargers. When Northeast Louisiana came after me as head coach, I jumped at it.

"Every once in a while I talk to Coach Bryant on the phone, or see him at conventions, and I remind him how he'd tried to keep me out of the business. He just gives me that long searching look, half smile, and says: 'Hell, son, you don't ever seem to want to listen to me.'

"The hell I don't," John Crow smiled now. "In anything and everything except that one thing."

Suddenly, John Crow slapped his desk smartly. "Hey, look, I'd like to talk about Coach Bryant and the old days until the cows come home, but this is a chance to get into some other things, like football in general. Someone asked me just the other day if players feel the same pride and tradition as they used to and I had to say no.

"I don't think they feel it as much any more. I just don't think the kids are as school oriented as they used to be, or quite as loyal to one another as they once were.

"I really don't think you can demand as much of them. And a coach wouldn't dare give them gut checks to see how much hitting they can give and take in practice, the way it was 25 years ago. They'd pack up and leave. Do you think Pat Dye at Auburn, could come in and give the same type of gut checks that Shug Jordan believed in? In fact, whoever takes over for Paul Bryant at Alabama is going to have a whole new act. Not that Coach hasn't mellowed a lot from his old days, but his attitudes towards loyalty and how a kid should make a complete contribution of his effort and spirit haven't changed.

"Sure, the kids today get up emotionally as much as they ever did but there's too much individualism around. Maybe it's the effect of too much television football. Too many heroes. Too much hero-type commentary by the TV broadcasters. Too much second-guessing and instant re-play for kids growing up and not respecting officials, coaches, and *authority*.

"People say that big money, and the need to fill stadiums will eventually kill football, but if anything ever kills it, it'll be the individualist. That's the villain in college ball right now, I think. The honors, the Heisman, the pro contracts, too much focus on *self*, if you know what I mean. The *me* generation as some people call it. In pro ball that focus is more understandable because of the fortunes they throw around for those guys.

"But we coaches in college football have to believe in something else and ask ourselves why does a kid play college football today. We think we know the answers if we zero in on the superstars aiming for that pro money, but ninety-nine percent of the kids aren't going to get up there. And I'd be happier, as a coach, if I knew exactly why they're playing—and still happier if it has anything to do with a belief in loyalty, desire, a spirit of sacrifice, affection for school and coach. Heck, if they can't *believe* in some positive things, why play the game, why fill those stadiums?

"For what purpose?" He paused. "But don't worry about it. It'll never happen. There'll always be football as we know it now. As long as Coach Bryant is around they wouldn't *dare* change its concept. And after he's gone his ghost would come back to keep things goin'."

Sitting back in his chair, John David looked across his desk and we both laughed. It was an amusing thought indeed.

# 9

# *Babe Parilli*

*"I was in the hospital recovering from a groin operation. At mid-week Coach came to my bedside and tossed me a whole new offense for Saturday's game. 'Learn it,' he said. 'You're going to play.' Hell, I couldn't even move!"*

—Babe Parilli

His name was Vito Parilli, but is there anyone in the U.S. who would know whom I was talking about if I didn't refer to him as "Babe"? Probably not. The name "Babe" had been tacked on him many years earlier, in the small town of Rochester, Pennsylvania, long before he had become an All America quarterback at Kentucky, then a pro star, and later an assistant coach with the Denver Broncos.

I had no way of knowing what a tremendous impression he would make on me, but I would come away realizing he was a man of solid character, a dedicated hard worker, a team man, a leader who had climbed the ladder of raw courage to greatness. In his lifetime, Babe Parilli has enjoyed only success, a traditional trait shared by so many of Bryant's boys. As a professional quarterback, he'd helped win a Super Bowl while with the New York Jets. As an assistant coach with the Pittsburgh Steelers, he molded Terry Bradshaw into a winner, and later repeated the same success story with Craig Morton of the Broncos.

And so it was another jet ride, this time four hours westward to Denver, Colorado to spend time with the man they also—and affectionately—called "Sweet Kentucky Babe." But call him what you will, he remains one of the most remarkable men in football and still another whose destinies were so unalterably tied to Paul "Bear" Bryant.

Parilli had gone to the Kentucky campus in the summer of 1948 as a shy, undersized and also unimposing 6–2, 170 pound freshmen quarterback prospect and left four years later as a marvelously talented, supremely confident two-time All America with an unlimited future.

Now he was being a gracious host. He had put me up in one of Denver's better hotels, and was taking me out to dinner. His black-gray hair framed his handsome Neapolitan face, his 205-pound bulk still providing him with a trim enough physique that was now as relaxed as his unhurried speech. Somehow, although he obviously worshipped Paul Bryant, it wouldn't be easy to get things out of him—but what would emerge would be completely honest and sincere. There would be no half truths, no distortions, no hesitancy in reaching back for fact and not fiction where Bryant was concerned. Now, in his office, he shoved aside a couple of cans of game films, as though clearing the decks for his single-minded purpose of talking about someone who may have been the most important person in his life . . .

"I guess you can say it was an *accident* that made it all possible. My parents were north Italian immigrants and their greatest expectations for me were to get a solid high school education, then a really good job in the mill, after putting in a few years as a steel worker. No, not as president of the mill, but maybe something in low-level management, at least a foreman.

"My best buddy, Skippy Doyle, had been our star tailback, and had already decided to go to Ohio State after sifting through a ton of big time offers. He'd kept turning down Kentucky, but finally consented to make a visit in the Spring of 1948, but only if they'd let him bring along his pal—me—just for the trip. I was a single-wing halfback in his school. I could throw pretty good but I'd never played quarterback."

The corners of Vito Parilli's mouth curled upwards as he reached back three decades. "I only weighed 170 pounds then, and there was no way Kentucky would consider me, but I had no way of knowing I was just going for the ride, and not to be considered as a football prospect. Even so, I didn't feel like going.

" 'C'mon, you'll enjoy the trip,' Skippy said. 'They'll reimburse us for our train ride.'

"Some train ride. We paid eleven bucks apiece, and found that our space aboard the train was in the mail car sitting on a casket. Eventually, somebody met us at the station in Lexington and took us to the athletic department. Coach Bryant came out of his office and asked Skippy to step inside, without even noticing I was there.

"They talked for two hours, and I never even got an introduction to Coach Bryant. A couple days later we returned to Rochester, Pennsylvania. Subsequently Skippy announced that, yes, he was going to Ohio State, but two months later a big sedan pulls up into our driveway and Coach Bryant and his assistant, Carney Laslie, got out. Next thing I know, Bryant is telling me he wants me to come down and visit the Kentucky campus.

"That sort of startled me and I told him I'd already been there. That really shook him up and for a moment he didn't know what to say, but he recovered quickly. Apparently what had happened after I'd visited with Skippy Doyle was that word must have gotten around that I was a good prospect and lots of people were out trying to recruit me. So, Bryant wasted no time and he said: 'This time we'll know you're there, and I'd like to fly you and your daddy down to see us.'

"My father couldn't get away but I went. I kind of liked what I saw, too, and because it was summer, there were a lot of Kentucky players working out and the coaches sort of had me working with them—running, throwing, everything. They worked hell out of me and then Bryant said he'd really like to have me as a quarterback. But I had to return home to play in a high school all-star game and I didn't make a real commitment. Day after that all-star game, though, Coach Bryant proved he was awfully serious. Carney Laslie showed up in another big limousine. He had a big tackle with him named John Netoskie, from Virginia, whom he just recruited. John was destined to be my roommate.

"What Coach Laslie did then was practically kidnap me. He said he was just taking John and me to a Pittsburgh Pirates baseball game. Later, I learned that Bryant had told him to get us back in that car and not to stop until we got to Lexington, Kentucky. I didn't even have any clothes, and in Pittsburgh I told Carney that, but he just smiled and said: 'We'll fix that right away. C'mon, let's get some.' An hour later we were all in that big Oldsmobile and on a 17-hour trip to Lexington with just a couple of pit stops."

Parilli shook his head and glanced out the window at the fleecy clouds hanging sharply etched in the blue sky over Denver. Then, silence . . .

I had to prod him a bit, now. Being at Kentucky, did things fall neatly into place? Was it a problem adjusting from high school coaching to what might be a pressure-packed situation under the intense, emerging genius of Bryant?

The question wasn't answered immediately, and then only by inference. "I had no idea," Parilli began softly, "no idea at all when I got to Kentucky I'd be just one of eleven quarterbacks. That's right—I said *eleven*. At first there was a sickening sensation in my belly, but from the first time Bryant talked to all of the quarterbacks I was determined that some day I'd nail the starting job. Gradually I became part of the Bryant philosophy of football. His quarterbacks were to always be the boss inside the huddle . . . the coach on the field . . . literally the focus of Kentucky offensive football . . . responsible only to him. And, by inference, he kept demanding that we seek answers within ourselves: Is that what we wanted? Is that what we'd set our sights on?

"We received special training in small meetings with the other quarterbacks through the use of a little game which was played daily in his office. Coach Bryant would pose a situation facing the quarterback and tell us the conditions that would have to be considered . . . where the ball was . . . the down, yards to be gained . . . the weather, wind . . . the type of defense and so on. Then he would ask one of us to call the play while another acted as referee.

"In essence, Coach Bryant became the opposition. More importantly though, in this performance he utilized the combined talents of Bryant the coach, Bryant the teacher, Bryant the psychologist and Bryant the salesman.

"A prime example of this unique training developed during these daily sessions of mental warfare occurred in a game with Georgia Tech. We were ahead, 7–6, the ball on our own 40-yard line and facing a fourth-and-one situation. The fans were screaming, my teammates on the sideline were waving to 'go for it' and finally Bryant gave his consent.

"Sending in the play to be used, Coach used Tom Fillion, a reserve fullback. When Fillion entered the huddle I asked, 'Did he tell you anything?'

"Tom said, 'No.'

"Again, I asked, 'Are you *sure?* Didn't he call any particular play?'

"Once more Tom said, 'No!'

"My palms suddenly felt sweaty. I was on my own. I called my own play—an off-tackle slant. But Fillion, the ball-carrier, slipped on the rain-muddied surface and the drive was stopped. Years later I asked Bryant, 'Why didn't you send in a play at that crucial spot?' He looked at me with a small, odd smile and replied that the play which I called at the line of scrimmage was the play he sent to the huddle with Tom Fillion. Evidently in the stress of the moment Tom had forgotten, and we both laughed. However, it all relates to the little game which we played daily. It taught us to think—and it kept us thinking.

"After awhile, Coach Bryant begins to infect you with another quality asset, *confidence.* Against North Texas State in my junior year, I received an injury to my groin and underwent an operation to relieve the pressure from internal bleeding. The next game scheduled was Louisiana State and at mid-week, Bryant came to me in the hospital with a whole new offense to be used against LSU, and tossed it on the bed.

" 'Learn them,' he growled. 'This is the game plan.'

"I could hardly believe it. I couldn't walk. I could barely move, and Bryant was telling me that he expected me to be the quarterback out there against LSU. He wasn't putting it in words but he was telling me that he believes you can do anything your mind desires.

"I got out of the hospital on Friday morning. I did some walking, gingerly, but that was all. And Coach told me I was to *play* the next evening (it was a night game) . . .

"On Saturday night he got me aside just before we went out for the pre-game warm-up, and said: 'Bigness is in the heart, Babe.'

"He told me that by using my mind and letting the heart do its job I could overcome my terrible soreness. Maybe so, but for one fleeting moment I wished I was back in Rochester, Pennsylvania, working in a steel mill where I simply could have gone on sick leave. But the feeling passed swiftly. You just don't quit on Coach Bryant.

"Besides, I was sort of fascinated by the game plan he'd established, with me in mind. Something we'd never done. A spread formation similar to the shotgun. I was to be set ten yards behind the center and allowed to drop back even further for additional protection.

"Just before kickoff Coach took my arm and in a low, raspy voice he said: 'Get in there and start throwing, and throw until I tell you to stop.'

"On our first drive we had the ball for seventeen plays—every one of them a pass. I was hurting with every step I took—hurting bad—but I kept throwing, even on fourth down, and we moved the length of the field. By the time the drive was over, LSU's big, ol' linemen were worn out trying to get near me because they had a 15-yard sprint on every play. Our offensive line was doing a great job of protecting me."

Parilli's face cracked a small grin which worked its way into a reminiscing chuckle. "Of course, before the game in the locker room they'd been issued a warning. Pat James, one of our toughest, said he'd personally maim any guy who let his man lay a hand on me. When Pat James talked like that you listened.

"So, by halftime, when I came to the sidelines with a 14–0 lead, my uniform was still fresh and unspotted. I think I could have played that game wearing a tuxedo. I received such fantastic protection that nobody touched me all day."

Suddenly Babe Parilli halted in mid-thought as another one tumbled in on his consciousness. "Let me tell you something," he said slowly. "To the end of my days I'll never believe that Bryant ever had any intention of jeopardizing my physical welfare that day. I have a hunch he consulted the team physician to see if the doc would flatly rule me out. And when the doc didn't— he probably said play it by ear—ol' Coach just went his psychological route and made *his* confidence *my* confidence. The man was a master at that . . ."

He fingered a playbook on his desk without looking at it. "In so many ways," he went on, "I can still recall those early days when they were converting me from halfback to a T-quarterback. Heck, my high school hadn't even used the T, let alone me being the quarterback, but Bryant must have seen *something* in me that I didn't know I had. I could throw the ball very well, as far as mechanics were concerned, but the other stuff, like taking the snap and dropping back, were giving me trouble.

"It was getting to me and making me have doubts. Coach Bryant would talk to me patiently and then one day he must have read my own question in my face, and he read that silent question and just said, quietly: 'Yes, you can.' From that moment on I began to shed my insecurity.

"But Lord, how we worked. There were no restrictions in those days on the number of practice sessions and in spring drills we were out there anywhere from 13 to 15 weeks. Bryant would scrimmage us three times a week and it took its toll. I don't think any coach could ever get kids to do that today. But we didn't know any better. Bryant was preparing us for war and it paid off for us. I think there were close to 100 freshmen who came in my first year. I'd hate to tell you how many of us survived until our senior year—maybe a dozen—but, God, the marvelous feeling we had, those who went the route.

"There were times I didn't think I would. I remember a big game where we were on the one-yard line, first down, with seconds to go in the half. We wanted that touchdown and we were going to score on a dive play. We didn't make it and before we could line up again the clock ran out. I looked up and saw Bryant running toward me. He was coming hard. I took off for the dressing room and he finally caught up with me, screaming his head off, demanding to know why I hadn't stopped the clock by tossing the ball out of bounds and really get better set for the play, or maybe call two of them in the huddle.

"I knew what my basic mistake had been. Our big left tackle, Lloyd McDermott had come to me in the huddle and asked: 'Babe, do you want me to go to the other side?' What he meant was to go to unbalanced right, and run the dive play over the two big tackles.

"I said: 'No, we won't have to.' A mistake. I should have put him over there and we'd have gotten in.

"Eventually, it cost us the game. Later I admitted to Bryant that I'd screwed up twice—by not taking McDermott's advice and by not killing the clock. He just frowned, grunted and gave me a little poke in the ribs. 'Don't worry—you'll never do it again,' he said. It wasn't a warning. He was just showing confidence in me.

"Speaking of his frown," Babe continued, "so many of us picked up things from him that stayed with us. After I got into professional football I noticed—in fact, people told me—that I was developing a perpetual frown as a reaction to just about everything. You take football and life very seriously once you've been exposed to Coach Bryant.

"Billy Neighbors, the great Alabama lineman, who later played professional football with me in Boston, told me he was always petrified that he'd be late for a team meeting. That came from life with Bryant. He never got over it."

Silence for a moment. It was a good idea to let the silence run, while he mentally dug into the past.

"The man was like a father to us. It was a low budget operation in those days at Kentucky. We had three old football dorm houses that were just terrible. Tiny rooms, hand-me-down furniture. Two bunks in each room. I think we had our sheets changed once a month. But it made us a close-knit group. A lot of guys came in from West Virginia or Pennsylvania coal and steel towns and believe me, they weren't raised according to the book of etiquette. Good kids, though. Coach Bryant smoothed off a lot of rough edges. Taught 'em table manners and politeness in dealing with people. Some of 'em came without a single suit of clothes. Bryant was the first coach in our conference to issue nice travel blazers to his kids. They loved it.

"Oh, sure, we cut up a lot, and Bryant expected it, but he let us know there were limits. He wouldn't allow us to have cars on campus—said it would take our minds off football—but we all managed to get some kind of old hunk of junk to drive around and Bryant looked the other way. My roommate, John Netoskie, gave up six Florida game tickets on the 50-yard line for a beat-up 1934 Plymouth. John Griggs, our center, latched onto an abandoned 20-year-old hearse and somehow put it into running condition. We kept those junkers hidden, but they got worse and worse and finally Coach stormed in and said, 'I want that junk yard cleared out!' Well, he knew we'd just stash them away somewhere else, but he'd made a point that anything we put together on wheels shouldn't be a menace to society, because he didn't try to find our parking yard again. We did upgrade the junkers, though.

"I never had one of my own. If I ever got a date, the team doctor used to lend me his Ford. That wasn't very often, though, because we were afraid to get dates. Bryant didn't like it. He didn't want you messing around much. There were only two things you were supposed to have on your mind: football and a decent grade in the classroom. Coach Bryant insisted on us having at least a C average, and anyone who had anything from a C on down had a tutor arbitrarily assigned to him by Bryant. He had a card out on every one of your classes and the prof would mark it every two weeks, either satisfactory or unsatisfactory, and Coach would assign tutors on that basis. There was no escaping his eye on you."

Babe Parilli looked away for an instant, then back at his visitor. "For which an awful lot of Bryant's boys are always going to be grateful."

# 10

# A Lesson Learned

> *"Bryant could watch the seven offensive linemen execute on one play during a drill and, as though he had a photographic mind, he could tell each of the seven what he had done wrong. And when he had you dead to rights you just had to develop confidence in the man's leadership."*
>
> —Steve Meilinger

At 6–2 and 228 pounds, Steve Meilinger still looks as though he could play tight end for Kentucky, where he was twice an All America in 1952–53. At a two-hour breakfast in the Campbell House Hotel in Lexington, Kentucky, his huge hands disposed of gargantuan portions of pancakes, bacon and eggs, toast and coffee.

His full face, just slightly craggy, beamed above a white sweater that exposed a colorful tan and green shirt. It was offduty dress for a Chief Deputy United States Marshal. Previously he had been an FBI Special Agent. And before that he'd played professional football for the Green Bay Packers and Washington Redskins.

Meilinger, self-professed as "one of Bear's boys," has two strong attachments—football as played under Paul Bryant, and law enforcement—but he was quick to reveal that on a limited time schedule it would be football that would be the conversational priority at this breakfast table.

*       *       *

"There's no doubt of it," said Steve Meilinger, "when I went to the University of Kentucky, Coach Bryant was my father away-from-home. And, lordy, did I ever need him. Because you're talkin', now to a guy who was tossed out of high school for a year after I was a freshman. Oh, I wasn't a hard-core hoodlum, or anything like that, back in my small home in eastern Pennsylvania, but let's just say I broke too many rules, disciplinary *and* academic.

"They let me back in but it cost me my senior year of football eligibility and I never officially finished high school there. I could have gone down the drain if I'd made the wrong move at that time. There were some southern colleges who said they'd overlook the fact that I hadn't finished that fourth year and they'd arrange for me to get a football scholarship anyway.

"But before I could get myself trapped in a bad scene like that, a friend came along and arranged a one-year scholarship for me with a military academy in Virginia where I could play football one more year. I accepted and that's where I attracted the attention of 40 or 50 big-time colleges. They swarmed all over me in the usual way—Notre Dame, West Point, the Big Ten schools, the Southeastern Conference schools—and I didn't know which way was up. Suddenly—God knows how or why—I found myself promising to go to the University of Pennsylvania. That was before the formal Ivy League was started, and Penn recruited right along with the big powers and with the same tactics.

"But I lived just 50 miles or so from the Penn campus and I was just wise enough to realize that I'd be home every weekend during the off-season, and there were home town distractions that could be disastrous for me. Still, I was actually stencilling my name on a foot locker in late July, ready to ship it on to Pennsylvania, when a car pulls up one day with two assistant coaches from Kentucky—Ermal Allen and Carney Laslie.

"They told me how much Coach Bryant wanted me down in Lexington. When Carney wound up staying in town for two weeks, visiting me day and night. I got the idea that Coach Bryant wouldn't let him return without me. Laslie was eating my mother's good, German cooking every night and she began to think he was part of the family. Then, after some phone calls from Bryant himself, I was dumb enough to do as Bryant and Carney Laslie suggested. Which was to take a trip down to Lexington with Laslie and then visit a big farm near Paris, Kentucky. I didn't know why in hell I was to visit this farm, but it was a beautiful showplace, and the owner treated me like I was a royal guest. What they did was practically kidnap me for two weeks, hiding me out there, away from the other schools until the term started . . ."

Meilinger paused for breath as he raked over the elements of the scene. "But what happened is, some other school got to my mother and pried loose from her where I was staying. But she tipped off Bryant and they moved me from the farm to another big home out in the country. All the while, Bryant and his assistants were assuring me they were doing the best thing for me, and I'd look into those pale blue eyes of Bryant's and I'd buy it all the way.

"So, finally, when school started, they brought me out of hiding. I'd already signed a Southeastern Conference letter-of-intent but they were still scared some other conference would sweet talk me away.

"I've never told anyone, publicly, what that first year was like, so this is a first. There was no limit on scholarships in those days so we had close to 110 freshmen at Kentucky. We'd all been told we'd have to work hard but we figured that was the usual thing to be told in college. Oh, boy! After the second day of practice you could hear cars around midnight pulling away from the dorm as guys started leaving. Guys would pack and just sneak off. Didn't even bother saying goodbye to the coaches. Of course, Coach Bryant wouldn't even have been interested in saying goodbye to quitters, and they sensed it.

"When I originally saw those 110 freshman I told myself I had very little chance to make it. But after two weeks my roommate, Jim Proffitt, and I would watch those guys making off with their suitcases and we knew the longer we stayed the better our chances would be. We began to be sort of infected with Coach

Bryant's philosophy that if you pay a big enough price you're going to get the more valuable merchandise in the results. For three years Proffitt played the end opposite me.

"My freshman year was uneventful aside from the fact that I stuck it out and learned a few things, although some of the coaches, I was told, were sort of licking their chops waiting for me to become a full-grown sophomore and a starter. The word was that I had *promise*.

"It took some doing to deliver that *promise*. In the first place, in pre-season practice before my sophomore year, Bryant took us over to a place called Millersburg, or something like that, which we learned to refer to as 'Hell Hollow.'

"We began our day at 6 A.M., without breakfast, just a pint or so of orange juice in the training room. Then we'd work out in shorts, just running sprints and drills. After an hour and a half of that we'd have breakfast. Then an hour of meetings, then an early lunch, another meeting and then practice for three hours in full pads. It was dreadfully hot in early September. We'd practice in that damn hollow and look up on the top of the hill where the breeze was strong enough to bend the trees half over, but there wasn't a breath of air down on the field.

"Wheee-ew!" Meilinger's reflective whistle provided another accent. "We'd always close practice with 50-yard sprints for the backs. And because I was the fastest lineman, Bryant always made me run with them. The gimmick was that the guy who crossed the finish line first would be allowed to go in first after practice. Turned out I was really the fastest man on the team. I always got to go in first, and I'm not sure how Bryant regarded that. He liked his linemen to work right up to the end of the day and here I was earning the right to be first into the dressing room. But he always would get ticked off because his backs weren't as fast as I was, so he always made them run full 100-yard sprints each day. But *everybody* had to run eighty yards up a hill to the dressing room after practice. When you got there you had to lay on the floor for thirty minutes before you got up enough strength to undress and shower.

"There was nothing to do at night, which is why Bryant picked that Godforsaken spot. There was one general store and a fillin' station in town. Bryant would let us walk into town at night to get a bottle of soda pop or an ice cream cone and then walk back to camp and go to bed. He used to tell us at meetings that some day, in some fourth quarter of a tough ball game, we'd thank him for what we'd been through in training, because the fourth quarter would pay off in a victory. Of course, we had no way of telling, then, how sweet a victory could be. Back in Millersburg we weren't even thinking of victory. We were just thinking of surviving the next day. But, by God, was he ever right.

"Anyway, let me get back to those coaches thinking I had *promise*. Well, I almost didn't *deliver* it because in spring practice before my sophomore season I found out what a guy could expect if Coach Bryant thought he was goofing-off or was a wise-ass. There was this practice day when maybe I was a bit of both. I'd told an assistant coach this was worse than prison. So the assistant coach told me to go off and just sit in the middle of the field by myself. There I sat for a half hour. When practice was over I got up and sauntered toward the dressing room. I took a quick shower and was ready to leave when a manager or somebody told me Coach Bryant wanted to see me. I walked into his office. He'd taken his shower and was just knotting his tie, standing in front of the mirror behind his desk. Without turning around he growled: 'We recruited you as a football player and not a goof-off trouble-maker.' And then in one motion he swung a forearm that knocked me clean across the room against a wall. I sagged down into a chair, like in a movie scene. No director could have staged it any better or smoother.

"I never moved from that chair. I was a big, tough kid but I knew if I twitched a muscle at him he'd be all over me in a moment. Then I heard that deep gravelly voice of his saying, very calm like: 'Get your ass out of here, turn in your suit and be out of this building in five minutes and off this campus by tonight. We don't want you around here any more.' "

Steve Meilinger shook his head and buttered a piece of toast. "Wow, I can still see me picking myself up outa that chair and heading down the hall. My head was spinning and I was trying to think of where I could transfer to. I got about forty feet when someone behind me called me. It was an assistant coach. Carl Simms. 'Come back here,' he was saying, 'The Man wants to see you again.'

"So I went back into his office. He was sitting behind his desk with his big hands folded on a can of film. 'I'm gonna give you one more chance,' he said. 'But if you screw up one more time on that practice field, if I just *point* towards the gate, you better be gone because I'll be right on your heels kicking your butt every step you take!'

"Now, I'll tell you, that man knew *exactly* how hard to knock me across that room . . . He knew *exactly* how to tell me I was through . . . And he knew *exactly* how much I would believe in him from then on.

"After that, I never questioned his methods, his attitudes or the way he handled me—or any other player. I think I could've been a helluva problem for another coach at another school and I was lucky enough to sense I should let Coach Bryant call the shots—right or wrong."

He grinned. "Hell, there was one time when he was *absolutely* wrong but I let him get away with it. Maybe because he did it with such a sense of humor.

"They'd built a tower alongside the practice field and for some strange reason, even after he'd ordered it built, he hated it. That wasn't the case by the time he'd mellowed at Alabama, where he uses the thing constantly. But at Kentucky he watched everything like a hawk from that tower but loved every excuse to come down from it. We were holding a long session of those one-on-one drills which we hated because Bryant made them into miniature wars and you didn't dare lose, so you can imagine what we put into them.

"Well, one of our varsity guys, Chip Carpenter, I think, had missed a couple blocks in succession and suddenly Bryant's hat comes sailing down from the tower and he's roaring after it, almost beating it down. That hat coming down was always a signal for us. He'd toss it and start running across the field toward whoever had sinned, and everyone would chant, softly, *Toot-Toot*, here comes the train.' Every time Bryant would get wound up for a charge we'd call him, *Toot-Toot*.

"So, there I was, ready to take my turn on one-on-one blocking against some big varsity tackle and Coach Bryant is under a full head of steam, with everybody softly chanting, *Toot-Toot,* which he never seemed to hear, by the way—but instead of zeroing in on Chip Carpenter who he'd caught dogging it, ol' Bear has ripped off one of his shoes and next thing I know he's busting me across the ass with it and I go flying about five yards off. I looked up at him and hollered: 'What'd I do?'

"He stands there with his hands on his hips, glaring at me, 'I've been watching you the last two minutes and haven't seen you make a decent block yet!'

"One of the assistant coaches is standing there giggling. 'That isn't true, is it, Coach?' I plead with the assistant.

" 'Don't go looking for mercy with anybody else,' Bryant snapped. 'You're dealin' with *me*. Now, get in there and put a real block on your man.'

"So I show them a helluva block and the assistant goes over to Coach Bryant and I hear him saying: 'That wasn't Meilinger who'd been missing his blocks, that was Chip Carpenter. You gave the shoe to the wrong guy.'

"Bryant just mumbled: 'Goddamn, I don't care. He needed it, anyway.'

"The man had powers of observation that were uncanny," Meilinger continued. "His assistants were responsible for drills for various groups: ends, halfbacks, defensive backs, linebackers and the others. Bryant would go from drill to drill. He could stand there and watch what was happening with offensive blocking drills, and maybe right nearby was a coach taking the running backs through formations, or whatever. Heck, Bryant could watch seven men do their stuff on offensive line play and as though he had a photographic mind he could tell each of the seven what he had done wrong on a single play.

"He'd put an arm around an end and say: 'If you'd taken that step to the outside, then fake and come back in, you'd probably have had no problem with putting your block on the linebacker.'

Then he'd make his point with the center, and go down the whole line. A man may not be born a football coach, but that kind of insight maybe *has* to be born in you. I know I couldn't do it, nor could most football players. To just stand there and in one look drink in everything like that. When he has you dead to rights like that you just had to develop confidence in the man as a teacher and leader."

I had to agree, and said: "He's still like that—maybe even more so. He stands up there on that tower at Alabama watching every drill that goes on and uses a tape recorder to remind him of things no one would ever dream he was observing. On a Thursday, he'll come in to a staff meeting and say: 'I was noticing the other day that quarterback so-and-so was not coming out from the center with the right rhythm and was taking too big a step backward.' And one of the coaches will say they've been working on it, and Bryant will grunt sarcastically and say: 'Yeah, I know. That was Monday and he's still doing it . . .' "

Meilinger's memory reached into another cranny of recall.

"Another thing, the way he accepted final responsibility for everything. Like during my junior year, I believe it was, when we lost three or four in a row—the only time that ever happened to him at Kentucky. He called the team into a meeting and said: 'Okay, you're not this town's team any more, or the university's team, or the state's team—YOU'RE MY TEAM, NOW. You've been taking the heat and the blame for those losses, but I'm really the one who got beat, not you. It was my coaching, not your playing, which cost us those games. So, now you're my team. The people in town don't want you any more.'

"Boy, did that ever choke us up.

"But that was Coach Bryant's sincere philosophy. He actually believed in that, and he made us believe it, too, and it took a big load off our shoulders in a difficult re-building year. And at practice during those weeks there was no frenzy or cursing or stuff like that. No additional work. Bryant was acknowledging things that couldn't be helped and was assuming all the responsibility. He'd wander around, pat us on the back for a good block during a drill and tell us, 'way to go, son; that's the way we'll hit 'em this week.' If you don't think kids re-act to an approach like that, you don't know young college football players, because, believe me, there are a lot of coaches who carry a string of defeats on their faces and in their whole outward attitude, and there's no lookin' up."

Steve Meilinger snapped his fingers. "Oh, yeah—before I forget. He was a master of getting you to achieve something you'd never dreamed you could do—if he needed it from you. It was after a third straight loss, just before we were going down to play Miami of Florida, and I got a message Monday afternoon that I was to attend a meeting. So I get there and I see it's a meeting Coach Bryant and an assistant are having with the quarterbacks. I hadn't the foggiest idea why he wanted me to sit in, but after a few minutes of X-ing and O-ing on the blackboard he turns to me suddenly and says: 'Steve, I want you to start learning these plays.' I told him that as an offensive end I already knew the plays, but he shook his head and said: 'No, I want you to learn 'em as a quarterback.' It was the only time in my association with Coach Bryant that I thought he'd come unhinged from his senses and I sat there sort of numb, just listening.

"A few minutes later Bryant ended the meeting, and as we walked out he put an arm around my shoulder and starts talking to me like a Daddy to a son.

" 'Steve, I know you've never played quarterback in all your life and that you're a heckuva offensive end, but I need you somethin' special. Our quarterbacks are small and we all know they can't run it worth a lick. In our Split-T, our quarterback has to run. You know that, I know that, the opposition knows that. Now, you're big and you're faster'n any back we have. All you have to do is learn some ball-handlin' and handin' off and I think we can win us some games—if you can cut it in practice this week.'

"I remember him takin' a long pause and me not saying *any-thing,* and then he adds: 'And I think you can do it, son, or I wouldn't be askin' it of you.' Then he squeezes my shoulder and I tell you if he'd have told me to go out and knock over the Chinese Wall with my bare hands I'd have done it.

"So all week I practiced at quarterback, and we didn't even bother trying a pass because I wasn't much at throwin' that thing. I was just going to hand off, do some runnin' myself and block once in a while, which I could do better'n anyone else, by the way.

"Hell, there were guys on the defensive unit, off practicing at their end of the field, who didn't know a thing about the switch until a couple days later. Bryant took the offensive unit over to scrimmage against the defensive starters. He had Herbie Hunt, our usual quarterback, running things while we stood watching with his arm around my shoulder. He'd point out how Herbie should have faked to a halfback and then cut into a hole, or how he shouldn't have run but pitched off. From that vantage point I started to make some sense of what I had to do. Then Coach Bryant told me to get in there and do it and the defensive guys stood up and stared open-mouthed. So we practiced like that for two days. Half the guys thought it was hilarious and I think the other half thought we should just cancel the game with Miami and spend the night drinking beer."

Steve Meilinger's big frame shook gently as he chuckled. "We went down to Miami and the game was on Halloween night. I'll never forget it. People who knew about it, including some of the press, said Coach Bryant ought to put on a goblin suit and go play with the ghosts because someone had obviously put the voodoo on him. I think for me they had nothing but pity.

"Bryant put me in there and said, 'Just run the goddamn ball,' and after five or six plays I got over the idea that this was Bryant's idea of trick-or-treat and we began ramming that ball right down their throats and it worked, by God, it worked. I made that Split-T work. My offense scored three times and Herbie Hunt came in once and tossed a touchdown pass just to make it a real Halloween. I think we beat 'em, 32–0, and the press described Coach Bryant as a Halloween genius.

"The rest of the year I alternated at offensive end and quarterback and even played some halfback and the press hailed Bryant as a rare molder of talent, and I made All America. At end.

"As I recall it though, I probably paid the stiffest price that any All America ever paid for it. Oh, don't misunderstand—because it was just one of those oversights Coach Bryant could get involved in because of his intensity. Sometimes he'd just forget what was happening, as he did in our famous 20-minute full-speed drills. First, I'd put in twenty minutes of continual high speed drills at offensive end, blocking or running pass patterns. Not a second of rest between plays.

"Then, because Bryant wanted me to work at halfback, too. I'd go twenty minutes of intensive running plays. Then he would work me into the quarterback drills, running and blocking. Remember, whatever your position was, there'd be a twenty minute high-speed drill every day. Well, hell, Coach Bryant must have forgot I was working three different spots and after a few days I was really being sapped and losing weight and he kept asking what the hell was wrong with me because my tail was dragging, and I didn't have the courage to tell him.

"Finally, one day I went over to the team physician. I told him I couldn't say anything to Coach about it, but I was running sixty-minute high speed drills every day, to everybody else's twenty, and any day now I was gonna collapse.

"Well, Dr. Angelucci was sure shook up and scurried right over to Coach to tell him. Bryant was startled. 'Good gracious,' he said, 'I never realized. We'll have to put a stop to that.'

"If I hadn't gone over to Doc, I think Coach Bryant would have lost me as a player because he was so intent on his drills he just didn't stop to think he had me alternating at three positions.

"Anyway, the Doc came over to me and gave me the keys to his car. 'Take a friend into town and get some quick beers into you,' he said. 'It'll work wonders as a revival remedy. But don't tell Coach.' Hell, if I know Doc, and if I know Bryant it was probably Bryant's idea, though he didn't dare let on."

Meilinger's visitor nodded understandingly and mentioned that for all of Paul Bryant's reputation as a very physical and demanding coach, there were former Bryant players and assistant coaches all round the country who swore he could be a big pussy cat.

"Oh, sure," Meilinger said., "He had his rules and he knew when it was okay for some of those rules to be broken. I recall dating a girl in Lexington whose father would lend us his country club card for an occasional Saturday night after a tough game. The two of us would be sitting there sipping a bourbon and Coke when Bryant would walk in. He'd pick up my glass, sniff it and say: 'I thought so, but have a good time.'

"Maybe at practice the following Monday or Tuesday, if you weren't looking too good he might say something about turning off your country club privileges and you'd get the idea and put out an extra good lick on the next few plays.

"On the night before a game, he wanted us to be in at 9 or 9:30 P.M. at the latest, and often he'd come by and just sit around in your room for a few minutes, just making warm, pleasant conversation, almost like tucking you in. He calmed a lot of butterflies in your stomach that way—especially for the younger guys.

"Before a game he'd often give us a prep talk that wasn't all frenzy and hysterical, stuff like that, but he had a way of soothing you, turning on your confidence and MAKING YOU BELIEVE HE WAS GONNA BE RIGHT WITH YOU ON EVERY BLOCK OR TACKLE YOU'D BE MAKING. He was uncanny, that way, but it was so human, so offbeat from what he'd been putting you through all week in practice that you suddenly knew he cared more about you than he did himself. I know it soothed me, but it also made me so nervous, wanting to live up to him, that I'd practically have tears in my eyes when I tore out there onto the field. I think it affected a lot of guys the same way."

Steve Meilinger hestiated. "Yeah, he was like a Daddy to us. We knew that although one of his hands could belt us across the chops, the other was always there to comfort us and to lead us. And oh, man, the mileage he could get out of that . . ."

# 11

# Bob Gain

> "*I'd called Bear Bryant down, right to his face in front of the other guys. They say he looked like he was gonna tear me apart, and I was daring him. If he makes a step toward me I'm gonna protect myself and to hell with the rest of my football career at Kentucky . . .*"
>
> —Bob Gain

Bob Gain is an unusual—and important—chapter in this chronicle because he represents a "minority opinion" on Paul "Bear" Bryant. He is one of the most sincere and forthright men I've ever met and it was a pleasurable experience talking to him at great length in the huge den of his lovely home in Willoughby, Ohio, suburb of Cleveland, hard by the shore of Lake Erie.

After fixing a couple of drinks, he deposited himself in a big, easy chair that barely accomodated his bulk. He wore blue jeans, a cordoroy shirt and blue socks. No shoes. He was a picture of relaxed comfort and his deep voice seemed compatible with his image, his background, and the fact that he was very successfully into the heavy machinery business.

Gain, the greatest lineman in Kentucky football history, was a two-time All America tackle and later an All-Pro tackle with the Cleveland Browns. He was one of Paul Bryant's true superstars. He ran a hand through his thinning, gray-black hair and his strong features came alight as he launched into a subject that was very meaningful to him: the early Paul "Bear" Bryant.

"Let me be honest right out front," Bob Gain was saying. "I'm not one of those guys who spends the rest of his life worshipping Coach Bryant. I know a lot of guys do, and that's fine with me because they have their reasons and they're entitled to them. Coach and I had our moments—the good ones and the bad—and I still remember them. And let me be quick to say I respected Bryant a ton. He had a job to do—he decided how he'd do it—and he *did* it, dammit, and was fair about it, and for that I give him lots of points. I just didn't see eye-to-eye with some of his methods and philosophy, if you want the fancy word, but I'll never regret that I was exposed to him because there's no way a guy couldn't firm-up under Paul Bryant and learn something about life, too."

Huge Bob Gain wasn't being belligerent or defensive about it as he launched into his subject and his inherent honesty shone right through. "Starting at the beginning, I enrolled at Kentucky in the Summer of 1947. It was a wild time to be playing big-time college football because of the situation that existed right after World War II, which I'll get to in a minute. There were a lot of schools trying to recruit me. I couldn't even count the offers, but I visited Notre Dame, Pitt, North Carolina State— some place just about every weekend. When Kentucky got on me, Bryant came over to see me after Carney Laslie, his assistant, had broken the ice.

"Bryant had no reputation of any kind, then. He'd just been a head coach for all of five months at Maryland when he took the Kentucky job. He didn't really amount to a hill of beans to me when he came around to recruit me. But there was something about him, a kind of low-key excitement that made me want to play for him. All the others made me feel *wanted,* if you know what I mean, but this young guy was sort of challenging me, too, and I guess I fell for it."

Gain laughed, and maybe there was a bit of cynicism in it, but there was undeniable humor in is reflection. "He was green and inexperienced and could do a lot of things he couldn't do later. Physically, I mean, and I guess we were all intrigued with the way he could get in there throwing a block, mixing it up with somebody to show how it was done. Wow! Was he ever physical! But under the circumstances it was definitely to his advantage.

"You see we had a tremendous number of guys on the squad. Not only were there a lot of freshmen but there were close to two hundred G.I. veterans returning from military service, all of them on the G.I. Bill to fall back on if they couldn't make it on a football scholarship. The government picked up the tab for all their tuition and books and a hefty allowance—at that time about $200 or $300 a month for room and board. So Coach figured any of these ex-G.I.'s who could make the grade would be saving the university a whole lot of money on scholarships, but he wasn't about to take one of them just because of that, and before he got through with them a lot of them figured it'd been a whole lot easier back in the tank corps or the infantry.

"A lot of them were too far out of shape, sportswise, to cut the mustard again. Some had lost their competitiveness and desire, even those who'd once been good ball players. Many were married and got flak from their wives. And many were 24–25–26-years-old and had previously played college ball or service ball and were by then much bigger'n us freshmen but Coach Bryant mixed us all together and put us through the mill with the same rules.

"That was one, helluva month of August, I tell you. Bryant was determined to run off anyone who didn't have what it takes. The freshmen were fighting for their lives—and to keep their scholarships—and the older guys who were really good, had no intention of losing a position to a kid and they beat hell outta us. And remember this new coach who was killin' us wasn't much older than some of the guys he was coaching. And for that reason he could never get mellow or buddy-buddy with anybody. He was still going through that formative period when he wanted to prove so bad that he could win, and Kentucky actually became the testing ground for his theories and approach to football.

"So, even when things got back to normal and he began getting normal-aged players again he just never readjusted his thinking.

From what I understand, what he did at a place called Junction, at Texas A&M, he just sorta refined them, know what I mean?"

Gain grunted and paused. "I know there's a line in the Bear's book that he wrote about his life where he says, *'They love me now for all of the things they once hated me for.'* "

Another pause and then a snort. "How about a claim of bullshit from Bob Gain? I know, now, what he was trying to do, and, by God, he pulled it off, but *'love'* him? Listen, he was close to being a genius as a coach because of the way he could organize and recruit and handle most people on a personal level and motivate the hell outa them, but he made some awful mistakes by over-working players. He blew a couple games that way. You learn this when you're growing up in football, from high school to college to pro, and looking back I can see how wrong Bryant was in his desire to separate the men from the boys. He carried it too far."

Suddenly Gain's face relaxed a bit, not in a mellowing posture but perhaps in recognition that there had been, after all, some moments that had been less than almost unendurable hardship— moments that had come close to humor and even high drama.

"Yeah, but it was a lot more fun my senior year because Coach knew what we had—and we knew what we could deliver. It was a matter of getting up for the tough games and holding our mental and physical edge for those we figured to romp. It was really an enjoyable season because I think Bryant was beginning to follow a real schedule of practice and realizing he had to save something for Saturdays. Y'know—don't lose it all on the practice field.

"So we got our timing down better. We really knew what the hell the plays were. But one day Bryant got pissed off about something and jumped me with both feet about missing a play. Now, the Bear was one of those 'even-if-I'm-wrong-don't-correct-me' kind of guys. Well, he gave me that goddamn look and was quivering. Most of the guys standing there were sure he was gonna hit me, but I never took any crap off him, and waited for him to make his move, if he was gonna.

"Now, back in the steel mill areas, when you call a guy a bad name or curse at him there's trouble. But I had a high school coach who'd put a guy off the team for a week for using profanity. But with this bunch at Kentucky, every other word was a curse word. Now, you've got to remember, I'm the only guy on the team playing both ways, and a freshman at that, too, and now Bryant makes a remark to me, saying: 'Dammit, Gain, you're horseshit like the rest of 'em!' And I thought 'screw you, you SOB. These other guys, they're only playing thirty minutes and I'm going both ways and you're gettin' down on *me?*' And most of the other guys, war vets, were three, four years older than me. At age 18, I was hittin' against guys 24 and 25, and that made a helluva difference and they rocked my goddamn brains my first year. At the end of the season I was walking around on my heels like a punch-drunk fighter.

"And so I called Bryant down at practice, right to his face and in front of the other guys. They say he looked at me like he was gonna tear me apart, and I was daring him. If he makes a step towards me I'm gonna protect myself, and to hell with the rest of my football career at Kentucky.

"But he glares at me and takes a different course. He says: 'Who the hell you supposed to get on that play?' So I named the guy I'm supposed to get. Then he starts calling off all eleven players and asks me who they're supposed to block. I knew every assignment of every player. I knew the play backwards and forwards. I called the blocks for the tackles, guards, and center. I know where all four goddamn backs are goin' and who they block. I'm spittin' it all out with a mad-on and I carry it even further. I tell him what the assignments are if the play is reversed or we do an option off it.

"He just stares at me, and says 'shit!' I knew I'd called his bluff. I also knew he'd have a lot more respect for me from then on.

"I said a little while back that Coach Bryant blew a couple of games for us because he over-worked us. Best example was our Orange Bowl game against Santa Clara in 1949. We went down to Cocoa Beach, Florida, for pre-game training, looking forward to having a good time and still win the ball game. To mill town and coal field kids like us, Florida would be a dream world. We flew down but if it'd been up to Bryant he'd have made us run—all the way down from Lexington. I know he wanted us to run back after what happened . . ."

The way Gain said it was proof of an everlasting experience etched deeply into his memory.

"Just a long punt away from us was that gorgeous beach but we weren't allowed to go swimming. 'You don't swim when you're in training,' said Bryant. 'Bad for you.' What was *good* for us was getting up at 5 A.M. and practicing until 7 or 7:30. Then breakfast, an hour break, and back to practice. It was like spring training when Bryant worked a squad with an eye to cutting the guys who couldn't produce. But, hell, we'd just finished a season and were still in good shape.

"We went down to Miami for Christmas dinner and Bryant said we were through with all contact work and would just taper off until New Year's Day. But the next day he blew his cork about us eating so much and ordered us to work it off by scrimmaging. But first he put us through a long series of wind-sprints, 18 or 20 of these 40-yard sprints. I'd have appreciated less approval and a lot less running.

"We went into that game with Santa Clara and were ahead, 7–0 at the half, but we just ran out of gas. In the second half we couldn't have beat Marymount Female Seminary, and Santa Clara won 13–7. I weighed 234 going into the game and 223 coming out. In the locker room, later, Bryant glares at us, all around, and says: 'As far as you seniors are concerned, I'm damned glad you're leavin'. As for you underclassmen, when we get back to Lexington we've got work to do.' It was like the ungrateful SOB had blown the game and was turnin' around to blame *us* for it.

"Paul Bryant was tough to take in those days, but I sure would've like to play for him at Alabama after he'd gotten Kentucky and Texas A&M outa his system. The whole thing at those places, I guess, was simply immaturity and a desire to prove himself. With maybe the wrong tactics.

"I learned something about life in producing what that sonuva-gun Bryant demanded of me. Like I say, he made me play both ways, offense and defense—the only guy who did that on a regular game-by-game basis. I learned that if you have it, you give it, if the goal means anything to you. I later found out it's the same in life. Sure, it'd be easy to say to yourself, 'hell, those other guys aren't coming close to contributing what I am. So why should I bust my tail for their glory?' It'd be easy to let down once in a while because you're tired or sore in every muscle. So, who're you letting down? Those guys aren't performing as you are? Coach Bryant? Kentucky? Hell, no, you're letting down on Bob Gain, who, in a sense, is more important than any of them. Know what I mean?

"There was a demand in his tone that challenged me to not be aware of his meaning.

"I became a starter the last half of my freshman year, playing with those older G.I. veterans. In my sophomore season I started going both ways. Bryant came up to me before the season started and simply said: 'Get your ass in shape. You're doin' double duty for us.' I didn't argue or show resentment. I was too young to know the real score. And for those three years I must have averaged 57–58 minutes a game. Those were long Saturday afternoons.

"Actually, Coach had a practice schedule all written down, but in those early days he never followed it. In my sophomore season he'd just throw the damn thing away and we'd start scrimmaging. He'd get mad at something or someone and he'd have everybody grab a partner and practice head-on tackles for ten minutes. Then it was back to scrimmaging again until after dark, with the lights on. One night we got in at 8:30. Plenty of nights we got in too late to eat because the players' cafeteria people had long since closed for the evening. We had to just scrounge around for liquids. Most of us were just too tired to eat, anyway.

"By the time I was a senior and an All America—I'd also made it as a junior—Coach seemed to be loosening up a bit. After three straight bowl games he was beginning to recognize the wear and tear of his crazy practice sessions. I understand he was tough at Texas A&M, but there's no way he was as rough on them as he was on us." Gain paused. "Except maybe for that wild Junction gig everybody keeps hearing about.

"But in my last two years at Kentucky—even while I'd had that All America fame—I could take just so much of Paul Bryant. One year the Atlanta and Birmingham Quarterback Clubs were going to give me a trophy at their banquets for being the top college lineman. I asked if Bryant was going to be there, too, and they said, 'Yes, sure,' and I told 'em to mail me my trophy because I didn't want to be there with him. Wrong of me, I guess, but I was a young kid and it wasn't until much later that I realized how much of himself Coach Bryant had put into his work and that all along he'd intended for us to share in any glory that might come out of it.

"I think what made me realize more than anything, how physical a coach he actually was, was something a pro great, Harry Gilmer, told me. Gilmer had been an All America quarterback at Alabama and he played professional football many years with the Washington Redskins. In my senior year he said: 'Bob, you're gonna love pro ball.' I asked him why, and he said: 'Hell, you'll last forever up there. We seldom have contact stuff and once the season starts we never scrimmage. You know what college teams do on Fridays—just run through plays and do some mild semi-bumping around just to establish position and timing . . . well, that's what we pros do most of the week.'

"I told him I couldn't believe it, that he was bullshitting me, and it would be all elbows, fists and knees in practice, just like the games. He laughed and said I'd find out. And I did. Professional football practice was kiddie stuff compared to my college days with Bryant. Of course, pro *games,*" he wore a thin grin. "*That* was something else."

Anxiously, I now braced him from a different direction, and caught him by surprise, after a fashion. "Was there ever a time when you felt you ever had the advantage over Coach Bryant— sort of beat him at his own game?"

There was a period of rumination, as Gain clasped his huge hands behind his head and pursed his lips slightly. "Well, now that you mention it . . ." His face broke into a widegrin. "Yeah, yeah, there sure was, and for some of us it made up for everything that had gone before.

"We were 10–0 for the season and figured to wrap up 11–0 against Tennessee in our final game of my senior year. We're playing them at Knoxville and for the first time in the century the thermometer goes down below eight degrees. There's been 18–20 inches of snow Friday night and they had to call out the entire Tennessee student body to come out on Saturday to clear the snow off the tarpaulin and get it off the field.

"We'd come over with our satin pants and summer gear, half T-shirts under our lightweight jerseys and no long stockings. About 10,000 Kentucky fans go to downtown Knoxville on Saturday morning and buy up every sweater and every pair of long-johns in the city. The Tennessee team, of course, was ready with cold-weather stuff but we were unprepared. It's never more than slightly chilly in Knoxville, and for football that's okay—but we go out there on the field and it's murder. We had seven or eight fumbles and our blood wouldn't even circulate in wind. We got beat, 7–0, and there goes our undefeated season. We trooped into the dressing room and Bryant looks glum but not as ornery as he might have been.

" 'It ain't all that bad,' he begins, 'because we're still gonna go to a bowl game. Either the Sugar or Orange. We'll take a vote on it right now. So, all those who want to go to a bowl game raise their hands.'

"Well, everyone is looking at me, it seems because I'm one of the co-captains and my hand stays down. I look at Coach Bryant while maybe three out of 44 players' hands go up—and not very quickly at that. Three yeas and 41 nays for Paul Bryant. He looked like someone had just punched him in the face when he wasn't looking. He couldn't talk. He just stood there, his mouth sagging open.

"I said, 'Coach, why don't you step outside for a couple minutes while we have a team meeting.'

"He nodded and without another word he walked out of the

room, still shaken. I got up on a trunk and said, 'Okay, fellas, we can't quit after a loss like this, robbing us of an undefeated season. We've got to make up for it but let's lay some ground rules. You guys stick by me and I'll put it to the Bear when he comes back in, and that's the way it'll be. Now, everybody in favor playing the number-one team in the country, probably Oklahoma, raise your hands.' "

Bob Gain, sitting in the comfort of his den near Lake Erie, nearly thirty years later, reveled in the recollection. "Yeah, we wanted Oklahoma. If you want to make restitution you do it against the best, not a team that had finished second, fourth or fifth. We were third, then. We wanted Oklahoma or nobody— and we weren't gonna sit still for another Cocoa Beach deal.

"We're gonna practice only once a day. There'd be no crazy, all-out scrimmages. There'd be just one scrimmage at the end of the week. Just enough contact to keep us sharp. We'd be allowed to swim in the ocean. And they'd have to fly us all home for the holidays for three days off at Christmas and then back down to Florida or wherever we'd be training.

"There were a couple other things I suggested, and all the guys were staring at me, their mouths open, and then they were all grinning at me and telling me, okay, you're the leader, go and tell him. So I opened the door and called Bryant back in.

"I told him what we'd decided, and what all the ground rules were to be. Nothing like what it had been when we went down to play Santa Clara. We told him we'd go south to either the Orange Bowl, Sugar Bowl or Cotton Bowl—wherever Oklahoma was.

"He was looking at me like I'd lost my mind and that we were nuts if we thought we could tell him how to run his show. But suddenly he knew we could because we had 22 or 23 seniors who were his key guys and there was nothing he could threaten us with for the future. Finally he got his voice back and said, 'But what if I can't get Oklahoma?' I told him, that's it—then we don't play anybody. That was it.

" 'That's it?' he echoed.

"I nodded. 'That's it . . . Now, we'll take a vote.' And we did, right in front of him, and forty-four hands went up.

"Bear said to give him ten minutes to make a couple of phone calls. He left, and we laid around still in our sweaty uniforms until he came back. He stood there a minute. Ol' Bear was gonna show us he had a sense of drama, too.

" 'Well, we got Oklahoma,' he said finally, 'in the Sugar Bowl.'

"We let out a cheer that rocked the place. It was as if we'd never just played Tennessee in that arctic stadium and lost our undefeated season.

"Well, Bryant went along with exactly the things we demanded and we had us some fun in New Orleans and didn't leave our game on the practice field. We worked out lightly but Coach did something he'd never done before. He had us watching Oklahoma films until we knew every second of all the game films we watched. And he had a reason for it that just wasn't tactical.

"That was a great Oklahoma team, with 31 straight wins, the longest in the nation at the time, but they had some guys who weren't exactly the most sportsmanlike in the world. In fact what they were was plain dirty, no names mentioned. We looked at this one game where they were playing Nebraska, who had a great tailback who could run and pass. We're watching the film and we see this Nebraska kid go down, and while he's sprawled with an arm stretched out, and an Oklahoma defensive end, I believe he was, walks over and steps on his hand and pivots on it with his cleats. The Nebraska kid jumps up and had to be restrained from going at the Oklahoma sonuvabitch.

"So, we notice this Okie bastard does anything. Elbows, knees, throws a little secret punch, steps on people and maybe a little biting in a pile-up for all we know. We do a whole catalogue of complaints on three or four of their guys and Bryant notices the fever we're workin' up as we cry out, 'See that! See what he did? Run that film back again!' We had things down to such perfection that we could tell when one of those Okies was gonna wind up and toss a punch and under what conditions of the game. We decided we'd all go after this one particular guy.

"So the day before we leave for New Orleans, Coach Bryant calls in all the seniors and says: 'I'm gonna tell you guys something. I know what's goin' on, but we're not goin' down there to have a brawl. We're goin' down to play a football game. Now, whatever you guys want to do within the rules, you have my blessings, if you get what I mean. You want to knock them into the fifth row, go ahead. You want to ring their bell, go ahead.' So, by the time we were ready to take the field on New Year's Day ol' Bear knew we weren't gonna take any shit from any Oklahoma player, and that we didn't consider them God and His Disciples who couldn't do any wrong. Sure, they were the perennial champs and, some said, the greatest team ever to pull on a uniform, with some of the toughest bastards ever seen, but we meant to stick it to 'em.

"The whole expedition was just as we laid it out for Bear. We took it easy, flew home for Christmas as we demanded, scrimmaged only once each of the two weeks we were in New Orleans and went into the game multi-motivated. We had to redeem that single loss to Tennessee. We wanted to knock off the number-one team. We wanted to prove to Coach Bryant that we could win our way where it would have been doubtful his way . . . And by now, there were a lot of guys who, deep down, wanted to win it for Bryant, too, and I could see that . . ."

A pause, a sigh, and a grin. "Well, we beat hell outa Oklahoma that day, 13–7, and the score doesn't reflect how we handled them.

"That was the highlight of my college career—and probably the high point of Kentucky football, to this day. We were crazy happy, and so was Bryant. Hell, we even gave him the game ball because he did a beautiful job of preparing us in our game plan. He said he was going to hang it right up in the middle of Kentucky Coliseum, high above the basketball floor. He meant to rub it in to Adolph Rupp's nose because Rupp thought the whole university was founded on Kentucky basketball success. Hell, Adolf even told me once that if it weren't for Kentucky basketball we wouldn't have a university and 'don't you ever forget that, son. We support you, we pay for you.' At one time, maybe, but Kentucky football under Bryant was beginning to pull more than its own weight. But I could tell, even then, that Coach knew he'd never get enough credit for football, as long as Rupp held the state of Kentucky in his hand. I knew he'd be leaving. Soon."

But the Kentucky experience—was it all bad? Was it true, as Coach Bryant once said, that you later wrote him a letter, telling him all the hell was worthwhile?

Gain nodded. (Was it grudgingly? No matter.) "Yeah, I think I did. Through no fault of mine, I think he felt hurt over something that happened while I was in the service. I was stationed in Tennessee. I was an officer—and I'd had a run-in with the commander. He wanted me to play for the base football team and I refused. Then he said, dammit, if you don't play you'll have to coach. We never did get along and something happened once—I won't go into it—where he really got down on me just before the big Kentucky-Tennessee game. Coach Bryant had invited me specially to a big party the night before and I wanted to go. We were getting to be pretty good friends by then and I didn't want Coach to think otherwise. But my commander hit me with some chicken-shit duty for the weekend—purposely—and I couldn't go. Soon afterward, I wrote Bear the letter.

"Now look—there were moments when I hated his guts and I know there were times he probably hated me, too, because I defied him. But good coaches don't try to make puppets out of people, and I think Bryant learned that from his experience with some of those Kentucky seniors that year. We were young but we still were entitled to a voice, to speak our minds. I used to get so damned mad because Bryant's assistants in those days never spoke up, and if they did, on rare occasion Bryant would get on 'em.

"Those young assistants would come around, all nervous, and I'd tell 'em, 'Hey, don't worry, we'll win this game,' and they'd say, 'How sure are you?' And I'd tell 'em, 'Goddammit, I'll win it all by myself if I have to.' And I guess there were times when I did win a couple of them by myself, even though I was a lineman. I was always in favor of the coaches letting the guys relax a little. There was no point in getting uptight by Wednesday because by Saturday they're going to have a letdown.

"When I look back at Bear Bryant I recall what a tremendously hard worker he was. He was making his mistakes, then, that he doesn't make now. But even so we believed in him because he saw the results. But methods differ. I played for years under Paul Brown at Cleveland, who never used profanity. He was a master of throwing the needle at you, giving you the barb with a single, short one-liner and get you madder'n a hornet without ever using a curse word. Bryant and his assistants never realized how we resented all the cussing then. If the president of the university ever came out to practice and listened to some of the vocabulary there might have been a quick change. He sure as hell wouldn't have learned anything about the English language.

"Yeah, Paul Bryant was a heckuva coach even then, and he got better as he went along because he learned how to handle young guys. And sincerely, too. I know there are a lot of us old timers who would have loved to play for him in his Alabama days. He made *believers* out of us, then. Today, I guess, he makes believers and *followers* who almost worship him."

# 12

# *The Healer*

*"The man simply made us believe there are lessons
to be learned in football that are difficult to teach
at home, in church or in school . . . How to fight
and fight back when you're being assaulted physically, emotionally or spiritually . . ."*

—Dr. Gaylon McCollough

There's a word that is over used in sports these days and, because
it is, it has become trite and almost useless in terms of proper
definition. The word is *class*. We've heard it, we've read it, and,
if you're like me, the last time you did you may have felt like
putting out a big yawn and muttering: "Yeah, sure . . ."

But every once in a while you encounter the real article and
it smacks you dead center with the instant recognition, and suddenly you have the translation right there, and nobody has to
fill in the background or the gaps or the reasons why, or *anything*.
You know what I mean. You've been there.

I was waiting in his office not only patiently but with a sense
of subdued excitement and, yes, a bit of drama, because this one
I'd heard about in so many ways and from so many people. He
came out, now, about 6–3, with wide shoulders but a narrow
body. Sandy hair, a long strong face and, if it were not for the
three-quarter length, white lab coat you'd see him as impeccably
tailored. His hand was extended graciously, warmly, and he

clasped mine in a way that said he was indeed glad to see me, even though he is a terribly busy man.

He was Dr. Gaylon McCollough, of Birmingham, Alabama, one of the most renowned facial plastic surgeons in the South, if not in the country. He is also a truly great representative and product of college football, and I hope I don't cause any embarrassment by talking about him this way.

He played center for Alabama in 1962–64. It was said of him that he wasn't blessed with a lot of ability but was indeed blessed with an over-abundance of heart, desire and motivation. I'd known him personally for two years, had known his background and had been impressed by the things I'd heard from people who knew him much longer and better than I.

And so I knew the word *class* was comfortable and functional in ascribing it to him.

Class? Why does it deserve to be important I thought? Why do so many young men aspire to this desirable but really seldom achieved characterization?

Class never runs scared. It is sure-footed and confident in the knowledge that you can meet life head-on and handle whatever comes along.

Jacob had it. Esau didn't. Symbolically, we can look to Jacob's wrestling match with the angel. Those who have class have wrestled with their own personal "angel" and won a victory that marks them thereafter.

Class never makes excuses. It takes its lumps and learns from past mistakes.

Class is considerate of others. It knows that good manners is nothing more than a series of petty sacrifices.

Class bespeaks an aristocracy that has nothing to do with ancestors or money. The most affluent blue blood can be totally without class while the descendent of a Welsh miner may ooze class from every pore.

Class never tries to build itself up by tearing others down. Class is already up and need not strive to look better by making others look worse.

Class can "walk with kings and keep it's virtue, and talk with crowds and keep the common touch." Everyone is comfortable with the person who has class—because he is comfortable with himself.

If you have class, you don't need much of anything else. If you don't have it, no matter what else you have—it doesn't make any difference.

Gaylon McCollough, M.D.—who played center for Paul Bryant at Alabama before going to medical school, an ex-athlete, family man, healer of humankind, sensitive citizen, and a Bryant loyalist—has class.

\*         \*         \*

His receptionist had instructions to hold all calls, and Gaylon McCollough was now doing something he enjoyed thoroughly: talking about football.

"When I was in high school," he was saying, "I had a difficult decision to make about college. Where should I go? Where did my professional future lie? Would it be Georgia Tech for architecture or Alabama for medicine? But then I began to be recruited by one of Coach Bryant's assistants—Bob Ford. He explained the Alabama system, its goals, what the program stood for, and the people involved. And particularly, he gave me an insight to the man who'd be the central focus of it all—Coach Bryant.

"And then Ford just casually mentioned: 'If you want to wear a national championship ring when you leave college—then pick Alabama.'

"I suddenly became excited and wrapped up in what he gave me to understand about Coach Bryant—and a national championship. Sure, other schools had tried to woo me with talk about their winning programs but none had mentioned the idea of taking dead aim at a national championship . . ."

Gaylon McCollough smiled and entwined his strong, surgeon's fingers into a sort of steeple. "I was ambitious and goal-oriented," he went on, "and it suddenly hit me that if I could enjoy national championship football under a man like Paul Bryant and still get the kind of education that would gain me admittance to medical school, I'd have the best of two worlds at Alabama. Well, four years later, on graduation day, I had a championship ring on this finger"—he wiggled it—"and an acceptance to medical school back on my desk.

"What a four years," he went on, softly. "Learning how to get along with others—learning how to motivate some people and be motivated by others—having Coach Bryant pound into me the fact that I *could* find time for football and the number of studying hours I'd need to make it to medical school. There were times I doubted it could be done, but I didn't dare let him know I had those doubts. He was only interested in winners.

"And during the early 1960s football was truly king again at Alabama after so many mediocre seasons. The campus came alive with enthusiasm and a whole new sense of success and belonging. And nobody, more than Coach Bryant, made *belonging* a sort of religion among football players.

"It was evident that he'd surrounded himself with terrific assistant coaches and players who shared a common goal—to win together. It wasn't formulized but his methods always left great and meaningful impressions.

"In 1963, my junior year, we had beaten Vanderbilt, 21–6, but undeniably it had been a sloppy effort on our part. On Sunday, word went out that we were all to meet at 5 A.M. on Monday in the players' conference room. Everyone was on time except an assistant coach who was a few minutes late.

"Bryant didn't say anything to him but he started to use him in demonstrations of techniques—Coach and the assistant—while calmly expounding on some of the fundamentals we'd blown against Vanderbilt. Then, finally, Bryant got onto an example of form-blocking, all the while lecturing like a professor in a classroom. Coach Bryant, himself, mind you, was doing most of the demonstrating, himself. Next thing we knew, he'd blocked the assistant right up into the fourth row. A lot of us got the message; practice that afternoon was going to be a barnburner."

McCollough smiled thinly, the memory flooding back to provide satisfaction as well as understanding. "After lunch, at the dorm that day, I noticed that five of my teammates were packing their suitcases and leaving for home. They'd decided that what lay ahead for the rest of the season was not for them.

But that afternoon at practice—would you believe?—Bryant merely told us to wear our sweat suits. There would just be a light conditioning drill. He knew his message had gotten across, and we understood.

"Coach Bryant was a man of many methods, some of them surfacing in the strangest and most revealing ways. Once we lost to Georgia Tech, 7–6, on a very controversial play called from our bench. Back in the locker room several of us sat with drooping heads, crying. Bryant, who had followed us in, stood in the midst of all and set things right, with just one line. He said he wanted to lead us in prayer, but it turned out to be a solo prayer on his part, and he started it with: *'Dear God . . . if I had stayed home today, these fine young men would have won the game. Amen.'*

"It was no act. I honestly believe—we *all* believed—that Coach Bryant was sincere in his actions. He felt his decision had lost the game—not the players. But we knew better, and we all resolved to work our tails off the next week in practice to renew the confidence in ourselves, our coaches and the student body. We said we'd come back strong—and we did."

McCollough paused, thinking. "Then there was the pre-game meeting before a game that was considered a toss-up. We may even have been the underdogs. Bryant had some thoughts he wanted to impart.

" 'One day in life,' he insisted, 'the world is gonna cave in on you. Twenty, thirty years from now you may come back and your house is burned down, your mother is in the hospital, the kids are sick, you're overdrawn at the bank, and your wife greets you with the news that she's going to leave you for your best friend. What're you gonna do? You gonna quit?'

"The man simply made us believe, over the four years we were with him, that there are lessons to be learned in football that are very difficult to teach at home, in church or the classroom. And I honestly think these lessons can be taught more effectively by coaches on the football field. How to work—how to sacrifice— how to *fight* and fight *back* when you've been assaulted either physically, emotionally or spiritually. As a parent I know it's very difficult to teach your children how to work. But they've got to learn because they're going to have to do it some day if they're going to compete and win. If my son plays football, the piano, or whatever—if he learns how to sacrifice, to work, and how to fight, then he's going to go through life on life's terms and be a winner.

"What did *I* learn from football?" He echoed the question. "Well, among other things it taught me about winning *and* losing. How to be humble while winning and gracious while losing. Not just satisfied in any way, even though you've given your best, but gracious and accepting.

"Sure, the whole world's aglow when you've just won, but when you lose, Coach Bryant has an angle for you. 'Look around you, because things are going to be different. The signs will tell you that. You'll note the intent and resolve in your teammates' voice, and the special way your Dad shakes your hand. You're being *told* something, son, and if you listen, you'll make it back.'

"The few times our Alabama team lost (only four times in four seasons while I was there) I realized Bryant was right. And when we got beat on a Saturday afternoon I couldn't wait until next week to prove myself. Why? Because I didn't enjoy losing. Losing made it tough to live with yourself when you played football for Paul Bryant.

"I can look all around me—in my community, in the hospital, at civic affairs, in politics—and I can see the things Bryant taught us. Among them was his very cogent appraisal of people we'd encounter. There would be those who sit—there are those who sit and observe—and, finally, there would be those who sit, observe and then make something happen. Well, those are the kind of people I prefer to be with—the guys who're going to bust their gut to help achieve a goal."

Gaylon McCollough snapped his fingers as something flooded back to mind. "Oh, yes, the pressure—he taught us how to deal with pressure—an enemy that can make any game or task seem extra burdensome. When I entered medical school, it wasn't just a mere transition. It was one tremendous adjustment. And, believe me, I had to start from scratch, and struggle, because I was unaccustomed to an intellectual environment which required me to attend classes and labs and study, sixteen hours a day, seven days a week.

"As hard as it was—and I saw guys crack under it, pack up and leave—I always remembered those practice sessions under Coach Bryant and what he always said about fighting back. Stress? Heck, I suddenly saw it as just another opponent I had to block or tackle. And after a while I began to notice that studying for medical exams was like practice sessions prior to a big game. So I treated them as such and began to formulate my own *game plan*. I'd anticipate a defensive reaction to a certain formation we'd run, and gradually I began to accurately gauge the professor's strategy on a test."

Dr. Gaylon McCollough leaned across the desk, his brow slightly furrowed. "Today, my continuing goal, as a doctor, is to be as good a surgeon as it's possible to be in my field. And I still approach each surgical case like a football game because both require a tremendous amount of very specialized preparation. Each human face that I see in an operation is going to be different— just as each football game is different. The coaching staff will always spend many critical hours studying game films before deciding their own game plan for the following Saturday; so must I study many pictures of my patients prior to surgery.

"In a game, a coach may be forced to alter his original plan because of a sudden complication he hadn't anticipated, yet he is able to adjust because he has planned for every eventuality. The same applies during an operation. And unless some catastrophe should strike, the operation should be successful because all of the proper procedural steps have been taken.

"Later, when I visit with my patients and notice that twinkling in their eye and that smile of satisfaction—I know that the surgery was worthwhile—and that's the purpose in my existence as a doctor. And the same is true for Coach Bryant.

"His responsibility as a coach is to prepare his boys to win on the football field. But most importantly, he wants them to be great people—after they leave football, after they leave him."

There was a small pause, accompanied by a shy smile as he leaned slightly toward his visitor. "And with only rare exception— very rare—has he ever been disappointed."

# 13

## Broadway Joe

> *"I can remember Coach Bryant saying before a game: 'Those ol' boys you're playin' just don't have the class you've got. Hell, y'all are wearin' genuine alligator loafers while they're wearing Thom McAns.'"*
>
> —Joe Namath

The helicopter appeared suddenly against the blue sky, and more than two hundred youngsters peered through their helmets as it approached the field, hovered, and then landed.

"O.K., everybody—supine!" said Bill Dockery, who grinned and fell on the grass.

The door opened and quickly Joe Namath walked out into a world he had never left.

These days he has been singing and dancing and starring in "Damn Yankees" at Jones Beach on Long Island. That is where the helicopter—at $375 an hour flying time—took off thirty-five minutes earlier. And it is where he will return in the afternoon to get ready for the evening's performance.

But at the age of 38, Joe Namath remains a part of the game that elevated him to folk-hero status.

He has commuted from Jones Beach everyday for the last three weeks (twice, bad weather forced him to land somewhere else or turn back) to work at the camp that he and Bill Dockery, a lawyer and former Jets teammate, started ten years earlier. Saturday will mark the last flight of the season. It is graduation day for the youngsters.

Namath's right knee, as it was during his playing days with the Jets, was heavily taped with an elastic bandage. He wore blue shorts, sneakers without socks, dark aviator glasses and a green sunvisor.

He wore a T-shirt, which he quickly took off. Then he plunged into the huddle.

"Give them room back there, move over," he barked to the players standing behind the huddle.

The young quarterback took the snap and moved back awkwardly.

"Don't look downfield when you're pedaling back. You know where they're going," he advised the quarterback, 16-year-old John Morris of Rochester.

Another quarterback lined up.

"Pretty good drop, pretty good drop. All right," said Namath. But he also told the quarterback, "You're not getting your hands on the center from the gitgo. As soon as you get to the center you put your hands on him. It gets the defense tense. They know you're ready to start, but they don't know when."

And so it went. He moved with a slight limp, from huddle to huddle, quarterback to quarterback.

"What happened to his knee?" an 8-year-old vistor asked.

"He used to get hit a lot playing football," the father replied.

*　　　*　　　*

I can vividly recall my first glimpse of Joe Namath. I was a student manager of the Alabama football team when I saw him saunter onto Thomas Field while visiting during his pro career. Waves of heat shimmered off the Astroturf as the Tuscaloosa sun beat mercilessly. It was only 9:30 in the morning but the temperature was already soaring up toward 100.

Immersed in this searing heat and humidity, Joe Namath, sweat pouring through his dark blue Alabama practice jersey, was jogging around the field. After about ten minutes, a couple of friendly receivers joined him as Joe picked up a bag of footballs and began tossing them to them with rhythmic, fluid movements. He began his warm-up slowly, and by the time he was fully loose it was like watching a human revolver. He took the imaginery snap, set up, cocked his powerful right arm and in a blur of throwing motion sent a perfect spiral humming across the field.

He continued his routine—a pass across the middle, squareouts, curls, post patterns. After forty-five minutes he was finished with his workout. He shuffled off the field with the now-famous Namath stoop, his head and shoulders dropping, and joined his old friend, former Tide student manager, "Hoot Owl" Hicks inside the Coliseum for therapy for his chronic knee problem. Later, Joe would have lunch at his restaurant in town and probably play a round of golf with some buddies at Indian Hills Country Club, or perhaps go fishing.

Now, a few years later, hard as it was for me to believe, here I was, chatting comfortably with perhaps the most famous football player since—well, why not Red Grange? Sure, why not? Is there a better candidate? Someone who through incredible performance and the sheer force of personality and charisma, has established himself as the ultimum persona gridironensis. Well, if the Latin is phony, the fact remains the same. Joe Namath stands alone. He was relaxing. Talking to me as though it was the most amiable if not important thing he could do that warm summer afternoon in Connecticut. And I'm not ashamed to admit it; I was one big ear.

*        *        *

"Wherever it is I've reached for myself, today," he was saying, "I might never know what was more responsible for it—my background in Beaver Falls, Pennsylvania, or the influence of Coach Bryant." A pause. "Maybe we should split it down the middle. First, Beaver Falls. That's hill country in western Pennsylvania, about fifty miles northwest of Pittsburgh, population 14,500 people on a crowded day. Steel workers, local merchants, a few farmers. Red brick town hall, three or four main shopping streets, one high school, the nearby river cutting through Beaver Valley. Hardly a vacation resort or a Shangri-la to come back to. But a helluva great town to grow up in, and then spread your wings.

"You grow those wings, fast, if you're a good football player, and that whole area—Alliquippa, Sharon, Ambridge, Farrell and other places—turned 'em out by the dozens, including guys like Johnny Lujack, Babe Parilli, Chuck Fusina, Joe Montana and I guess I can include myself.

"Nobody had money or status. You had to work and hustle for both. Hustling made you resourceful; work made you hard. I was hustling by the time I was 11 or 12, running errands for the pool room, collecting and selling bottles. However, there was Namath & Alford Enterprises, junk dealers deluxe.

"We kept the stuff in my cellar, and one day my Mom ordered us to clean out the place, so Linny Alford and I borrowed (maybe we swiped it for a while) one of those kid wagons with a handle— you know the kind they made then—and we started to haul our stuff to a nearby junkyard.

"Just then an old, 'professional' junkman with a rickety, horse-drawn wagon came clopping up our street, shouting: 'Scraps and rags . . . I buy scraps, junk and rags.' He stopped when he saw our first wagon load and we asked if he was interested in a deal. Eventually we agreed on a price—which would not exactly keep us in luxury—and he took our stuff away.

"The next few days we scrounged the whole town, searching for stuff the old junkman might be interested in, and it might take three days to get a load big enough to offer the guy. And there'd always be these big negotiations that made us feel like wheeler-dealers. We'd demand six bits, he'd counter with sixty cents. Linny and I would stand off in a huddle and try for 70. He'd say 65, not a penny more and we'd take it. I think the old man enjoyed those negotiations more than the few cents profit he made.

"But then we put the *hustle* on the old man . . ." Namath displayed a small grin which was half apology and half merriment as he recalled the scam. "We started re-claiming a lot of the stuff we'd previously sold him through a simple procedure of *midnight liberation* at his junkyard, and re-selling the same stuff to him. But suddenly it was September and we had to leave the junk business for football. Both Linny and I joined the best kids' sandlot team in the world—or at least in Beaver Falls, Pennsylvania. There were three neighborhood teams in the town. One was made up of the *rich* white kids from the best neighborhoods; another of the poor black kids from the wrong side of the tracks; the third team was composed of me at quarterback, Linny at scatback and nine other little black kids who were our buddies. Our record in the first year of the franchise was something like 112 wins and no losses against all comers, playing every day after school and six more games on weekends. That kind of record takes some doing.

"I was only twelve then, but I already knew I'd be the star quarterback in high school. It was something I'd set as my goal and I was either good enough or lucky enough to turn out to be the most sought-after high school quarterback in the area. I visited Michigan State, Arizona State, Notre Dame and Maryland and one or two others, I think. I liked 'em all, but I settled on Maryland who wanted me very much.

"But the Maryland admissions office didn't. I had to have a College Board exam score of 750 to qualify for an athletic scholarship, and for various reasons I won't get into, my high school academic career found me a few points shy. I hit 730 the first time I took the test, crammed for a second shot at it and made 747. No go. And there was no way they could get around it at Maryland. But the Maryland coach, Tom Nugent, was a nice guy and had made a call to Alabama and explained the situation to Coach Bryant. Next thing I knew, Howard Schnellenberger, one of Bryant's assistants, was at my doorstep. What he told me intrigued me (including the fact that 747 would get me into school) and a few hours later I'd packed a single suitcase and was off to a town called Tuscaloosa, which sounded pretty much like a joke when you said it, but at least I knew there was a state called Alabama, somewhere in the South."

I asked Joe what his first introduction to Coach Bryant was like. Joe then paused to reflect for a few moments. "My first encounter with Coach Bryant?" he echoed. "Let's see . . . Oh, yeah." He shrugged and smiled. "How could I forget?"

Another pause. "One of the managers took me to football practice after I was all signed up in the registrar's office, and there was Coach Bryant up in that famous observation tower, watching and frowning and yelling a lot. Suddenly he noticed me and waved for me to climb up the tower to him. He introduced himself, I greeted him and we started talking. I couldn't understand what he was talking about—and we must've talked for fifteen minutes—and out of the entire conversation I only understood one word: he kept saying something about a *Stud,* apparently talking about the ballplayers in the field. I was lost, but I managed to look reasonably intelligent and kept nodding. Then he started yelling down at practice again and I mumbled a goodbye and left.

"Pretty soon after that, once I started practicing with the freshman team, I got to understand Coach Bryant. He made sure I understood him. The freshmen were scrimmaging one Monday night and I ran to my left on an option play, and I started to pitch out, somebody tackled me and the ball fell loose. I didn't even make a scramble for the ball. Heck, I couldn't; the guy who had tackled me was still holding on to my legs.

"Bryant, all excited, rushed out in the field and yelled, 'Dammit, Namath, it isn't your job just to pitch the ball out and lay down there on the ground and not do anything. You just don't lay there!' He kept grumbling, and I started walking back to the huddle, just half listening to him, not looking at him, and suddenly he grabbed hold of my face mask and nearly lifted me off the ground.

" 'Namath,' he said, 'when I'm talking to you, boy, you say, 'Yes, sir,' and look me in the eye!

"I said, 'Yes, sir, Yes, sir,' real quick. He scared me half to death. From then on, if Coach Bryant just said, 'Joe,' and if I was sixty yards down the field, I'd sprint to him, stop a yard away, come to attention and say, 'Yes, sir.' He'd taught me my first lesson in respect and attentiveness. It would not be the last . . ."

*       *       *

Clem Gryska, the current assistant athletic director at Alabama, who was Namath's freshman coach, tells a story which, after he'd repeated to Bryant, gave the Tide coaches an insight to the confidence their quarterback recruit felt within him. "It was during our freshman game with Tulane and we were getting our tails whipped, when Joe came over to me and took me by the arm. 'Coach,' he said quietly, 'I want you to go over to the bench and relax and don't worry, because we're gonna come back and knock their ears off.'

"With Joe driving them calmly and expertly, those frosh did just that, and I knew we had a star in the making. There was just such believability and security in his tone when he took me by the arm that I knew we had a winner."

*       *       *

Namath took time out to wave at a friend who'd come by the camp, then sifted back through the years again to his days at Alabama. "Coach Bryant knew how to handle every mood a player could have. My sophomore year, when I was starting at quarterback, we were having a terrible day against Vanderbilt and much of it was my fault. Bryant got smart and pulled me out of the game. I was really angry as I came off the field and hurled my helmet to the ground, and it bounced right at Bryant's feet. He looked at it calmly, for a moment, without expression, then came over and sat down next to me on the bench and put his arm around me.

"To about 50,000 fans in the stands it must have looked as though he was dispensing some fatherly and coachly cheering-up—don't worry, kid, we'll get 'em yet. Cheering me up . . . ? Hell, he was damn near squeezing the back of my neck off with that huge paw of his.

" 'Boy,' he was saying, 'don't ever again let me see you coming out of a ball game acting like that. Don't ever do that again, or you're gone.'

" 'Dammit, coach,' I said. 'I wasn't mad at you or anybody else. I'm just disappointed at myself for playing so badly. I deserved to be yanked outa the game.'

"He drew his head back a tiny bit and gave me a long look. 'Okay, Joe. I understand.'

"That was a truly great moment between us. An awful lot was said and an awful lot didn't have to be said. My relationship with him was growing every week.

"Believe me, Coach Bryant is some kind of man. Sure, I hated him at times, but outside of my family and a few close friends there's nobody in the world I respect more. At times, he worked us so hard that you just couldn't believe it. We certainly couldn't, but we responded to his methods. And I know that if I'd been a tackle or a guard at Alabama, I wouldn't have lasted through college. Those guys used to come in after practice and sometimes walk straight into the showers with all their gear on like zombies— they were so beat. I felt guilty just being able to stand up.

"Victory, though, is what Bryant believes in ahead of everything else, and he measures everything on that basis. Often, he has been asked whether I was the best quarterback he ever coached, and he says no, because Alabama lost four games in three years with me as quarterback; Pat Trammell ranks first with Coach Bryant because Alabama lost only three games in the three years Pat played quarterback.

"I think the most important thing I learned from Coach Bryant was that if you wanted to be first class, you've got to act first class. He always felt his team should have the best of everything, from the dorms we lived in to the hotels we stayed in on the road. He wanted to make sure we believed we were the best— not cocky, but confident, I can still remember him saying before a game, 'Those ol' boys you're playin' just don't have the class you've got. Why, hell, y'all are wearin' genuine alligator loafers while they're wearin' Thom McAn's.'

"Bryant also, had a knack for throwing out funny lines at the most serious moments. Once, when the *Saturday Evening Post* came out with a story that claimed the 1962 Alabama-Georgia game had been fixed—both Coach Wally Butts of Georgia and

Coach Bryant won a lot on money in a lawsuit over that story—Bryant got hold of an early copy of the magazine and read the story out loud to us before spring practice. He got to the part where the magazine was trying to say that we'd been given the Georgia plays in advance and, because of that, we'd held them to only 37 yards rushing in the whole game. That's when Bryant stopped right in the middle of that section. He looked up at us and shook his head. 'Why, hell,' he said, 'that's just too damn many yards to give 'em at their best!'

"Coach Bryant and I have a very close relationship. I respect the man, and I like him—to play golf, for a drink, to talk—every chance I can get. And I know how much it must've hurt him when, in my junior year, he suspended me from the Alabama football team. It must have hurt him almost as much as it hurt me. I had broken some of his important rules and I knew it.

"The day I was asked to come to his office, Coach Bryant was waiting with his assistant coaches. 'Every coach except one,' he began, 'thinks we ought to punish you, but not suspend you. But I've made up my mind to suspend you, 'cause you've broken the rules, and I can't change that decision. If I did, or if the University changed my decision, I'd have to resign at the end of the season because I'd be breaking my own rules. I know we've got two big games coming up and I know we need you, but if I let you play, I'd have to retire, I just couldn't live with myself.'

" 'Well, sir,' I replied, 'I don't want you to do that.' I could understand the position he was in. I felt miserable but he was right, I was wrong. He had reduced it to its simplest terms.

"Coach Bryant suspended me and I had to move out of the athletic dormitory. I missed the last game of the regular season, against Miami, and I missed the Sugar Bowl game against Ole Miss. Both games were on national television and it really hurt to miss them, but Steve Sloan, who was a sophomore then, and Jack Hurlbut, a senior, took over the quarterbacking and did a heckuva job and Alabama won both games.

"After missing those games, I behaved myself all winter, and in the spring Bryant let me come back out for football. I worked like hell and won back the starting quarterback position. Following my senior season, after I had signed with the Jets, I walked up to Bryant and said, 'I want to tell you—you were right. You did the right thing, suspending me, because it made me a lot better person. And I want to thank you.' "

Finally, I asked Joe what football and the game of life had taught him . . .

"First of all," he began, "everyone on a team is different. They're all human beings and so they act differently in different situations. And a quarterback must know how to deal with each guy to get the best out of him. The coaches have already done that, technically, but the job on the field is for the quarterback.

"With some guys it doesn't do any good to holler at 'em. They have a certain kind of pride which, when they get beat on a play, automatically cranks them up for a better job on the next play. All the quarterback—me, anyway—has to do is check with them to see what actually happened. But you don't have to get on them. They take care of it themselves.

"Other guys are inspired by another guy yelling at them. They get chewed out by the quarterback and that fires them up. They say, 'Okay, this play I'm really gonna kill my man.' Some guys lose their orientation and start making mental errors. Sometimes you can shake those guys out of it. 'You want to play out here? Then start thinking or get off the field!'

"Every guy is different and every situation is different, and all you can do is try to react to what is really going on. Whatever happens, the quarterback reacts accordingly. You just can't decide to be a tough guy and start screaming at people—no matter what. But you can't stand around and let things slide when guys are messing up, either. You have to get a sense of every minute of the game.

"As a quarterback you have to know when to step in as a leader, even ahead of the captain. You have to have a complete feel of this particular game, pick up on the pace of it, find where the momentum is and learn how to handle it. It's like a rock band. The drummer has to take care of the beat—get things rolling when they slow down or knock things off if they get too frantic. A quarterback has to feel the flow of the game and move things around to keep the pace going right.

"One of the first things I learned from Coach Bryant is that every game is different. Every game is a new adventure. You have to find out what type of game it is—how the guys are reacting to the situation and make things go accordingly. If you've got the game under control then you have to keep things cool and orderly, and moving efficiently. You don't do anything to interrupt the flow.

"But if things aren't happening out there, you have to get some spark ignited. If we'd been stopped a couple of times, I try to find out what's the matter, and so do the coaches. Maybe it's the game plan. Maybe the defense is doing some things we didn't expect and they're really messing us up. You hope you're able and capable enough to adjust while the game is going on. It's too late when you start checking the film the next day."

Suddenly he tapped his chest and leaned into his thought. "And what if the one who makes the big mistake is you? That's the time when you need confidence in your ability, mentally and physically to do the job. Mistakes or errors are made in all walks of life—not just football. What you've got to do when that happens is find out exactly how and why it occurred. Then you're better prepared for a similar situation if it should arise. Let's not make the same mistake twice, is what I'm saying. You just go back to work. It may have still ticked me off when I thought of an error during a game. I'd say to myself: 'How could I have done that?' But when it was time to go on the field again with the offense I'd just think: 'Forget it, buddy—let's go get 'em.'

"When I came out on the field I was ready to roll. And the way I wanted to do it when playing football is the same way I want to be in my daily life. I want it to be smooth, to operate with no excess motion of disturbance. It's all a matter of style. That's really what Coach Bryant was always trying to teach us, whether he, or we, understood that. How we prepared, how we performed and how we lived our lives was just a sense of style, really."

It was getting time for Joe to leave. Broadway was calling. He picked up a football and tossed it to a crowd of youngsters.

They leaped for it like Yankee Stadium fans chasing a Reggie Jackson home run.

He waved and got into the helicopter, and soon they were off. The helicopter dipped so Namath could wave again.

Walking back toward the car, watching Joe's copter make its way toward Jones Beach, I couldn't help thinking of his final words before he departed. "Bryant's boys have something special going for them."

I think I know what he meant.

# 14

# Four from Alabama

> *"There was much skepticism in the Black community of Tuscaloosa when I was considering Alabama . . . Some folks didn't think Alabama was the place for black players even though the color line had already been broken . . . They thought I'd be better off at a Black school. But how could they know how I felt that night when Coach Bryant called me on the phone?"*
>
> —Sylvester Croom

They were four of the finest football players at Alabama in recent years. All four were All America selections.

Lee Roy Jordon was a linebacker from Excel, Alabama, who had played for Bryant in 1960–61–62; later was an All-Pro with the top-ranked Dallas Cowboys and is now in the lumber business and the registered cattle business. Paul Crane, was an All America center from Pritchard, Alabama and started for the Tide in 1963–64–65. He played with the World Champion New York Jets before an injury cut short his career, and, after assisting Paul Bryant at Alabama, became a top assistant under Steve Sloan at the University of Mississippi before entering private business in Mobile, Alabama.

Johnny Musso, perhaps one of my favorites, was a two-time All America halfback from Birmingham and was known as "The Italian Stallion" during his starring years of 1969–70–71 with the Crimson Tide, and later became the top running back in the

Canadian League before joining the Chicago Bears of the NFL. Today Johnny has become very successful in the commodities futures and is one of the youngest businessmen to ever earn a seat on the Chicago Board of Trade. And Sylvester Croom, an All America center in 1973–74, represents the modern generation of Bryant's players. Sylvester had a brief professional football career with the New Orleans Saints and is now an assistant coach at Alabama.

*       *       *

"Naturally, I have a lot of memories of those days playing for Coach Bryant," Lee Roy Jordan explained, "but the one that seems uppermost in my mind isn't something that was dramatic or exciting, or stuff like that. It was a simple speech which Bryant made to the freshman class in 1959, my first year. He sort of let his eyes roam around the room, letting his gaze fall on just about every one of us. And what he was saying went something like this: 'Now, y'all are freshmen and you're starting out on a road to you ain't sure where. But I'll tell you one goal you'll reach if you'll just listen to me and do as I say . . . If you'll follow through with the program I lay out for you and if you work at it the way I demand you do—you'll be national champions before you graduate. And that's a promise from me.'

"Now, hell, how many coaches can dare *promise* a bunch of freshmen a national championship even before they've pulled on a pad. A lot of kids these days, sophisticated and all that, might be a bit cynical and even suspect they're bein' conned, but if you could have seen the look in Coach Bryant's eyes and hear that somethin' special in his tone, you'd have gotten chills up and down your spine the way we 18-year-old kids got.

"Yes, sir, I'm sayin' I did. What that man did was make believers outa us on Day One. Now, you can laugh and you can snicker but I was *there*. And, yes, sir, when we *did* win the national championship two years later, the first thing that ran through my mind was that Coach Bryant had promised something and had *delivered*. Of course he pointed out to us at our banquet that we'd done the delivering ourselves, but hell, I knew better . . ."

Jordan shifted his ample bulk and frowned reflectively. "He could reach you in so many ways, ranging from rage and anger to sarcasm, to open challenge, to humor, to gentle philosophic understanding. The same man. It kept a lot of guys off-balance but mainly it worked.

"Against Georgia Tech in my sophomore year we made more mistakes in the first half than anyone could think possible. We scurried into the dressing room draggin' our tails, trailing Tech, 15–0, and sinking fast, expectin' Bryant to take us apart. But he sensed that we'd made just too *many* mistakes to harp on them; it'd only have a negative effect. So he very patiently pointed out some things he wanted us to do differently and said that if we did them that way, we'd win the damn ball game.

"We latched onto his confidence and scored twice and were behind only 15–13 with a couple minutes left. On a fourth down we were faced with a fairly long field goal situation and Bryant called over Richard O'Dell on the sidelines. Our kicking game had been poor for several weeks and nobody had much confidence in our field goal kickers. So Coach Bryant put his arm around the shoulders of little Dickie O'Dell, who'd fooled around in practice, doing some kicking, but had never tried kicking a field goal in a game, and Bryant told O'Dell he was sending him out there to kick a field goal.

"Coach let O'Dell know there was no question in his mind that O'Dell couldn't put it smack through the uprights. Which Dickie O'Dell proceeded to do, winning the game for us, 16–15. That's called instant transfusion of confidence. O'Dell never again was called upon to try another field goal but for that one time there was no way he could miss.

"After winning the national championship in 1961 we were picked to repeat the following year. We were sailing along with eight straight wins and had another title all locked up—but we let Georgia Tech upset us, 7–6, in Atlanta and you never saw a bunch of guys get so low. Coach took the blame for the loss and we let him take it for no reason except that he insisted.

"So we moped somethin' awful the following week in practice. Coach Bryant came up with the cure. On Thursday, he told the starting team to leave practice early and go to the film room and grade ourselves on the Georgia Tech game film, with special instructions to very carefully watch our two-point play which was to determine the outcome of the game.

"So we went in and looked at that film and gave ourselves a grade on our performance, without knowing what the coaching staff had previously given us. Coach had kept those results to himself that week, for some reason. Well, sir, we were very kind to ourselves and we all took pretty high marks. But then we took a good look at that two-point play. With the score 7–6, in favor of Tech, Bryant, always going for the win, had given us orders to go for two. Well, on nine possible blocks on that play, no one made a decent block and Jack Hurlbut wasn't able to convert for the two points.

"There was no way we were going to let Coach Bryant take the blame for that loss. We all knew who'd blown it and we tore up those good grades we'd given ourselves. Later, Coach simply asked us if we had enough challenge left in us to really get up for our big, traditional finale with Auburn, and salvage the season. We went bonkers and beat Auburn, 38–0, and were picked to play Oklahoma in the Orange Bowl. They were favored and President John Kennedy had visited them in their dressing room before the game. In his pre-game talk, Bryant simply mentioned that. He didn't *comment* on it. He knew he didn't have to. We played the greatest game of our career and whipped Oklahoma, 17–0, and knocked *them* out of number-one contention—which, I think, was won by Southern Cal."

Lee Roy Jordan paused a moment while he tugged gently at an ear. "One of the things that annoyed some of the guys at first—but they eventually learned to appreciate—was the fact that Bryant always seemed to be a part of your personal life. He insisted on you going to church as often as you could. He let it be known that he expected you to say your prayers once in a while, that you minded your manners and just generally doing things your Mom and Dad taught you.

"After a game, Coach always sought out the players' folks outside the dressing room to shake their hand. It wasn't just to make 'em feel important. It was his sincere nature. He was a parent, himself, and he recognized these folks as *parents,* not just as parents of some football players.

"Speaking of those moments after a game, Bryant once told us how *winners* felt. They could go up to their Dads after a game, shake their hands, look them in the eye, kiss their moms, hug their girlfriends and go out and enjoy a nice, big steak. But when you lost, that steak wouldn't taste as good, you'd feel ashamed to face your folks and the hug from your honey just wouldn't feel the same.

"The one thing you knew for sure about him, he'd be with you all the way if you tried to be your best. If you were on the third team, but a good student, he'd stick with you. If you were a great player but struggling with your academics, he'd stand up for you. But if you did poorly in both, then you were in trouble, because one way or another you weren't doing your best.

"For years after I graduated—even after my years in professional football—I used to go back to him for advice. He was my business advisor, counselor, spiritual guidance—and friend. What more can you ask of a man?"

\*       \*       \*

Paul Crane knew what he was going to say, but the dubious look on his face made it appear as though he were fighting a contradiction. And he was. "You take a look at Coach Bryant and what you seem to see is a pure, physical, sort of stereotyped football coach. Hard, tough, just a minute away from meanness. And then you look back, and think back, to some of the things he'd say over and over again and you'd almost have to say, 'will the real Coach Bryant stand up?'

"I think basically Coach was a teacher or preacher at heart. A dozen times I've heard him say that the physical, the spiritual and the mental are the three main areas of your life. He'd tell us that that's what football is all about but we'd better carry those commitments over into life, long after we'd stopped playing football, or we'd be fall-on-your-face failures.

" 'Relationships,' he'd growl. 'Relationships with people. Mutual appreciation and support. They win games. They get your life's work done.' You'd hear him talk about guys he played ball with at Alabama and you'd swear he was talking about his family. You'd hear him talk about the hard work, how they suffered together and gloried together, and how those were the people he had the fondest memories of.

"He made me aware that when you're caught up in the heat of a game you realize just who you can *depend* on, who's willing to pay the price. He hammered at us that we had to learn— and feel—the utmost confidence on the guy next to you or making the play with you. He had us believing that the guy may get whipped and the play might not work, but on the next play that guy would work twice as hard and never quit. But the way Coach Bryant laid it on you, you were left with an awful burden. The burden of knowing that that guy was feeling the same way about *you,* and you wouldn't be worth much if you let *him* down. Some might think I'm corny, but they've never played ball for Coach Bryant."

Crane doodled with a pencil on a notepad for a couple of seconds, then looked up. "There was nothing going on with his football teams he didn't know about. He knew, for instance, that a kid has been going to church every Sunday, for years. The kid suddenly stops going. Who do you think learns about it, real mysteriously, and gets that kid back on the track? Coach's view was that you don't have a hit-and-miss arrangement with God. If you don't *believe,* that's your privilege. But if you *do* believe, you pay your spiritual dues.

"Same with a kid's family. Coach Bryant expected you to telephone your parents now and then, and write to them every once in a while, and he'd ask you if you had or hadn't recently, and by God you'd better not lie to him. A guy could make an awful mistake in a game, and Coach would practically skin him in the dressing room, but if he saw the kid givin' his Mom a kiss after the game, the kid was practically forgiven."

He was silent for a long moment. "If it hadn't been for Coach Bryant I wouldn't have been able to have gone into coaching. I'd played for the New York Jets, and later was injured, and knew my career was over. I'd worked for an advertising company in Birmingham for a while and enjoyed it. I thought I could make a fine career of it. But there was this feeling I couldn't get rid of—that I wanted to work with kids, and the best place for that was in football coaching.

"I talked to Coach Bryant about it and said I was at a crossroads. Football or advertising. Heck, he saw right through me. There was no crossroads at all. I guess I kept mentioning the idea of working with kids. Later he phoned me and asked if I was ready to come to Alabama as his assistant.

Crane chuckled. "Was I ready? Heck, I was almost packed before he hung up the phone." A pause. "And *that's* when I started learning about coaching football."

"When I left Alabama a couple seasons later to take a position up the ladder with Steve Sloan at Ole Miss, I felt I was leaving behind a big hunk of my life and soul. But I'm just one of the dozens of Bryant's boys all over the football landscape who feel the same way. Actually, it's a marvelous feeling."

*     *     *

Johnny Musso was very emphatic about it. "You only have to prove yourself once to Coach Bryant—by his standards—and when you've done that, he knows he can count on you—that you've done what he knows he can count on you—that you have the stuff to be a winner when it counts. It's his way of believing in *you,* and when you get the feeling that he *does* . . . Well, I tell you, you get a lift that stays with you as long as you're associated with him. And even *after* that. For me—and a lot of other guys that belief is so real you can taste it.

"On the football field, the opportunity to prove yourself to Bryant usually comes during spring training in a controlled situation. If Bryant thinks you're going to be the kind of player who can make it under him he'll place you in a situation where a lot of things are adversely going against you. Especially when it's hot and you're tired.

"He'd stack the cards against the offense by not allowing substitutions, but every time you dragged yourself back to the huddle you'd see a fresh defensive player running onto the field. Yet the offensive players with no rest were supposed to prove themselves above and beyond the call of duty. On these days there'd be no alumni, no visitors of any kind on the sidelines. Just players and coaching staff, with all the coaches tight-lipped and cold-eyed, particularly Coach Bryant, who wanted to see who was dying out there and who could rise like Lazarus from the dead and keep hitting.

"I remember working so hard I didn't think I could run another play, especially if it was designed for me to carry the ball, but somehow I always found a little extra in reserve. Especially if I saw Bryant's eye on me. And then one day toward the end of spring training Bryant would place the offense in a situation where it sort of worked against itself. It would begin with him putting the ball on our own 30-yard line, and the offense was supposed to drive the ball down field as far as possible. Then, on fourth down, you'd punt and race down to cover the kick. But nobody else took over. The same offensive team would turn around and start driving the ball upfield again. What it meant was, if you had a good drive previously and a good punt to the 10-yard line, you were then confronted with a 90-yard march going back the other way.

"If you proved yourself, according to those standards of his, you got a reward that zinged into your very soul and stuck with you a long time. Coach Bryant would just slide up to you, maybe put an arm on your shoulder, and mumble: *'You looked good out there.'* Five words. But knowing what you'd accomplished in terms of his demands, those words could mean the making of a football player. He had made a believer out of you and you were in damned select company."

Musso paused, and the heavy black brows began wrinkling over the black Italian eyes. "I don't know if this was deliberate on his part, or whether he did it unintentionally—but he had this knack of keeping you off balance. So, eventually I began to expect the unexpected from him. There were times when you had a great practice or had a helluva game, and although you didn't expect a medal you sort of looked forward to being patted on the back. Well, sometimes—in that situation—he'd just grunt at you and say: 'Well, that's a *little* better,' or maybe: 'C'mon, keep it goin', keep it goin',' as though you'd been slacking off.

"Yet there were times when guys felt discouraged and were dragging their tails, and were due to be chewed out. But, instead, he'd come over and remind you of some great moments or games you'd had, and he'd insist they'd come back again. He's just a fabulous judge of people and of the kind of motivation they need at a particular time. And another thing . . . once the cards have been stacked against you and you've been confronted with a lot of adversity and you've come through, Coach Bryant will never place you in jeopardy again. Why? Because you've already proved you have the guts and determination to win when the chips are down. He knows that any fall off on your part would be due to pure mechanics and not a lack of desire of motivation. The guy has already passed Bryant's test and both parties firmly believe in each other."

He shook his head. "The man was a genius at drawing the best out of you on the shortest notice. I'll never forget in my senior season, just three weeks before our opening game against Southern Cal, Bryant walks into a squad meeting and announces he's switching our offense from pro-type to the wishbone-T set. We sat there for a moment, stupefied. If a coach decides to change his entire offense he does it in spring training when he has several months to work on it before the season opens. And here's Coach Bryant telling us everything is going to be different—every blocking assignment, all the execution, all the reads of the defense—*everything.* And we have to master it in three weeks.

"Coach Bryant knew what we were thinking. But without any expression on his face he just nodded and said: 'If I didn't think we could do it, I wouldn't be asking you to.' Well, when you're 20-years-old and playing for Coach Bryant, what more do you need? We knew it took a lot of guts on his part to make such a drastic change before the toughest opening game Alabama had ever played, and I think it was the biggest calculated risk Bryant ever made.

"Over the years, with quarterbacks like Joe Namath, Steve Sloan, Kenny Stabler and Scott Hunter, the pro drop-back passing game had worked well. Those guys could really throw. We had Terry Davis, however, a gifted athlete who wasn't a brilliant passer but he was quick and could read defenses beautifully. A natural for the wishbone, and I don't think many quarterbacks ever ran the wishbone quite like him.

"Well, Bryant's offensive conversion was a big secret shared only by the team and staff. Practices were closed to everyone. Then came the day when the Southeastern Conference Skywriters Tour came through on their annual one-day visit. These were the important sports writers in the Conference area who chartered a plane and visited each school for a day. On this day Bryant had us running our old pro-set offense. Sure as day, we looked sloppy and rusty and all the writers went back home and reported that Alabama wouldn't be much of a team in 1971.

"In our dressing room after that day's practice we all yakked it up because we'd pulled off the greatest hoax in Alabama football history. But Bryant came by among us and told us the last laugh could be somebody else's unless we had the kind of season that came out of the hoax. It sobered us considerably."

Musso grinned. "There are football writers and fans who think that modern Alabama football fortunes were born in that three-week pre-season period—and in the Southern Cal game that opened our season.

"We beat Southern Cal, with our new offense clicking beautifully, and we went on to an 11-0 regular season record. And it all started with Coach Bryant walking into that pre-season meeting and telling us we could make the switch in three weeks. As I look back on it, now, there couldn't have been a guy on the squad who didn't believe him. Man, you just don't know the depth of unspoken communication between Bryant and an Alabama football player. It's downright mystical."

*　　　*　　　*

"Going to the University of Alabama was not really something I'd looked forward to," Sylvester (Sly) Croom was saying. "In fact, I hadn't even thought about it when I was attending Tuscaloosa High School and playing football. I'd been in the first group

Bryant dispatches some words of wisdom to his prize pupil, Joe Namath, during the heat of battle against Texas in the 1965 Orange Bowl.

Bryant and Curt Gowdy relax together prior to filming of a hunting trip for *The American Sportsman.*

Bryant celebrated the 1966 Orange Bowl victory over Nebraska with Steve Sloan (*left*) and Ray Perkins (*right*).

Bryant, always pointing his men toward victory, interrupts 1963 game against Florida to dispute an official's decision. The official eventually admitted his error.

At the 1961 National Football Foundation and Hall of Fame banquet in New York, President John Kennedy and General Douglas McArthur listened as Bryant told them of the pride in having players like Pat Trammell (*behind Bryant on podium*).

Bryant's success led the Alabama faithful to believe that their legendary coach could really walk on water.

When Bryant received word that the *Saturday Evening Post* was going to publish their "fix story," he went on television to challenge their lies.

Bryant had to suspend Joe Namath from the team in 1963, but Namath came back to lead the team to a National Championship the next season.

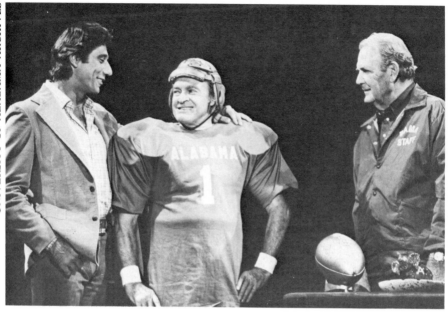

Joe Namath, Bob Hope and Bryant ham it up during filming of a Bob Hope special in Tuscaloosa, Alabama.

Bryant and Auburn coach Pat Dye, both ex-farmboys, take a break during recruiting season for a hunting trip.

**Bryant** watches his squad from his legendary tower, passing out tidbits of information.

Johnny Musso, often nicknamed "The Italian Stallion," was twice an All America halfback for Bryant in the early 1970s.

Bryant, singer Anita Bryant and co-host John Forney on Bryant's highly rated weekly television show.

Bryant and Notre Dame's Ara Parseghian serve as honorary cooks at Sugar Bowl luncheon prior to their memorable New Orleans shoot-out.

Rev. Billy Graham (*middle*) visits with (*left to right*) football coaches Pat Dye, Bryant, Danny Ford and Jackie Sherrill at "America's Tribute" to Bryant in Washington, D.C. in 1982.

Bryant strikes a familiar pose during his
team's pre-game warm-up.

Notre Dame's Dan Devine and Bryant relax during an off-season outing. On the field,
however, Devine held a 2–0 edge in winning which gave Bryant plenty to worry about.

Bryant and Darrell Royal of Texas accept Bluebonnet Bowl trophy after a 3–3 tie in 1960.

Bryant accepts congratulations from LSU coach Jerry Stovall in 1981 following another difficult battle in Tiger Stadium.

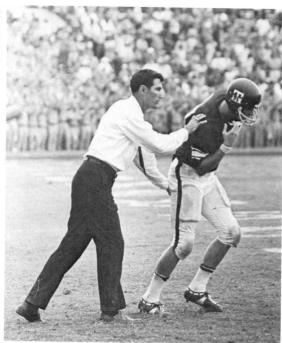

Gene Stallings of Texas A&M defeated his former coach in the 1968 Cotton Bowl.

(Left to right) Jim Owens, Jerry Claiborne and Phil Cutchin eventually left Bryant's staff to take head coaching jobs.

Steve Sloan built winning teams at Vanderbilt and Texas Tech. He is now attempting to rebuild the football fortunes at Duke.

John David Crow rebuilt Northeast Louisiana into a winner. He is shown here after a golf outing with Bryant and Alabama assistant Clem Gryska.

Bryant receives phone call of congratulations from President Reagan after breaking Amos Alonzo Stagg's record of 314 wins.

Crowds filled the cemetery on the day of Bryant's burial.

Bryant at home on his tower.

HIS PERMANENT HAT RACK

COLLEGE FOOTBALL

An editorial cartoonist attempts to portray the impact that Bryant's death had on the game of football.

of black kids who were integrated into Tuscaloosa Junior High School in the 1960s. It was certainly a new, if not slightly nervous, situation for me because I didn't know what to expect.

"All things considered, it was a pretty smooth transition but then I went on to high school and I thought: 'Well, now I want to play football here. Will it be okay? Will it lead me anywhere?' I knew I'd be going on to college. My father was an assistant high school principal and our family was education minded. Would I be good enough to make it at a big-time school? Should I try it at what we used to call a 'white college' or should I take the conservative road and try it at a black college?"

Sly Croom paused while he collected some of the pieces of his recent past. "As it turned out, even though I became one of the so-called stars at Tuscaloosa High School, there weren't a lot of scouts beating at my door. They only people who seemed at all interested in me were Georgia Tech and Alabama A&M. And after Georgia Tech made their first approach they never followed up on it.

"Very frankly," Croom continued, "I didn't know where I stood as a potential college football player. In high school I played fullback, tight end, and even some offensive guard. But no one was wooing me, although when I was a junior there were a couple of former Alabama players, doing some student teaching at my high school, who came around to talk to me. One was Mike Ford, who'd been an All America defensive end, and the other was Danny Ford, an All-SEC offensive tackle. They weren't related. Danny Ford, of course, is now head coach at Clemson.

"Anyway, both of them suggested I think about my going to Alabama. They thought I had the physical part of it but what they were really hinting around at me was whether I thought I was a winner. They told me you had to be a natural winner, deep in your heart, if you ever expected to play for Coach Bryant.

"Just the mention of Coach Bryant's name by them was enough to make a black kid like me break out in goose bumps. Me play for Bear Bryant, at Alabama? I just let it simmer in my mind.

"By the middle of my senior year I was having a fine season, which was when Georgia Tech and Alabama A&M approached me. As I said, nothing came of the Tech interest, but A&M was willing to take me. Nothing but silence from the rest of the Southeastern Conference. It didn't tick me off; what it did was provide some motivation for me. If I knew I was a winner—and I think I knew that—then, heck I *could* play for Alabama. And just about the same night I decided that, the phone rang and it was— guess who? The voice, a deep, brass rumble, said, 'this is Coach Bryant at Alabama,' and I don't think I said anything back. I think I just nodded silently into the telephone, unable to speak. He went on to say that Danny Ford and Mike Ford thought I was good enough to play for Alabama. Did I think I was? If I did, he'd sure like me to join up.

"Well, it wound up that I said I'd be happy to come to Alabama, but there was a lot of skepticism in the black community of Tuscaloosa. There were some folks who didn't think Alabama was quite ready for black football players, even though the color line had already been broken one or two years earlier by a couple of very fine black players. They thought I might do better at Alabama A&M.

"But how could they know how I felt that night when Coach Bryant called me on the phone? How could they make the judgments I had made about the honesty, sincerity and concern that came through in the deep rumbly voice when he spoke about education and preparing myself for a place in the world community through football *and* the classroom.

"He didn't say anything about his discipline and tough methods. He didn't have to. His methods already had made him a legend. And I couldn't believe there'd be any difference between white and black on the football field.

"And was I ever right. From the first day as a freshman— and freshmen weren't eligible for varsity by then—I could tell there'd be no such things as white players and black players under Coach Bryant. There'd just be *football* players. I tell you, it was instant belief on my part, and I was in awe of him. Not only as a football coach but as a human being. Heck, there were a half dozen blacks on the squad by then and any one of us could look into the mirror after a shower, our bones aching, and tell ourselves we sure were black and Coach Bryant didn't know it.

"Coach Bryant turned me into a center. I made All America and along the way, on that Alabama practice field, I got complimented and booted in the tail, in turns, by Coach Bryant and I was grateful for every moment I spent under him.

"You know something? As many times as I went to his office to talk to him about any problem I might have—and there were plenty of them—I never had to wait more than three minutes before he'd see me. His players simply came first. In fact, he once cut Darrell Royal short on the telephone—not rudely, but timewise—because he knew I was waiting to see him."

Sly Croom re-settled the tinted aviator glasses on the bridge of his nose. "When I was drafted by the New Orleans Saints he told me to give it the best shot I could—and if things didn't break right for me in the pro's I should consider getting into coaching. Well, I only played seven or eight games with the Saints and it didn't work out. Next thing I knew, I had a phone call from Coach Bryant asking if I'd like to be one of his graduate assistants that season. I was elated that he asked me but told him I thought maybe I'd be better off starting on a master's degree in educational administration. He said that was a good idea—and that I should consider doing both. At the same time? He said, sure, why not, if I wanted *both* of them bad enough, and if I had the drive and desire to work that hard."

Sly Croom allowed a thin smile to cross his rugged face. Now that it was all past him he could afford the luxury of a slightly pained remembrance. "So I signed on as an assistant coach and checked in as a graduate student. I worked with the team every day until 6 o'clock, took a quick shower, grabbed a hamburger and a glass of milk—or maybe just time for a hard-boiled egg that I kept handy—and hustled off to a 7 o'clock class four nights a week. Believe me, there were days when I felt like chucking one or the other—football or the master's program—but every other day Coach Bryant would drift over to me and say, 'how's it goin'?' and I knew very well he wasn't talking about football—and I knew if I quit that master's program or even come up with poor grades he'd have my tail. You don't let Coach Bryant down, once you make a commitment to excellence. That's what comes across every day you're associated with the man."

Sly Croom's smile was broad and satisfied. "So, now I'm an Alabama football coach and I have that master's degree in educational administration, and some day there's the strong possibility that it'll be education full time for me—and guess who'll be happier than anybody if that comes to pass. Believe it, friend. . . . It'll be Coach Bryant."

# 15

## *The Leaders*

> *"There was a piece in the paper about a Houston pitcher who had died of a melanoma, starting with a mole on his leg. . . Suddenly I was looking at a black mole on my arm. I knew that couldn't mean me but my wife insisted that our doctor take a look at it . . ."*

—Jack Pardee

It is only a co-incidence, of course, that many of Paul Bryant's finest football players come from small towns, just as Bryant, himself, did. Bryant quite possibly had a special feeling for boys from small towns. Not only did they have some affinity with his own backwoods beginnings in Arkansas, but he once said that a boy from a small town was more likely to come to college unspoiled, uncorrupted, and unconsiously ready to be molded for bigger and better things.

Jack Pardee could only dream about the world beyond Cristoval, Texas, a town of five hundred people in the sand hills of west Texas. It was sheep and oil country, and Pardee started working as a roughneck in the oil fields at age fourteen. The experience convinced him there had to be more to life than roughnecking. He decided he'd finish high school, where he immersed himself in sports. It was Class B football for him, because his school had fewer than one hundred students. It also meant that the same boys had to play on all teams—football, basketball, baseball and track. Class B football was also the 6-man game. You had to be exceptionally good—and versatile—to attract college scouts to a 6-man football prospect. Texas A&M found Jack Pardee somehow, and he became the first and only player from a 6-man team to make All America.

After an illustrious professional football career as a linebacker with the Los Angeles Rams and Washington Redskins, Pardee signed on as a Redskins assistant coach, then he had a stint in the ill-fated World Football League. In 1974, he became head coach of the Chicago Bears and built them into a winner. Four years later he returned to Washington as head man, taking the Redskins to the playoffs and earning Coach-of-the-Year honors. Today, he is an oil executive with Runnels Mud Company in Midland, Texas.

Steve Sloan, from Cleveland, Tennessee, a "big" small town of 20,000, as a high school quarterback had made a big impression on every major college scout in the South. Narrowing his many choices to home state Tennessee, Georgia Tech, and Alabama, he finally opted to go with Bryant. An All America quarterback who led Alabama to national championships in 1964 and 1965, Sloan played briefly for two years with the Atlanta Falcons and then took aim at college coaching. Presently reviving the Duke University program, he previously had built winning programs at Vanderbilt, Texas Tech and Ole Miss before Duke lured him away to the hills of North Carolina.

Ray Perkins, of Petal, Mississippi, pop. 6,000, knew from the time he was a high school sophomore that he wanted to go off to Tuscaloosa and play football for Paul "Bear" Bryant. As a Tide end he was All America in 1966 and had a bright career as wide receiver with the Baltimore Colts before a knee injury ended his playing days. He was an assistant coach at Mississippi State for one season before joining the professional ranks where he was an assistant with the San Diego Chargers New England Patriots and the San Diego Chargers before the New York Giants tapped him to re-build their fortunes. In December 1982, Perkins left the championship contender Giants to succeed Bryant at Alabama.

\*      \*      \*

"To begin with," said Jack Pardee, "I don't think Coach Bryant ever tried a player at as many positions as he did with me. I was a sophomore when he came to Texas A&M, and I was in on that gut-wrenching episode at Junction, where he was he was looking for *football players.* He must have thought I was a *player,* all right, but he sure went around Robin Hood's barn trying to find it out.

"He tried me at halfback, at fullback, at end, at defensive end, at tackle, the defensive secondary, and even at center. I only lasted a day at center because it was obvious I could never make a proper snap, so Bryant gave up on me pretty quick on that one. He had me doing all the specialized work at those other positions, but instead of me being discouraged he gave me the feeling that he truly believed in me and in my ability but was just looking for the right spot for me. I'm sure, with any other coach, a lot of guys would have packed it in but, honestly, I never felt that way. I *knew*—and I knew that *he* knew—I'd be playing football for him. Golly, how he could get you to believe in something. Y'know, I probably never would have been an All America under any other coach, but Bryant. What an experience it was, finding yourself being molded as a player and a person under him."

Pardee picked up a pencil from the desk which was the nerve center of the Washington Redskins operation and rolled it between his fingers, studying it. "Incidentally, I think Coach Bryant's second year at Texas A&M, was one of the greatest coaching jobs ever done. The first year—when he had so little to work with—the team lost nine out of ten games and had gone through the hellfire of Junction. How he kept the program from disintegrating and making everyone believe better days were coming was a major miracle. But in that second season of his—when Charlie Krueger, John David Crow, and Loyd Taylor were sophomores—he had us believing we'd set the world on fire. Well, by golly we almost did. It was a heckuva blaze, anyway. We lost the opener and the finale but we won everything in between. Nobody expected us to win that opener at Los Angeles against UCLA, the defending national champion with at least three All Americas returning. And there we were, losers of nine of ten the year before, walking into the lion's den at the Los Angeles Coliseum on Friday night before the game, for a workout.

"We'd never played at night, before. We stared around us and I think a lot of us just tried to stay close to Coach Bryant just for the sheer comfort of it. Yeah, we were scared witless but we didn't dare let him see it, or know it. You don't ever, *ever* let him know you're scared. I think he'd outright kill you. You can lose, but you can't be *scared*, know what I mean?

"I was the starting fullback and Bryant had gotten together a great game plan. Yet, in the Coliseum, the night before the game, we were running some dummy plays without pads and helmets. I must have been still staring around the stadium one time on an option play and I must have gone the wrong way, because John David Crow and I crashed head-on. They carted both of us off to the training room and for a while they thought neither of us would play the next night. Bryant was beside himself, bellowing about how could a dumb thing like that happen and I never did tell him I was so awed by just being there that I'd gotten fuzzy and forgetful. Well, we both played the next night but I was more frightened over what Coach Bryant might do to me, than by that great UCLA team. I kept imagining he had his eyes on me and wasn't watching anyone else. I had one of the best games of my junior season and we ran that UCLA team all over the field—pushed 'em up and down—but we lost 21–0. They gained very little ground on us but Ronnie Knox, their great quarterback, tossed three TD passes. Three plays were the difference.

"The following week we went up to Nebraska and creamed 'em, scoring 27 points in the first half. We were off on an eight-game winning streak and lost our last one to Texas, but by then we had faith in what we were doing and *believing* in what Coach Bryant was doing with us. And when the season was over, the true value of the famous *mustard seed* incident stood out in front of us for all time, as a symbol of what Bryant's faith message could do . . ."

Now there was a long pause as Pardee visibly hesitated, as though debating seriously as to whether he should expand on what his memories had not seized upon.

"I was just thinking . . ." He finally began. And then he committed himself. "I don't know how many folks remember that battle I had with cancer. And I don't think anyone besides myself could ever know how the faith which Coach Bryant helped instill in me, pulled me through. You just can't stop fighting for something you believe in, he was always telling us. You don't even consider the odds, he always pounded at us. Brother, you don't even know how many times those words always came back to me.

"I couldn't have asked for more in my football career. I'd come from a little ol' six-man high school team in scrub-poor West Texas to make All America at Texas A&M. I'd made it big in pro football for seven years, with the Rams, including All Pro. I had a fine wife and four great kids and a few good years left in professional football. We'd just bought a new house. One morning I was having breakfast and reading the morning paper. There was a piece about a pitcher for the old Houston Colts who had died of something called a *melanoma,* starting with a mole he had on his leg. They described the mole and suddenly I was looking at a mole I had on my arm.

"I knew that couldn't mean *me,* of course, but my wife, Phyllis, insisted I stop in at our family doctor just to let him look at it. The doctor said it didn't look suspicious but he'd take it off, anyway. Believe it or not, a good friend of mine had stopped into the doctor's office while I there. He was a writer at a Hollywood movie studio and he was getting some background information about something he was writing about a football player whose life was being threatened by cancer. My writer friend, the doctor and I all smiled over the coincidence of my visit and the doctor told me to go home and don't worry about a thing.

"A couple of days later the doctor phoned and asked me to stop by for a cup of coffee. He had never asked me over for coffee before . . . something was serious, so I dropped everything and got on over there. He told me the biopsy report had come back from the lab and it was positive. The black mole on my arm was cancerous. Suddenly I felt as though the toughest blocker in the NFL had just caught me in the pit of my stomach.

"I asked him what everybody would ask in that situation: 'Was he *sure?*' Could there be a mistake?

"Quietly he assured me there was no error, and even before I could follow up with the normal question of how serious, what next, how long, and stuff like that, he was telling me he'd already been doing some checking about treatment and was convinced that a program they had at the UCLA Medical Center was as good as any place in the country.

"So I checked in there the next morning and a couple of the doctors laid it right on the line for me. They said they didn't know too much about treating this type of melanoma at that point, but they'd recently developed a new technique which they thought was promising. They didn't have too much history on it due to its recent development. I think they called it 'isolated profusion,' which meant nothing to me but it sounded like a heckuva weird procedure when they explained it to me. But I said, heck, I want to see those kids of mine grow up, so let's go. Football was the last thing on my mind, right then, but I couldn't help thinking about what Coach Bryant used to say . . . *'That you can win and you can lose and most of the time it's the believing that's the difference.'* Well, Coach had been right so often that I decided to believe—to *know*—that this thing would work and I'd beat it.

"Now, I don't want to try to explain all the technical aspects because I might get something bolixed up, but to begin with they said I might be in the operating room 10 or 12 hours.

"They were going to open the incision where the mole had been removed and insert some sort of drug. Then they were going to put me on a heart-lung machine to breath for me while they lowered my body temperature by packing me in ice. From what I understood, the chemical they were going to use was too strong to be injected into the whole body. The idea was to isolate my right arm from the rest of the body through this freezing technique. But because of my body size it took a long time to reduce my body temperature which is why the procedure took eleven hours. I may not have everything lined up with the proper X's and O's here, but whatever the game plan was, it worked.

"They put me into physiotherapy because I had almost immediately lost the use of my right arm, and I was climbing the wall, trying to get some movement out of it. But even before I could get a ripple out of it, I asked the doctors if I could play football again if I got the strength back. They looked at me for an instant, sort of blankly, and then one of 'em said: 'sure, why not?' My mind worked over two things. One, they really didn't think I might play again, or two, there was no hope for me and they might as well let me down gradually.

"I started on a program of physiotherapy and weight training to restore muscle and motor activity in my right arm. It was a month before I sensed any kind of improvement. I spoke to Coach Bryant on the phone and must have mentioned that it would take a miracle to come back. Because he growled: 'Make your own miracle.'

"I'd had that surgical and drug procedure on April 20. The Rams' training camp opened in early July. I'll never know whether it was the good Lord, or whether I'd followed Coach Bryant's instructions to make my own miracle. But I played that season. Not particularly well, *but I played*. The team didn't have a good year and I figured at least I'd be better for the following season. But I was 28-years-old and maybe the cancer would come back, or at least I'd be limited in my playing ability while it was in remission. What should I do with the rest of my active life? I decided to give college coaching a whirl, and Gene Stallings, my former teammate and the new head coach at Texas A&M, took me on as an assistant.

"But after a year at A&M, with me taking part in its strength and conditioning program, I had the urge to play again. I went back to the pro's and put in eight more of the best years I had as a player. Fortunately, the cancer never returned, and when I was offered a chance to enter pro coaching I jumped at it."

Pardee's craggy face broke into a small smile. "Football couldn't be better to me than it is here, running the Redskins. Long ago

I found out that whatever success you have, as a player or coach, you pay a tremendous price for it, one way or another. And, as Coach Bryant once told me, if you want or need something terribly difficult, you just go out and make your own miracle."

*　　　*　　　*

Steve Sloan, a man whom I'm privileged to call a close friend, was one of Paul Bryant's most brilliant quarterbacks at Alabama. Now he is head coach at Duke. "Having played for him and coached under him for several years, I suppose I could bring dual insights to this business of remembering Coach Bryant," he said softly. Sloan had taken time out during a busy recruiting season to talk to me about his former coach in his new headquarters at Duke in Durham, North Carolina.

"Strangely enough," he was saying, "both insights sort of take a parallel course toward the same conclusions. Life under Bryant as a player, and under him as an assistant coach, is really the same thing. He is concerned—no, make that consumed—he is consumed with two things. Making you want to win and making you want to be a better person.

"I have never, never seen a man so opposed to losing. I'm not talking about people who get sick over it, or who impose an irrational ugliness on other people when they lose. That's negative living. Coach Bryant's approach is positive. He gives you— player or coach—the idea that, just as the human body has antibodies and builds immunity against certain diseases, so does he (Bryant) have a sort of low tolerance and immunity within him to losing.

"I know, for sure, that it's a physical thing for him. Yet I sometimes thought there was something worse than losing as far as Coach Bryant was concerned—not performing up to your best. I remember our 1965 game against Tennessee, when we should have won by two or three touchdowns. Tennessee played inspired ball and we were sloppy, and they tied us, 7–7. Coach was really going to unload on us in the dressing room after that one. In fact, he beat us all to the dressing room door to make sure everyone would have to file past him.

"But when he got there, with us trailing right behind him, he discovered that the door had been locked from the inside. Without missing a beat, Coach Bryant drew back, lunged and knocked the door right off its hinges. We went in past him and he spun on his heel and left. There was nothing he needed to say.

"Whenever I think of Coach Bryant's approach to football— and to life—I think of eight words spoken by Henry Ford in a meeting in Detroit convened by President Hoover in 1928. It was a meeting to challenge outstanding young people from all over the U.S. There were several speakers but when Ford got up he said only eight words. I think it was the greatest eight-word speech in history. He said: *'There is no such thing as no chance.'*

"Coach Bryant always instilled that into us—and he also turned it around. In football, as far as he was concerned, there was no such thing as *chance,* in the sense that you could leave something to chance. Victory came from a sense of purpose and preparedness.

"Let me give you an example of how Coach Bryant prepared. You've heard it said that football is a game of third downs. And it is. Every third down situation is critical because most games are won by the team which makes the most third down conversions. We always called it 'third down and clutch yardage.'

"Well, Bryant always seemed to be able to anticipate something extra, in practice, for the type of drills we needed to win a particular game. On Tuesday, before a big game against Mississippi in 1965, we had a terrible practice. So Coach called an early morning Wednesday drill on short yardage situations. All week he and his assistants had studied Mississippi's third down defenses. When do they stunt? When do they blitz? When do they expect us to pass, or go wide? The offense must come up with a play or plays to use against the expected defense, particularly on third down.

"And always, Bryant knew there was the intangible factor. What would his team do when confronted with adversity? Will it fold at the crucial moment or rise to the heights needed at that time? And what makes coaching so intriguing is that the overall importance of the play isn't really known until hindsight becomes operative. A winning season can hinge on a single play. A bowl game may rest on it. You just never know.

"I think Coach Bryant always knew. So, let's get back to that game with Ole Miss in 1965, after that special Wednesday morning practice. With about two minutes left to play, we trailed 16–10. We got the ball and as the offense went on the field, Bryant slapped a couple of us on the rump and said softly: 'Remember, now, when it comes to third and clutch . . .'

"It was another case of instant transfusion. We had ninety yards to go and we had to keep it alive against a ferocious Mississippi defense. Four times we were faced with 'third and clutch.' Once, Jerry Duncan caught a tackle-eligible pass. Then, Ray Perkins made a fantastic catch for a 30-yard gain.

"I think on every third-and-clutch I'd involuntarily glance toward the sideline, and there'd be Coach Bryant standing solidly motionless, with his arms folded, or his hands resting on his hips. It's seem as though he were staring straight back at me. Lord, what a feeling, and what rapport a quarterback would have with the man at that moment.

"So we were still alive. Up came another third and clutch. Steve Bowman plowed into the middle and made the first down by inches. A half minute later Les Kelly did the same thing. Four 'clutch' situations in a row. We scored. Then, with five seconds left on the clock, David Ray kicked the extra point for a 17–16 victory. We went on to win the national championship that year. Just because Coach Bryant knew how to prepare for 'clutch' yardage—and how to stand there on the sidelines and imbue a team with his own winning desires. It's a combination of talent and genius that doesn't exist in any other football coach."

*　　　*　　　*

"I'm sure everyone who played for, or coached under, Coach Bryant remembers him for different things," Ray Perkins stated, "although I'm equally sure they all share some thoughts in common. I can still recall his impact on me long before my senior year in high school. I was only 15, and just beginning to play high school football, but I already was hung up on going to Alabama and playing for Bryant. A lot of kids in the South—if they were any good at all—wanted to play for Alabama and the real reason was Bryant. His name and reputation were magic. But in my case I was in for a disappointment."

Perkin's face broke into the beginning of a bitter smile. "I was recruited by exactly one school—Southern Mississippi. Nobody saw me as their fullback of the future, which was what I played then. But one day an Alabama assistant coach—Dude Hennessey—came around to scout our game against Columbus, Mississippi. Columbus had a couple of big backs Alabama was interested in. Hennessey had never even heard of me. But I had a particularly good game that day, and instead of going to the Columbus dressing room he came over to ours and offered me a scholarship to Alabama. I was excited—shoot, no, I was *stunned*—and I'll never know how I got the nerve to tell him, 'Thanks very much, but I'd like to hear it personally from Coach Bryant.'

"Hennessey said okay. I think he knew how I felt and went along with it. So, the next night I got a phone call from Coach Bryant who told me he'd like me to come to Alabama. I heard that slow, rumbling voice come over the wire and I almost had to pinch myself that it was all for real. After all, it was something I'd been dreamin' about, and for all I know, it was still a dream, but your hands don't sweat when you're dreamin', and mine sure were while I was holding that phone."

A small muscle twitched in Perkin's face and his eyes narrowed ever so slightly. "I'll tell you what I *did* know for real at that moment," he recalled. "I was sure that if I should play for Coach Bryant I could play for anybody. I liked his winning ways.

"Now, there was a time when Coach Bryant would never have taken a player who'd told him he was getting married right after high school graduation, which I planned to do. But he understood and didn't blink an eye when I told him. I said I'd be bringing my wife with me and she'd get a job, and with my scholarship and her job we'd manage just fine. I think he was impressed with my seriousness or he mightn't have gone for it.

"Anyway, we enrolled at Alabama, and it didn't take long for me to understand how Coach Bryant could develop a closeness with his players. It happened in spring training, my freshman year. I got a head injury which was going to require surgery. The team doctors didn't think I'd ever play football again, and you can imagine how my wife and I reacted to *that*. So they took me to the hospital in Birmingham. And you know what

Bryant did? He brought my wife to Birmingham and put her up in a hotel for nine days . . . And he, himself, stayed in Birmingham all that time, too, and came to see me every day while they did the surgery and then ran a lot of tests. When the doctors were finished, they still doubted I'd play again. One minute after they told me that, Coach Bryant was telling me I'd still have my full scholarship for four years and that I had nothing to worry about.

"So I was red-shirted my sophomore year and Coach Bryant kept my spirits up by telling me strange things happen with football injuries and very often nature could do what doctor's couldn't. And wouldn't you know that by the following fall, the doctors said I could play again, and I had three great seasons there.

"I was president of the A-Club during my senior year, so I had a lot of opportunities to meet with Coach Bryant in off-field situations and I got to know the man in ways a lot of his players never did. I'll never forget one thing he said to me: 'If you want to be successful, you've got to find people your success means something to and touches them in a positive way.' When you think about that for a moment—think real hard and deep about it—it gives you a whole different perspective of success. I've never forgotten it."

Perkins shook his head in a gesture of wonderment. "It's hard for outsiders to understand the bond that always exists between Coach Bryant and his former players and coaches. A few years ago he gave a reunion in Tuscaloosa for his 1961, 1964 and 1965 National Championship teams. Someone said they contacted almost one hundred people. Ninety of them showed up, from all over America, from the South, the Midwest, the Northeast and even from California. What a reunion! Dinners and lunches. An Alabama film session. A golf tournament. All kinds of great moments together for three days. Do you know of any other coach who ever pulled off anything like that?"

"Well, no," Perkin's visitor admitted. But maybe because there was only one Paul "Bear" Bryant.

There was instant agreement there.

# 16

# *Tackle Eligible*

*"I was in the shower, and Sang Lyda came run-*
*ning in and said, 'Coach Bryant wants everybody*
*out of the shower and into the dressing room.' I*
*didn't know what was going to happen."*

—Jerry Duncan

After all of the miles that had been traveled, all of the great personalities that had been encountered, and all of the stories that had been told, there were still several resources that needed to be tapped until I was completely satisfied with the knowledge of how Bryant and his winning men had become so successful.

Call it perhaps a lesson in character building, Horatio Alger style. I knew, however, that the stories that these men had shared with me, the many conflicts that they had encountered in life, and how they were resolved, would have a positive impact on my life for a long time to come.

So in the famous words of Willie Nelson, I was on the road again visiting famous football legends of the past. The first stop on the second phase of this fascinating adventure would be with Jerry Duncan, now a successful stockbroker with Dean Witter Reynolds, Inc. Those who knew Bryant and his winning football men best say that Duncan and Dee Powell (who was with Bryant at Texas A&M and became his line coach at Alabama) were the toughest players, physically and mentally, he ever coached. Even today, at the end of spring practice, they still give "The Jerry Duncan I Like To Practice Award" to a promising Tide player with an outstanding winning attitude.

It was mid-afternoon and the giant stockbroker firm, located on the seventh floor of the First Alabama Bank Building in downtown Birmingham, was settling down after another big rally in the often hectic marketplace called Wall Street. The "big board," as they call it, was flashing the closing figures for the day. The secretaries and other salesmen were moving quickly from one office to another checking and double checking the final tallies.

Within minutes I knew that the afternoon's interview would finally take place. But time passed ever so slowly.

Why?

My notes in front of me indicated that Jerry Duncan had been recruited to Alabama by Clem Gryska, current day assistant athletic director and recruiting coordinator at Alabama and the person directly responsible for Coach Bryant's successful football program. Duncan had been raised on a dairy farm by his father in Sparta, North Carolina, a rural farming community of approximately 3,000 people where he had been a standout halfback at Sparta High. The competition among the small North Carolina schools was nothing to brag about, and along with Duncan's relatively small physique, there were few schools interested in his football talents.

North Carolina State, however, took a chance and signed him to a scholarship but later backed out after checking Duncan's grades. Georgetown offered him a full scholarship on the nearly impossible condition that he could make the basketball team, too. Finally, Alabama, who had won the national championship the previous season, showed up from the middle of nowhere offering the Sparta native a one-in-a-million chance to come to Tuscaloosa, Alabama, and make good on all of his dreams of glory.

Finally, it was 3:15 P.M. and the receptionist was leading me down the hallway to my long awaited interview with Jerry Duncan, the man who had come to Alabama as a stand-out halfback, was converted to one of Bryant's "itty-bitty linemen" making Bryant's controversial "tackle-eligible" play so successful in the mid-sixties and later overcome a near crippling bout with arthritis.

Anxiously, I looked forward to the moments ahead.

*     *     *

In the fall of 1964, Alabama was voted the national championship following the close of the regular season. Then in the Orange Bowl, Texas beat Alabama 21–17 after Joe Namath failed a quarterback sneak attempt from less than a yard away, late in the game. It was that disappointing loss that would set the stage for Bryant's Crimson Tide in 1965.

"The Spring of 1965 was the most difficult spring I ever went through. It was a rebuilding time. We had lost a lot of our offensive line. It was really a demanding spring, one of those that people have heard about under Coach Bryant when things were really rough. There were a lot of people who left, and I was almost one of them. He reminded us every day of being stopped inside the one-yard line against Texas.

"We'd got to the stadium for a scrimmage one Saturday, and practice wasn't going like Coach Bryant wanted it to. The students were in the stadium sunbathing, and Coach Bryant told us to go to the dressing room. After we'd been there for a few minutes, Coach Bryant told Sang Lyda, the team manager, to get the students out and lock the gate. The students left thinking practice was over, and then we came back out, and the fur would really begin to fly, and Coach Bryant was right there in the middle of it."

At the end of spring practice in 1965, Duncan was a second team guard. "You always went by to see Coach Bryant before you went home," Duncan explained, "and Coach told me, 'You're not a very good football player right now, but I believe you've got a chance if you'll dedicate yourself and stay in shape all summer.' So I loaded and unloaded trucks at Baggett Transportation in Birmingham and worked out at Ramsey High in the afternoon. It was tough, but when I returned to Tuscaloosa I was in top condition."

Fall practice turned out to be full of breaks for the North Carolina youngster. On the first day a first-team tackle failed to run the mile in the prescribed time and he was denied a uniform. The coaching staff them moved Duncan from guard to tackle in a back-up role. And in the first practice the man with whom Duncan was competing for the starting tackle position went out with a knee injury. Now, Duncan finally had his chance.

Bryant, in the meantime, moved into the athletic dorm that fall to ride herd on the 1965 Tide. "I ran into him in there a week or ten days before we played Georgia," Duncan explained, "and he told me, 'I sure am proud of the way you've been doing Jerry.'

"I said, 'Thank you, coach. I've been trying.'

"He said, 'Trying hell. I expect you to get a lot better.'

"And with that he turned and walked away. I never really did talk to Coach Bryant any when I was playing for him. About all I said was, 'Yes, sir.' And that was all that needed to be said.

"We didn't have many athletes in 1965, but Paul Crane was a great one, and so was Ray Perkins and Dennis Homan. I never did think Steve Sloan was all that good, but all he did was get the ball across the goal line and win. Not only was he a great player, but a great person and tremendous leader.

"Most importantly, the thing we had going for us was Coach Bryant. We would have killed for him. He intimidated us enough to make us think we weren't any good, and all along we wanted to prove to him we were. That's the reason we won so much, because we weren't going to let him think we weren't any good. Coach Bryant knew from the time I got there until I left that I wasn't worth a damn as a football player, but I was going to show him I was, and I hope in some way I did."

The Crimson Tide opened the 1965 season ranked number-one in the pre-season polls. But in their first contest against Georgia, Alabama lost, 18–17.

"We had all kinds of opportunities to win, even as bad as we played. When the time was running off the clock and we obviously were going to lose, the offense was walking off the field, and some of us were crying and sobbing, and Coach Schnellenberger ran over to where we were and slapped somebody on the head and said, 'All right, get your ass up and throw your head back and run off this field like a champion.' And that's what we did.

"In the dressing room Coach Bryant told us, 'You're not worth a damn. We've wasted a lot of time. You've let the people down who wore this crimson jersey before you. Now we're going back to Tuscaloosa and get to work, and I'm going to try to save you.'

"At 8 o'clock Sunday morning, the team was assembled in the film room and Coach Schnellenberger said, 'Okay, we're going to watch this film, and then we're going to go outside and throw up, and then we're going to watch it again and throw up again. We're going to watch it over and over and over.'

"After we watched it over and over and over, we went to the practice field and practiced what seemed forever.

"I knew how those guys felt after practicing for Coach Bryant at Junction. Afterwards, I did a little bit of soul searching, trying to decide how important football was to me. Finally, I called my daddy and said, 'I'm coming on home. They're just about to kill us down here. I've had all this I can take. We got beat Saturday, and I just feel so bad.'

"He had seen the game on television, and he said, 'Well, you should have gotten beat, the way you played.'

"That really made me feel good. I said, 'Well, I think I'm coming home. I'm tired of football.'

"He said, 'Well, if you want to come up here and milk these damn Holstein cattle for the rest of your life, come on.'

"I got to thinking about milking those Holsteins twice a day for 365 days a year, and football didn't sound so bad, after all."

In the second game of the season, Alabama bounced back and defeated Tulane, 27–0, and began making preparations for their annual showdown with Ole Miss.

"The first team was working on the punting game during the last period Tuesday, and Coach Bryant came down off the tower as he always did for the last period," Duncan recalled. "I'll be damned if somebody didn't break through on the right side and almost block the first punt. Coach Bryant said, 'Line up and do it again.' Then somebody broke through on my side and almost blocked it. Coach Bryant just went bananas. He said, 'Get your butts off the field. Just go find your girlfriends and hold hands, if you can find one that'll hold any of your hands.'

"Later, while in the shower, Sang Lyda, the team manager, came running in and said, 'Coach Bryant wants everybody out of the shower and into the dressing room.' I didn't know what was going to happen. Everybody walked out, and he said, 'I want everybody in full gear and on the practice field in the morning at 5:15. Right now you're going to get your ass beat by Ole Miss Saturday night and I'm going to try to save you.'

"I said, 'Oh, my God.'

"Coach Bryant told us, 'Any player that's late, pack your bags and go home. Any coach that's late is fired.' That night Coach Dude Hennessey slept in the dressing room so he'd be there when all the rest of them got there.

"Wayne Cook, the starting tight end, said, 'I'm not going.' Some of us got together and called Coach Pat Dye and said, 'Wayne Cook's getting ready to quit. He's not going to be out there in the morning.' Coach Dye went to the dorm and got Wayne up and got him dressed and got him to the practice field. He told him, 'You're not going to quit. I'm not going to let you quit.' Wayne got his uniform on and turned out to be one of the best football players on the team. He was probably the best blocking tight end I've ever seen.

"When we got there at 4:30 to dress, Coach Bryant was already out on the field, walking around the track. He had on his street clothes, but he had on those big army boots that he wore. I never will forget those boots. They looked like they were size 20, and if you ever had one of them up the side of your rear end it felt like it, too. And I have.

"We got dressed and went out, and he took the first offense and put the ball on the 40-yard line and said, 'We're going to knock it in.' In about three plays we scored. Then he put the ball on the five-yard line and got the first team defense out there and said, 'Okay, we're going to stop them.' They nearly killed whoever was lined up in front of them. We probably weren't out there fifteen minutes. We went to work and did the job."

Against Ole Miss and trailing, 17–16, Alabama had to come from behind to win. Steve Sloan led an 89-yard march in the closing minutes. "In that drive, either two or three times we went on fourth down," Duncan said. "On third down and 14 we threw the first tackle-eligible pass that I caught, and it got seventeen yards. Of all the tackle-eligible passes I caught, even the one against Mississippi State that went for a touchdown, that was the one I remember the most because it really kept the winning drive alive. I can still visualize Johnny Vaught running up the sidelines hollering, 'Tackle-eligible!' He was the only one out of 70,000 people, besides us, who knew it was coming. But his players didn't hear him."

The Crimson Tide began to play with a reckless abandon after the Ole Miss game by manhandling LSU, South Carolina and Auburn. But the 7–7 tie with Tennessee will always linger foremost in Duncan's mind.

"We had the ball near the Vols' goal with seconds to play, and Kenny Stabler passed out of bounds to stop the clock—on fourth down. That definitely stopped the clock and stopped any chance we had of winning. There was a lot of confusion. At the same time Stabler was throwing the ball out of bounds to stop the clock, David Ray was lining up to kick a field goal, and Ray Perkins was in motion. It was anything but a well-executed play.

"In the dressing room after the game Coach Bryant told us, 'You'd have been better off if I'd stayed in Tuscaloosa with the rest of the coaches and just sent y'all to Birmingham. You probably would have won because I don't think we contributed very much today. I still think you can be national champions, but it's not going to be easy, and we're going to have to get some breaks along the way.' "

Prior to the Orange Bowl game against Nebraska the AP poll had ranked Michigan State first, followed by Arkansas and Nebraska with Alabama in fourth place. Earlier in the day UCLA beat Michigan State, 14–12, in the Rose Bowl, and LSU beat

Arkansas in the Cotton Bowl, 14–7. It was announced prior to the Orange Bowl evening contest that the winner of the game would be crowned national champions.

And before it was over, the Alabama-Nebraska display was a high fisted shootout but Bryant's men prevailed in the final result, 39–28.

"Nebraska was much more talented and had more great athletes than we did. It was the kind of game Coach Bryant thrives on. He knew we weren't as good as they were, and he told us so. He told us there was no way we could line up and play with them, but we were going to do things differently that night. We were going to play wide open football. We weren't going to be conservative. Sloan was going to throw from our end zone or the 10-yard line or wherever we were if we felt like we could get a man open, which was something Coach Bryant hadn't done before, at least not with this team."

Duncan himself didn't realize the magnitude of the game. "Unbeknownst to me, Coach Bryant had told Sloan he wanted to open the game with the tackle-eligible play."

"We won the toss, elected to receive and got the ball. Suddenly in the huddle, Sloan called a tackle-eligible, and I froze. I was the only one who didn't come out of the huddle, it scared me so bad. I was afraid I would drop it. Here we were playing before 80,000 people and millions on national television, and the least they could have done was told me they were going to open up throwing at me.

"Anyway, he hit me, and I think I could have scored if I hadn't fallen down. The Nebraska secondary rotated exactly like we wanted them to rotate. As a matter of fact, they over-rotated. They rolled up on double coverage on the opposite side of Dennis Homan, and I had one man out there and Ray Perkins to block him, but I fell down after I caught the ball and gained only about twelve yards. On the next play we ran the tackle-eligible screen and gained about seventeen yards."

All in all the Crimson Tide amassed 518 yards of thrilling offense in the Orange Bowl contest, including 196 yards on Sloan's twenty pass completions. Bryant himself got wrapped up in the post game fever and called it one of his team's greatest wins.

The next morning the AP sportswriters gave their nod of approval and voted the Crimson Tide another national title, their third in five years.

\*　　　\*　　　\*

These days Duncan keeps his hand in football by being part of the radio broadcast team for the Crimson Tide games and serving as a part-time scout for the selection committee of the Birmingham Hall of Fame annual post season bowl classic.

Off the field, however, Duncan has had to meet head-on one of life's most difficult hurdles. He has incurable rheumatoid arthritis, having been afflicted shortly after his playing days under Bryant. These days he is faced with frequent pain and often requires heavy dosages of medication. The joints located where the toes meet the feet have since been removed. His shoe size, which used to be size 11, is now size 8-½.

"With this arthritis thing, there have been so many times I just wanted to sit down and quit," Duncan said. "But I believe having been under Coach Bryant and having been disciplined by him has helped me. It prepared me for the pain and the mental anguish.

"I remember one time somebody went to one of the assistant coaches and told him Coach Bryant had been running us too much and we were bruised and tired. 'Can't you ease up on them a little bit?' The assistant asked Coach Bryant.

"That day at the meeting Coach Bryant came in and said, 'Somebody tells me ya'll are tired. Well, I'm tired, too. I'm tired of listening to all of that crap. I'm 50 years old. I'm tired of ya'll. I'm tired of working. But what am I going to do? Let me tell you something: If you think you're tired now, just wait fifteen years when you owe the bank $50,000 and you come home one day from work and your house is on fire and your wife has left town with the drummer and you've got three kids to take care of. What are you going to do? Quit?'

"I've thought about that a lot since then. Winning just means too much to me—whether it's in football, in business or in life.

"Quitting. There would just be no way."

# 17

# *Ageless Wonder*

*"My first impression of him was, 'This must be what God looks like.' He'd walk in the room and you wanted to stand up and applaud. He gives this speech to the student body and I thought he was going to get elected president."*

—George Blanda

The scrapbooks are stored way back in the closet, behind the place where the winter coats go in the summer and the summer coats go in the winter. They crackle when they are opened, as if the pages were made out of onion peelings. The corners are totally decomposed and some of the stories pasted inside are no longer readable. They come from an era that is gone with the wind, when football helmets were still being made out of leather and more schools played the single wing formation than the T-formation, which was considered just a little bit radical.

One of the great ironies in sports is that while athletes may be disturbed, annoyed or outraged at the curious things newspapermen write about them, they all clip out the stories and tenderly place them in scrapbooks. No active football player has more scrapbooks that George Frederick Blanda. His wife says she starts a new one every generation. And there is as much truth as humor in that remark. The first ones, though, are the most interesting.

It seems incredible that a contemporary of Doc Blanchard, Glenn Davis, Doak Walker, and Johnny Lujack would still be throwing his body around a football field more than a quarter of a century later. But those four people were Heisman Trophy winners during the four years that Blanda was an undergraduate at the University of Kentucky. Think of it, and enjoy the warm excitement of having your brain boggled.

Open those museum-piece scrapbooks and step way back in time. It is 1945 again. The great crusade against Fascism is grinding to a merciful conclusion. Patriotism is everywhere. There are flags behind the bar in Youngwood, Pennsylvania. There are also gold stars hanging in mothers' windows. The movies that appear in the town's lone picture show are so wholesome they squeak. Lynn Cari is falling in love with some soldier home on leave or John Wayne is being confronted by Sessue Hayakawa, who says, with a rattlesnake sneer, "Why, so, you are surprised I speak your wrangwrige. I was educated at a college in your country . . . at UC-R-A."

Harry Truman fills the White House with piano music and some of the choicest language anyone has heard in Washington since Andrew Jackson was president. There is a drastic shortage of athletes. And the Chicago Cubs and Detroit Tigers are winning pennants with an incredible collection of old men and 4-Fers. When they come together in the fall, Warren Brown, the Chicago columnist, will write: "I don't see how either team can win this World Series." Matters are so grim that the St. Louis Browns— remember them?—have a one-armed outfielder and everybody is saying, "Gee, he really isn't bad." Everything is relative. At the moment, Pete Gray really isn't bad.

Television has not yet been inflicted on society, its development held up by the war. So professional football does not dominate Sunday afternoon. There are only a few teams, the Pittsburgh Steelers, the Green Bay Packers, the Chicago Cardinals, the New York Giants, the Chicago Bears, the Philadelphia Eagles, etc. But they do not get much newspaper coverage outside the cities where they play. So the men of Youngwood spend their Sundays listening to Pittsburgh Pirates games on the radio and drinking

Polish Champagne—two shots of rye whiskey in a glass of beer.

This is gritty, drab bituminous coal country. High school football takes everybody's minds off the low quality of their lifestyles. Crowds are large at games. The entire town shows up. Stores close and houses empty for road trips. The traffic is bumper-to-bumper from Youngwood to Bentleyville and back. Only the police force remains behind. Players are named Stankovich, Kurowski, Stepko, Jurik, Puskarich, Ciereij and Blanda, the sons of men who spend ten hours a day crouched over where the rain never falls and the sun doesn't shine. Blanda is the tailback for the Youngwood High School Railroaders, of all exotic nicknames. He is what romanticists of the period refer to as a "triple threat," which means he runs, kicks and passes with equal skill. Not only that, he plays defense. In one game he comes frighteningly close to kicking a field goal on the kickoff. The ball hits the crossbar and falls back onto the field.

"But my big sport was basketball," said Blanda, looking at the scrapbooks. "And I was also crazy over track. In fact, I was the whole track team. It's true. I was a discus and javelin thrower and I also put the shot. I didn't have a coach. All I knew I got out of books in the library and I didn't know much. I was so dumb that every time I'd throw the javelin I'd get this terrible whiplash across my back. I didn't know any better.

"I'd go to the interscholastic meets and they'd say, 'Introducing the Youngwood High School track team' and I'd be the only guy there. I didn't even have a uniform, just dungarees, T-shirt and sneakers. I guess it would have been funny as hell, except that I'd usually get first in all three events.

"In one big meet, I got fifteen points and finished second in the team standing. I was a one-man team. I had a buddy of mine go with me to track meets. I'd carry the shot and the discus and he'd carry the javelin. He used to say that he was the manager for the Youngwood High School track team.

"Don't think track isn't dangerous. One day I was standing around the field and somebody yelled, 'Hey, George, watch out.'

"I looked up and there was this javelin flying through the sky and it was headed straight for my middle. Anybody else jumps back, right? Well, I was just a dumb Polack. So I jumped up.

That's right. That javelin hit me right in the upper thigh on my right leg. I came about this close to being the 'Queen of Pennsylvania.' That damn spear could have got me right in the groin."

So in May of 1945, George Blanda was recovering from his injury, the only athlete ever to be wounded in action at the Western Pennsylvania Interscholastic League track meet in Clairton, Pennsylvania. It has been his dream to go to Notre Dame. One afternoon he was on the playground, limping around, playing basketball and moving about as slow as you would expect anyone to move who was just recently punctured by a spear. And along came the Notre Dame football coach, who has a scholarship for this Slovak kid.

"Which one is George Blanda?" he asked.

"The dark-haired kid with the defiant jaw," a bystander replied.

"Him? The one that's moving so slow? When does the bus go back to South Bend?"

"After that I just about made up my mind I'd go to the University of Pennsylvania and be a genuine Ivy Leaguer. I had offers from Purdue, Pitt, Penn State, NYU, and William and Mary. I had received letters from lots of other schools. But I decided that I was going to go to the University of Pennsylvania. A fellow who lived over in the next town, a place called Greensburg, was an assistant coach at Penn and he hung around our place. Finally, he talked me and Lou Kusserow, who ended up going to Columbia, into visiting the University. I'd played high school basketball against Lou. He was from another small town in the area, Glassport. We took our exams. I passed and I guess he did too. And it looked like I was going to go to Penn. I planned to enter in time for the summer sessions, which started in July.

"I'm home one day and this guy comes to the door. I don't know him from Adam, but he's a scout for the University of Kentucky. He's got a train ticket. He tells me it's a train ticket to Lexington and I want you to go down there and look the place over. If you like it, tell me and I'll get you a scholarship. Well, hell, I don't know anything about the University of Kentucky. In fact. I didn't even know where Kentucky was.

"I thought Kentucky was all the way across the country. Up

until I was 17, I was never further away from Youngwood than Pittsburgh, which is about 30 or 40 miles away. I thought they were still fighting Indians west of Pittsburgh.

"I didn't want to go down to visit. But I don't know how to tell the guy I don't want his ticket. So I take it and thank him and close the door. I'm all set to go to Penn. I'd already told the head coach there, George Munger, that I was coming. They had some fine football teams there then. Chuck Bednarik was there. I guess maybe down deep in my mind I really didn't want to go there. I'd heard that you had to join a fraternity and keep up a social front. And I'm just a Slovak kid from a coal town and all I know is Polish sausage and boiled cabbage.

"The people at Penn had been impressing on me that there was a class structure there and it would be a good chance for me to move up socially. And that didn't really thrill me. I wasn't really looking for that, coming from my background. I just wanted to get an education. I was good in mathematics and figured I might want to be an engineer. I didn't know what an engineer was, but it sounded good. I figured I'd go to Penn anyway, because their engineering school was supposed to be pretty hot. I figured I'd just learn to live with the society stuff. So I decided I wouldn't bother with Kentucky. One afternoon, my old man caught me by the scuff of the neck—he was a pretty hardnosed guy—and he says, 'When you going down to talk to the people at the University of Kentucky?' I told him I wasn't going. He said, 'The hell you're not . . . so, go down there and look the place over.' Well, needless to say, if I hadn't gone he would have knocked the hell out of me.

"So I go from Pittsburgh to Cincinnati on the train. I'm a young, 17-year-old kid and I've got eyes this big. When I got to Cincinnati, I managed to get lost in the train terminal. Finally, I found my right train. I figure it'll be another long ride from Cincinnati to Lexington, so I better get some sleep. How did I know it's only an hour to Lexington? The conductor's shaking hell out of me and I'm trying to wrassle him.

"I got off the train and looked around. Thank God you can see the University from the station because there was nobody there to meet me. Nobody! So I start walking and I feel like the world is about to swallow me up. I keep thinking, 'I wish the hell I'd never left Youngwood!' And, 'What am I doing in this place?'

"After about an hour, I find the athletic department and I go looking for the head football coach, who was Bernie Shively at the time. He never heard of me! I said, 'I'm George Blanda!' He says 'What are you doing here?' I told him somebody gave me a ticket to come down and visit the school. He wanted to know what I played. I said, 'I'm a football player.' He said, 'Okay, this afternoon we'll have a little workout. Take you out and see what you can do.'

"I told him I was a kicker and a passer—you know, a single-wing tailback. So I went out and threw the ball around, punted and place kicked. It wasn't a tryout exactly. They just wanted to see what you had. At that time in 1945, with the war not over yet, they'd take you if you were breathing. They're looking for anybody. I could always throw the ball a long way. I probably could throw the ball better than I do now. Maybe I wasn't as consistent or as accurate, but I was hell for distance. I could really whip the ball. Immediately, they're impressed.

"I told them I was going to the University of Pennsylvania. Well, now Coach Shively knows my name. He has me stay around for about five days. They took me to the Kentucky Derby and I was impressed with that. I'd never seen horse racing before. Somehow I let it drop that I really preferred to play basketball. Now Coach Shively goes looking for Adolph Rupp, the basketball coach. He asks me to come to one of his tryout sessions. I guess Shively said, 'Give George some bull.' He knew I could play football for Kentucky, but he guessed that probably I wouldn't make the basketball team.

"Well, he was right. So Rupp let me work out and after it's over the Great Adolph Rupp motions me over and says, 'I think you can make our basketball team if you come to school here.' I always was a better basketball player than I was a football player and I knew I was better than any of the guys he had in there for this tryout.

"That got me thinking about Kentucky. But you know what the clincher was? They decided to buy me two suits of clothes. I'd never owned a suit in my life. So I picked out two suits— one blue and one brown. Then Shively really went to work on me. He had all these big players coming back, bigger than guys I'd seen at the other schools. And he starts telling me how Kentucky is going to go to the Cotton Bowl and the Sugar Bowl and I'd get a chance to see the nation. When you went up East, the coaches and athletic directors didn't talk about a thing except how great it would be to go to their schools.

"I said, 'Well, this is the place to go. If they give me two suits and promise me we'll go to the Sugar Bowl or the Cotton Bowl, I'll go to Kentucky.' That's all I got. I was never a pampered high school athlete. If you played poorly in those western Pennsylvania towns, you couldn't run fast enough to get away from the lynch mob. If you did well, the people looked up to you and said, 'He's a good athlete, that George Blanda.' But there was none of this slipping you $10 for having a good game. They expected you'd have a good game. Nobody ever took you out for a meal. Hell, there was no place in Youngwood to buy you a meal anyway. You were better off eating at home. We weren't pampered at Youngwood and that was good training, because it got me ready to play for Bear Bryant.

"Bear Bryant! There was a wonderful coach and wonderful man . . . a mean sonuvabitch, but a wonderful coach and man. The Bear taught me discipline, respect and dedication. He'd run your fanny right into the ground. Those practice sessions of his were . . . Well, when they were over you wanted to collapse. But the Bear wasn't that merciful. He wouldn't even let you die. He'd make you run back to the locker room. He'd tell you to turn in your suit if you didn't sprint. I picked up a lot from him. He was just as mean as my old man. But they both taught me how to compete.

"All the pampering I ever got was those two suits. That's all I ever needed. Other than that I got just what the NCAA allowed—room, board and tuition. One time I thought I should be getting a little something under the table. I'd heard all these stories. I mentioned it to Coach Bryant. He came up over the top of his desk and grabbed me by my eyeballs.

" 'You want what?' he yells.

" 'Just joking, Coach,' I said and got the hell out of there. That taught me a great lesson about greed. After that I didn't care if other people got more than I did. I was getting my college education paid for and I was getting help finding summer jobs. So, I figured I was damned lucky.

"They hustled me into school in time for the summer semester, because they didn't want me going to Penn. Naturally, there was a summer workout for the football players. About the fifth practice session, I tore the cartilage in my right knee. I was pretty upset about it. But at the time they didn't know anything about knee injuries. I'm not so sure they know much about it now. They just taped me up and I played my first year that way—freshmen were eligible for the varsity then. Needless to say, I didn't have a first-class year. My grades weren't that good because I was worried about my leg and I kind of let my classwork slip.

"Oh, yes, that first . . . we didn't go to the Sugar Bowl or the Orange Bowl or the Cotton Bowl. We won two games and lost eight. I was mad at myself. I said, 'George, you damn fool. You made a stupid decision and now there's nothing to do but hang in there and make the best of it.' I figured maybe something good would happen. Then, flash! They brought Coach Bryant in from Maryland. Well, that suited me fine. I'd heard a lot of good things about him. I had started out as a quarterback in the T-formation as a freshman and halfway through the season we switched back to the single wing and I played tailback. I didn't like all that switching around. Everything I had heard about Coach Bryant led me to think we would go to one formation and stay with it.

"Wow! My first impression of him when he came down in January of my freshman year was, 'This must be what God looks like.' He was a very handsome man, tall and smooth. He was the most energetic man I'd ever seen. He'd walk in the room and you wanted to stand up and applaud. He gives this speech to the student body and I thought he was going to get elected president.

"He called all the players in, one by one. I got a little worried, because I figured that, having gone 2–8 the year before, there wouldn't be too many of us around. He asked me how I felt and I told him my knee was killing me. He got me right to a doctor. I laid off spring practice, of course, and came back that summer. I went into that operation scared. I'd heard all kinds of stuff. A lot of guys told me that they might go in there and screw things up so bad I'd end up with a stiff leg. I made it all right. I had to drop out of school for the January-to-March quarter. I went home to Youngwood and I ran. I ran in that miserable weather for five or six miles a day. I figured I'd better work because Coach Bryant didn't strike me as the kind who would run an easy practice. Then I came back in the spring quarter and they were working out. I just hung around and watched."

One interesting thing occurred because of the knee operation. Blanda decided that it would be a good idea to take a tumbling class to build up the knee. The course was co-educational. That was fine because there was a certain brunette that he was very anxious to get close to and she was enrolled. In the same class is Miss Betty Harris, a Lexington girl who does not happen to be brunette. She was a blonde, very bright and shiny. It was all right with her because she had her eye on another guy.

"Would you believe it," she asks. "The girl George was after and the guy I thought was so cute fell for each other. In desperation, I looked around the room and here's this football player working out on the side horse. We made a marvelous couple. I was majoring in dance. That's why I took the class."

The two of them developed a meaningful relationship, long before the term became popular. However, there was one small hindrance: Paul "Bear" Bryant, who was now the sole proprietor of George Blanda's body and, he presumed, George's soul as well. Kentucky football players did not smoke, drink, curse or carry on with women, not even one they were in love with and wanted to marry.

"Enjoy how warm and soft that little hand you're holding going across campus is," Bryant was fond of telling his players, "because the memory of it is going to keep you company on the bench this Saturday."

One afternoon, Betty Harris and another girl who was also dating a football player on the sly, left their jobs at the University library, and climbed to the top of the stadium where they could eat their lunches and get a little sun. It was summertime and even the bluegrass was begging for relief from the Kentucky heat. Suddenly they heard noises on the playing field below. Coach Bryant had driven the team out for a special practice, it being nice and humid and all. Then, the girls were aware that Coach Bryant was aware that they had been seeing a couple of his athletes. But nobody was letting on. However, if they showed themselves, George and the other player would have had to turn in their suits. So they figured they could outwit Bryant. Of course, this was a tactical blunder, one which they'd share with numerous opposing coaches. The varsity scrimmaged in the heat. Then everyone who was still alive went through hours of special drills. By sundown when they all went sprinting off, the two girls were an inch away from a good sunstroke.

"I tell you that summer was hell," says George, who remembers it with more fondness than does his wife. "It was right after the war. You got all the returning servicemen who played in 1941 and 1942. You got all the kids from the 1945 team, freshmen and sophomores, mostly. And Bryant had people coming in from all over the country. He'd been the coach at the Bainbridge, Maryland training station and he knew where every stray athlete was hiding. Shoot, he'd bus them in. He'd get guys who had played on service teams and still had eligibility remaining. It was like you'd do now scouting and signing pro players.

"We must have had five hundred to a thousand kids come through there on tryouts. It was very competitive. It was the survival of the fittest, all right. It was like the old joke about having three teams—one there playing, one coming and one going. I think we practiced football eleven months that year. Coach Bryant brought in the Notre Dame box formation. I guess he figured he wanted to find the meanest Polack on the club and make him the blocking back. I qualified. I didn't like it. I'd always been a kicker, a passer and a runner and I liked the action. I didn't like moving around, blocking for somebody else.

"Hell, I sulked. He knew it, too. So he dropped me to the second unit. I tell myself, 'Okay, coach, you're going to see some action.' I kept hitting people and hitting people. I smacked one halfback so hard, he kicked me in the face when he got up. They were using Harry Ulinski, who later played with the Redskins, and Jerry Claiborne, who's the coach now at Kentucky, ahead of me as blocking backs on the varsity.

"I finally won the job late in the year. Next season we went to the T-formation and I became the quarterback. It was tough recruiting T-quarterbacks in those days and I could throw the ball. Coach Bryant figured he'd better give me the job because I didn't want to hit anybody. He said he thought they had invented the position just for me.

"I wasn't what you'd call a skillful passer, I was a thrower. But I could get the ball up there. He wanted a quarterback who was a leader and he had found out I had a mind of my own.

"There was one pre-season scrimmage—they called it the Blue and White game—when we were still using the Notre Dame box. I was calling plays and we were down on the two-yard line, getting ready to score. I get in the middle and decided, 'Shoot, we weren't going to shift this time.' I'll just take the snap directly from the center, send a man in motion and throw him a pass. Make up my own play, in other words. I throw the ball in there and, as I expected, no way it's going to be completed. We lose the ball on downs and by the time I get to the sidelines, Coach Bryant, who had been watching up in the press box, is already there. He got down that quick. He's right there!

"He grabs me and he says, 'You little . . . ,' well, never mind what he called me, 'I'm the coach of this team and until you're smart enough to be coach of a football team, don't go making up any plays. If you do I'll have you back in that little Pennsylvania town you come from so damned fast you'll think you never left it.' That taught me a hell of a lesson. The year before we'd had this easy going coach, Bernie Shively, who kind of encouraged individualism. And in high school we occasionally made up plays. But Bear . . . ooooh, boy! I never crossed him again. That man had you running so many 100-yard dashes, I think after my senior year, he had me down to 175 pounds. My mother thought I was sick or something."

During Blanda's senior year he got some practice making miracles. Kentucky had a 3–3 record heading for its worst season under Bryant. And Bryant was making ugly noises at the troops. The Wildcats were matched against Villanova and they got the ball on their own 42-yard line with just 44 seconds left to play. They were behind Villanova by a 13–6 score. The customers figured it's time to leave. Kentucky lost 11 yards in three plays. It was now fourth down and 21.

The Villanova line was charging with all the fury of Yangtze River pirates and Blanda couldn't find an open receiver. A tackle had one arm wrapped around George's funny leather helmet. Just as he went down, he got the pass off to halfback Jim Howe in the flat.

At midfield, Ulinski threw a block that got Howe into the open. Only eight seconds remained when Blanda stepped in and kicked the extra point that threw the game into a tie, 13–13. Kentucky did not lose another game all season. The morning after the Villanova game, *The Louisville Courier-Journal* mentioned something about a miracle and said that George Frederick Blanda, age 20, senior, Youngwood, Pa., was probably the man most responsible for making it happen.

"You think that earns you any special concessions from Coach Bryant? You figure that he's going to pamper you after that? Hell, no," says George, rubbing a finger over the clipping that tells about his undergraduate miracle. "At scrimmage the next week, I pitch out to a halfback, who just misses the ball entirely. It's a bad pitch and he's out of position, anyway. It just flops on the grass and neither of us make a move for it.

"So Bryant comes out and says, 'You bastards, both of you, start running around that track until I tell you to stop.' That makes me feel about that big. But we're both wrong, so we start running and running and running. Finally, this halfback leans over and says, 'Screw him, George, let's turn right at the exit by the gym and keep on going.' The Bear lets us run and run. About the fifteenth time around, I'm thinking, 'Is it really worth it?' I forgot how many laps he let us run. It was way past sundown when he finally waved us in. And we were heroes of the game the week before. What do you figure would have happened if we had screwed up?

"The Bear was a demanding sonuvagun. He still is, although he tells me he's mellowed some. I owe my longevity in the game to him and his coaching philosophy: Hard work equals success. That's the only way to make it. Hell, I didn't like his system at first. I wanted to be a goof-off like everybody else. But you could see Bryant get results. We were 2–8 the year before he got there. From that point we went from 7–3 to 8–3, his second year. There was proof that hard work would get you some place. Bear Bryant laid the groundwork for my whole life," says Blanda. "The only thing he was wrong about was when he told George Halas I probably never would make it as a place kicker in the National Football League."

# 18

# Bum and Jerry

*"Then he went around the room, patting 'em on the back with his hands. He told 'em, 'Damn, this is great. Now they'll see what kind of mamas and papas we've got. They'll see what we've got in us.'"*

—Jerry Claiborne

Paul Bryant's dedication to victory was total. "When you win," he often told his players, "the air smells sweeter, your food tastes better, and your girlfriend looks prettier."

Hanging in his clubhouse, Bryant had a favorite poem which best described the many lessons he taught his boys, hoping one day it will help them rally in the fourth quarter of a game or in life, when the going is always toughest.

The last paragraph of Bryant's poem told them: "Life's battle don't always go to the stronger or faster man, but sooner or later the man who wins is the fellow who thinks he can."

And these days two of Bryant's boys seem to think they can do a whole lot of winning, Paul Bryant style. So I went to see them, to learn more about them and what Bryant had taught them.

First on my trip was a visit with O. A. "Bum" Phillips, a modern day folk-hero in NFL football. Bum was a standout high school coach at Nederland High where he supposedly had a record of 90 wins and 2 losses, before becoming an assistant to Bryant at Texas A&M, and later was an assistant coach at Oklahoma State, then joining Sid Gillman at Houston where he later became head coach and rebuilt the Houston Oilers into the pride of Texas, even going one up on America's team, the Dallas Cowboys.

These days, Bum has a new coaching assignment, where he is rebuilding the football fortunes of the New Orleans Saints, aiming them toward the pinnacle of success, a feat which the town of New Orleans has been long overdue.

Afterwards, my sights were set northward to visit the recently named coach of Kentucky, Jerry Claiborne, who was returning to his alma mater where he had once been a part of Bryant's glory days. There he had played under Bryant and later became an assistant to him at Kentucky, Texas A&M and Alabama before taking the head coaching reigns of Virginia Tech and Maryland where he built them into big time winners.

It was a difficult task for Claiborne to return home, attempting to rebuild a program since fallen into despair. And then if he did turn it around, could Claiborne's football team compete with Kentucky's first two loves: basketball and horse racing?

It was a tremendous challenge for Bum and Jerry. However, I looked forward to learning from both of them.

*     *     *

Ever since he was old enough to pitch hay and ride a horse, Bum Phillips would rather spend an hour around the barn than sit through a Tom Mix double-feature at the local movie house. Celluloid cowboys were never his kick. He saw right through their pretty faces and primped kerchiefs.

"They were always kinda phony; that's why I really didn't care for cowboy shows," he recalls. "Now take John Wayne, Jimmy Stewart, Glenn Ford and Chris Wills, they were different. I could sit and watch them. They were real people.

"But Tom Mix, Roy Rogers and that crowd, they were a kind of drugstore type. That jumping onto a horse from behind can get your ribs broke or get you killed. First of all, that would take a whole lot of training and there ain't no horse gonna stand there and let somebody jump on her back from off a building."

You don't fool Mother Nature or real cowboys. Bum's paternal grandfather was a Texas Panhandle cattleman named Joe Phillips, who worked a dozen years along the famous Charles Goodnight Trail during the 1870s.

Bum described him warmly as "just a nice, plain ol' cowboy."

These days Bum is rebuilding the football fortunes of the New Orleans Saints after having done the same for the Houston Oilers where he became something of a western folk hero among the Texans.

According to one NFL owner, "the Houston Oilers were the joke of the National Football League in 1972 and 1973 when they put together consecutive 1-13 seasons. The critic's standard line was that the Oilers were doing okay; they won one game in 1972 and came right back with another victory in 1973. After Bum took over the coaching reigns, the the Oilers began telling the jokes."

Bum has been described as a Will Rogers clone. He has a story for every occasion and an occasion for every story. He hasn't met an Earl Campbell, or a George Rogers, he doesn't like. When his autobiography was being planned, Bum wrote Darrell Royal at the University of Texas stating that somebody would be contacting him for assistance.

"P.S. Probably won't be over three pages unless I lie a lot," Bum scribbled at the bottom of the letter.

In reality, all he has to do is talk. "The pros are boys just like high school players," he will tell you. "They're just older boys, that's all."

About coaching the B-squad at Nederland High School, he says, "I think you learn somethin' in that atmosphere, where you have to teach 'em how to tie their shoes and everythin'."

Bum can spot a counterfeit a country mile away. It's one of those inherent traits from an era of American history when cowboys were "free and full of the zest of darers." Something inside Bum tells him John Wayne was perhaps the perfect cowboy.

"He was a symbol," Bum says as if stating a fact, rather than delivering an eulogy. "He was what I thought a cowboy ought to be like. He was fair to everyone and he didn't dress up pretty. In the movies, he was always killin' the Japs and savin' the wagon train. I either liked him or the guy who wrote his scripts.

"I think he was something like he was portrayed, at least that's what I've always heard. He didn't act; he reacted. He wasn't a put-on."

Bum is something of an NFL iconoclast, but in a palatable sort of way. His personality greets you ahead of his opinions. He is a man of strong convictions and no pretenses. In other words, he is as easy to listen to as dentist-chair music and he gets his message across without blitzing.

The fat has been trimmed off his philosophies. The window dressing is gone. Superfluous testing and meaningless numbers have been junked.

"What does timing somebody prove?" Bum asks again. "Okay, some guys ain't as fast as other guys. But we can't say, 'We're gonna time you-all but we ain't gonna time you,' because that makes it look like we don't trust you-all. If they're on your team, they're on your team. You can't let 'em think anything different for a second."

There is a sensitivity and urgency for togetherness about Bum that can be traced to his childhood. He grew up during The Depression. He wasn't spoiled by material gifts, just coddled by kin.

"We were poor-poor," he recalls. "Poor in the sense of money, but rich in many other ways. Daddy drove a truck from Beaumont to Houston twice a day, 16 to 18 hours a day, six days a week. He did that seven straight years without missing a day.

"He never asked nobody for nothing. That was his job and that's what it took—two trips a day. He couldn't make a livin' by doin' it only once. We didn't have any money; but then, nobody around us had any.

"That's why I don't believe people who say, 'You better chaperone your kid, take him fishin' all the time or he'll grow up wrong.' I'd see my daddy only every now and then because he was workin'. If it comes down to makin' a livin' and bein' a buddy to your kid, you better make a livin' or you won't have a kid to be a buddy to.

"My daddy didn't work on Sunday, so we usually went to the creek for a fishfry. The men played dominoes and the women cleaned the fish. It probably didn't cost five bucks to feed all 20 or 25 people in the immediate family. We had fun. We didn't know anything else. We didn't know there was a Disneyland."

But now that he knows there's a Disneyland, Bum really hasn't changed much. Success, financial security, even NBC-TV closeups haven't affected his hat size or altered his principles. Which by the way sounds very much like his former boss at Texas A&M, Bryant.

"When I was at Nederland High watching his practices and later as his assistant there was one thing about Coach Bryant that I noticed quickly. He doesn't coach football. He coaches people.

"When I went to work for him—and I say for him because you sure don't work with him—the feeling was that he could get more out of people than anybody. Others may know more about football, but I think, I know, I've never been around anyone who knows as much about people.

"We used to have those conferences before practice at A&M. Coach Bryant would stick his head in, and in the middle of a sentence everybody would stop and look at him. Total quiet. He'd walk in, real slow. Sit down. Take out a cigarette. Tap it on his fingernail, and light it. And as often as not he'd smoke the whole damn cigarette without anybody saying a word. We'd just sit there and wait.

"Some of these guys had played for him for four years, and coached with him I don't know how long. I don't mean they were scared of him but they respected him, like I did. If he was going to say something they damn sure wanted to hear it. He never had to say, 'Let me have your attention. He already had it.'"

Bryant's last game at A&M was the Gator Bowl against Tennessee. It was to be played after he had already announced his plans to go to Alabama. Needless to say, nobody had any heart for the game. Coaches and players were confused, not knowing what was in store, and the workouts were lousy. The Aggie alumni were plenty upset, too. Bryant was definitely in a predicament.

Finally, he called his staff together and told them they had to do something. He told them, "If we don't get their attention we're going to get killed. We're not ready to play Tennessee."

"That afternoon at the team meeting," Bum picked up on the story, "he waited until all the players were in and selected, and then he made his entrance. He must have paced up and down for five minutes, with nobody saying anything.

"Finally, he let loose. He said, 'You know what they're saying about you, Crow?'

"Crow just looked up, startled, like a kid being jabbed. 'They're saying you don't care anything about this game. They're saying you just want to make sure you don't get hurt so you can sign a big pro contract.'

"Next he turned on Charlie Krueger, our All America tackle.

" 'Krueger. You know what they're saying about you? They're saying you don't give a damn about this game. All you're worrying about is which all-star game you're going to and how much money you'll make.'

"After that, he began moving from player to player picking on the starters.

"He told Roddy Osborne, our quarterback, 'Osborne, you're not thinking about this game. You're thinking about the banquet you're going to speak at.'

"He singled out Richard Gay and told him, 'You're not thinking about football. Football can't do anything for you. You're thinking about getting married and falling into a $50,000-a-year job.'

"John Tracey, our tight end, was next in line and he told him, 'Tracey, you know what they're saying about you? They're saying you won't even go on the field. You've been hurt all year and you're feeling sorry for yourself and you probably won't even suit up.'

"He went on down the line singling out others. Finally, he paused, walked back and forth some more, and nobody was saying a word. As a matter of fact it was too quiet.

"After a while he just stopped in the middle of the room, turned and faced them all. He told them, 'And do you know what they're saying about the rest of you? Nothing. They don't think you'll play enough to even mention.'

"Then he told 'em. 'And who do you think they are?' Pointing at himself, he told them it was him who didn't think they wanted to win. Suddenly, he had everyone's attention. His point was made.

"At practice that afternoon, things began to pick up a little. The first period was kickoff coverage and nobody was wearing any pads, just helmets and sweats, and the whistle blew and twenty-two guys converged at midfield in the greatest pile-up you ever saw.

"I'll tell you. It was a scene that John Wayne would have been proud of."

*       *       *

There were three bears at the Sheraton Washington Hotel on Monday evening, March 8, 1982. Two were stuffed and one was getting along in years. The 6-foot stuffed bears were in the lobby, each bearing a taped tag commemorating a historic football game. The bear on the left was for Paul Bryant's 300th victory as a college football coach, the one on the right honored the football fans' fancy; Bryant's 315th, over Auburn the previous November 28th, the victory that gave him more than any college coach in history. The third bear, of course, was Bryant himself, the 68-year-old Alabama football coach who earned his nickname by wrestling a bear as a youngster and whose admirers say he's grown tougher since.

A thousand former Bryant players, friends and partisan fans paid $125 per plate to honor the man called "Bear" in an event called "American's Tribute to Paul 'Bear' Bryant." At the head table, under a re-creation of the scoreboard from the record setting Auburn game, sat the Rev. Billy Graham, comedian Bob Hope, College Coach-of-the-Year Danny Ford, college coaches Jerry Claiborne of Kentucky, Jackie Sherrill of Texas A&M and Pat Dye of Auburn, along with the governor, both senators and all of the Congressmen from Alabama.

They convened, according to Senator Jeremiah Denton, because "in Alabama, Coach Bryant is second only to God. We believe on the eighth day, the Lord created the Crimson Tide."

This was no farewell. The mention of Bryant retiring never crossed the lips of the assemblage. Businessman Holt Rast, who flew up from Birmingham for the tribute, said discussions of Bryant's departure are not met with pleasure in Alabama. "It's sort of like talking about dying," said Rast, who played under then assistant Coach Paul Bryant in the late 30s. "We all know it's going to happen someday, but we don't discuss it."

For his part, the towering, craggy-faced Bryant said he would keep coaching until he is no longer wanted or could no longer contribute. "I wouldn't feel right about losing," he said at a VIP reception before the dinner. "I plan to get better. I sure don't want to go down any."

The man he beat to become the winningest coach doesn't think there is much likelihood of Bryant ever giving up voluntarily. "He's still tougher than anyone in the business," said Auburn Coach Pat Dye. "How long can he go on? I don't know. Forever."

So they settled down for dinner for 1,000 at the Sheraton.

Then President Reagan phoned from the White House to offer congratulations. Reagan said he's read in Bryant's autobiography about a game in which Texas A&M was down, 12–0, with three minutes to go and without the ball, but came back to win.

The President said he understood there was a pile of angry telegrams in Bryant's hotel room when he got back, from people who hadn't listened to the end of the game. "I've been hearing from those same people," Reagan said.

In the ballroom those who came to pay tribute to the coach listened to a Dixieland band, ate filet mignon and paid their respects to a gray-haired gent who's never quite grasped the meaning of the words "to quit."

Then, afterward, when the toasting was over and all of the former players were gathering together for their own private parties, it was my pleasure to sit down with one of Bryant's favorites, Jerry Claiborne, who had recently taken over the reigns of rebuilding the football fortunes of his alma mater, Kentucky.

"Bum Phillips once told me that Coach Bryant doesn't coach football," Claiborne began. "He coaches people.

"When we were coaching together at Texas A&M, our 1956 squad was undefeated, with only a tie to Houston, when it came to our traditional Thanksgiving battle with Texas. The game was to be played in Austin and our boys, (remember A&M was an all-male military school) were looking forward to the trip because after the game they could meet all of those pretty coeds."

Claiborne gave a slight smile. "But Coach Bryant had another idea. He told 'em this time there would be no courting. We'd just play the game and head home for the holidays.

"But before the game Coach Bryant displayed one of the smartest coaching ploys that I'd ever seen. Usually, at Memorial Stadium, the custom for the visiting team was to run out onto the playing field at game time with the Texas band playing—*'The Eyes of Texas Are Upon You.'* The student body and all of those Texas alums would raise hell and by the time your squad reached the sidelines everyone would be on the sideline holding hands, having lost their courage.

"Coach told us, 'Unh-unh. I don't want any *'Eyes of Texas'* on *me.* If they insist on playing it we'll wait 'til they finish before we go out.'

"He didn't take any chances either. When we were dressed and ready, he just told everyone to relax and wait. The referees even sent a man to get us.

"But he told 'em, 'I ain't heard *'The Eyes of Texas'* yet. We ain't coming out 'til we hear it.'

"Reluctantly he left. And we just waited. And waited.

"A few minutes later someone came back, knocked on the door, and asked Coach Bryant what was going on?

"Coach looked like he was getting a real mean on. He told that Texas official, 'As soon as they play that damn song and the Texas team is out there, we'll come.'

"They had to delay the kickoff a bit, but Coach made 'em play their song, and Texas was already on the field when we came out. They looked awesome. But so did we.

"Just before the half, we had a 21–0 lead but Texas still had a lot of fight left in 'em. Coach decided to give the first team a rest, which was the lucky break that Texas needed. They had seven points on the scoreboard in no time. But we were living on luck, too, because Jack Pardee returned the second-half kickoff for a touchdown.

"Those Longhorns never gave up. Everytime Coach would try to rest the first team, Texas would rally. We were still fighting for our lives at the end of the game, which we finally won, 34–21.

"The Aggies hadn't beat Texas in Memorial Stadium in nearly 32 years. But before the game, while we were having our silent prayer in the dressing room, Smokey Harper, our trainer, raised up right in the middle of it and said, 'I hope you gentlemen pray you got some guts out there so we don't screw this thing up again, because we're better than they are.'

"If I was a betting man, I'd bet that Coach had clued Smokey on what to say to get us all fired up."

The party in Buddy Payne's suite was getting full speed. There were A&M players, Kentucky players and a few like Congressman Claude Pepper from Florida who just wanted to be there for the cameradrie. Coach Claiborne and I just edged over to a corner in the room and continued our conversation.

"Probably the greatest example of Coach Bryant inspiring a team in the middle of a lost cause occurred in 1960 against Georgia Tech. Next to the Rice game of 1955, when we were at Texas A&M and down, 12–0, with only three minutes to go and came back to win, 20–12, this Georgia Tech game was no doubt one of the greatest comebacks that I'd even seen.

"We were behind, 15–0, at the half, and had made only one first down during two quarters of play. Later Coach described how bleak the situation actually was. 'When we came in, I didn't know what to do or to say. You have to have a plan, but I was fresh out. If we were down, 6–0, I was going to really get after them, make them look me in the eye, but I wasn't prepared for this. I knew they expected me to blow up, rant and rave and chew some tails.' "

Claiborne got this twinkle in his eye, a clue of satisfaction that coaches often reveal on special occasions, as he explained Bryant's great strategy amidst this difficult hour.

"But Coach Bryant didn't get a mean-on as expected. When we got in the dressing room at halftime he just asked, 'Where are the Cokes?'

"Then he went around the room, patting 'em on the back with his hands. He told 'em, 'Damn, this is great. Now they'll see what kind of mamas and papas we've got. They'll see what we've got in us.'

"All of us just looked at him in disbelief, trying to figure out what was happening. But coach knew what was going on. He got up on the blackboard and explained what was happening on the field, what plays weren't working and *why*. Then he told 'em if he had done as good coaching as they had playing then we wouldn't be in the fix we were in, but don't worry because if everyone would work together, we'd all get things straightened out and come back to win in the fourth quarter.

"He had everybody sold.

"And it was a heckuva second half. Coach was busy trying to direct our game plan and dodging liquor bottles being thrown by the Tech alumni. On the field we were beginning to look like a team, too, except when the fourth quarter began we were still behind, 15–0.

"But when you're fighting for your life that only rallies you onward. We were on the 6-yard line and it was fourth-and-12 to go. Coach must have been all guts when he called for a hook pass. He thought it would be good for 15 *clutch* yards. But Bobby Skelton, our back-up quarterback, called the wrong play and nearly threw an interception.

"Coach Bryant really got hot. He yanked Skelton out of the game and let him have it. He told him 'You little . . . you'll never play another minute for me as long as you live.'

"Coach didn't realize it, but he was fixing to have to eat his words. Tech couldn't punch it in, so we got the ball back. And immediately Pat Trammell got us going with a 30-yard strike near midfield.

"Then, on the next play fate took its course and Trammell

got hurt. All of a sudden Coach was on the spot. He had just benched Skelton, telling him he couldn't play. Now he's the only quarterback we got. No doubt Coach took a hard swallow before he called on Skelton to go in the game.

"Matter-of-factly, he motioned for Skelton to join him at his side. When he arrived, Coach Bryant put his arm around Skelton, trying to instill confidence in him like I'd seen Coach do so many times before, and told him, 'All right I'm going to give you one more chance to redeem yourself.'

"For the remainder of the game Skelton looked a pro. He converted fourth down plays four or five times on the first drive and took 'em in for a touchdown.

"Still behind, 15–7, Coach Bryant gambled and called for an onside kick which we recovered, and within a moment we had punched it in for another touchdown making it 15–13. The 2-point conversion was no good and up on the scoreboard time was becoming crucial. We just had to do something to win.

"Which we did. Instead of another onside kick, the kicker put this one in the end zone. Tech took over on the 20. And for four straight plays the defense held and we used four of our time-outs after each play, hoping to keep them from taking up too much time. After the punt, we got the ball at their 45-yard line.

"Now all we needed was a lot of prayers and a good scoreboard keeper.

"On the first play, Skelton called on Butch Wilson, our halfback for a sideline pass. Running his route, Butch got knocked out of bounds by the defender, which should have made him ineligible. But nobody realized it. Not the referees, not the Tech coaches, not even Butch. He just kept running his route. Skelton saw what was happening so he let it go, and Butch ran under it and romped down to the 12-yard line.

"Quickly, Coach motioned for our last time out to be taken. Normally, the 12-yard line that would be a more chip shot for Tommy Booker, our field goal kicker, but he was hurt.

"But Coach had prepared for every eventuality. He called on Richard O'Dell, a reserve end and kicker who had never kicked for us in a game. Coach simply called him over, patted him on the fanny and told him, 'Get out there and kick one.' Kinda like O'Dell had done it a hundred times before.

"Well, needless to say, Coach knew how to pick 'em. O'Dell's kick wasn't a pretty sight, but it went through the uprights and we won the game, 16–15."

Looking around the room, full of Bryant's former players, I seemed to notice a lot of those Richard O'Dell types, guys who had been called upon to perform near impossible feats and then did.

"After the Georgia Tech game," Claiborne explained, "there wasn't much those boys wouldn't do for Coach Bryant when he called upon them."

I think I understood why.

# 19

# *Pitch and Catch*

*"Then he stopped for a moment and just looked out the window of his office. After a moment he turned to me and said, 'Knowing that you gave it your all and not making All America is something you can live with the rest of your life. But not having the chance is something that will linger with you for a long, long time . . .'"*

—Dennis Homan

It's an hour's drive from Tuscaloosa to the small, rural community of Marion, Alabama. According to the United States census of 1980, Marion was the home of 4,467. Twenty years earlier, the population was 3,807. Preparing for the drive to Marion, where Kenny Stabler and Dennis Homan were holding their annual summer football camp for boys, I tried to imagine these two football greats, wondering how Father Time had been treating them in their athletic prime?

Marion lies on a rough line between Tuscaloosa and Selma (the town made famous by Martin Luther King's historic civil rights marches in the early sixties), but growth, like the interstate highways, has passed the city by. There are still pockets like this nestled away in the South. Turn right at a paint-flecked sign, proceed seven miles and leave the present.

"Kenny will be glad to see you if you want to make the trip," Dennis Homan said on the telephone, in a voice that sounded strong, assured and personal.

To find Marion, you drive eastward from Tuscaloosa on broad highways probing into the west Alabama countryside. Most of the time U.S. 82 winds its way through some of the greenest pasture land that one has ever seen. And on a clear, early summer morning the open country dazzles the eye, a glinting blue dappled with white. That in an instant is the difference driving here among the pines, the elms and the oaks as opposed to the Birminghams, the Clevelands, the Houstons and the New Yorks. The air is clear. A man sees sunshine. He realizes that the big cities have grown more dirty and more dark.

Everywhere the South bears its special markings: Indian names, mammoth plantations with their white columns, and county courthouses located on the town square. At Brent, halfway point on my journey, there were several lumber mills and a run-down factory made of red brick.

Down the road I continued, watching the green countryside rise and fall. Fortune found my way when I came upon a slow moving, oversize farm tractor in the process of commuting from one field to another. For five miles, I followed it down the narrow, two-lane highway. As I neared the town, I pulled off the main line to telephone the camp from a roadside booth. It was 9:15 A.M.

"Where are you?" Henry Pitts, Stabler's attorney and long-time friend, asked.

"About two miles from town at a country store that sells gas. Alabama Route 5."

"Good," Pitts explained. "Stay on 5 until you come into town. There'll be a sign on your right. Just follow it and it'll bring you toward the school. We're on the parade ground at Marion Military Institute. You can't miss it."

"I hope not."

Marion is one of those sleepy paced towns that the South is famous for hiding away from the rest of the world. It closes down at noon on Wednesday, yet manages to attract everyone to town on Saturdays as if it were a holiday of sorts. It also boasts of two colleges. Judson is the elite women's liberal arts college. And Marion Military Institute is one of the oldest military prep schools in the nation. It claims more than 170 generals and admirals among its alumni. During the mid-seventies, Marion served as the training camp for the Birmingham Americans of the ill-fated WFL. For one week during the past four years, it has since served as host to Kenny Stabler's summer football camp.

Finding the school and its military parade ground was a relatively simple task. Noting not to interfere, I took a seat among the bleachers which were crowded with several townspeople. They seemed in awe of what was taking place on the field in front of them: all of the professional players like Ray Guy, the all-star punter; Manny Sistrunk, the standout defensive end for the Oakland Raiders; Richard Todd of the New York Jets, and many others. Separated in eight different groups were the youngsters who all seemed to be listening to Kenny and his staff as they barked out their instructions.

One hour. Two. The warm summer sun began to make its presence felt. Finally, at 11:40, Stabler walked to midfield and with his whistle signalled for everyone to assemble around. Then in a few minutes Stabler blew his whistle once again and the group took off across the field in a trot toward the dining hall. At last, lunchtime and a chance to visit.

\*         \*         \*

These days Kenny Stabler is playing quarterback for the New Orleans Saints, directing the offense made famous by George Roger's electrifying romps and gallops and being coached by O. A. "Bum" Phillips. Kenny is considered with mixed opinions by the NFL media. Having guided the Oakland Raiders into the winningest record in pro football, a Super Bowl victory in January 1977, earning All-Pro status and having been selected as the Hitchcock Award winner in 1976 as the best player in pro football, without a doubt, Stabler has proven his abilities as a football player. It is, unfortunately, Stabler's often carefree lifestyle, off the field, that has given him the adverse notoriety.

Dennis Homan, however, is just the opposite. Having been Stabler's roommate during their college days at Alabama, one might make a "Mutt and Jeff" comparison of the two. Homan was an All America for Bryant in the mid-sixties, as was Stabler.

And the two of them, Stabler at quarterback and Homan at end, formed an awesome passing duo, playing on Bryant's 1965 national championship squad as sophomores, then led their team to an undefeated season and Sugar Bowl victory over Nebraska in 1966, and an 8-2-1 season in 1967, which included a berth against Texas A&M in the Cotton Bowl.

After graduating, Homan was drafted by the Dallas Cowboys where he became the starting split-end, ahead of superstar Bob Hayes. Later, he was traded to the Kansas City Chiefs and played for Hank Stram in their glory years, which included a Super Bowl championship. From there, Dennis closed out his playing days with the Birmingham Americans of the WFL and led them to the only championship of that league's existence. Today, Dennis is a very successful pharmaceutical salesman, a deacon in his church and an active speaker for the Fellowship of Christian Athletes. Without a doubt, Dennis personifies the type lifestyle that parents want their children to live.

\*     \*     \*

We sat outside under a big oak tree located in front of the administration building of Marion Institute—Homan, Stabler and I—waiting for the afternoon session to begin, talking about the great lunch which he had earlier, and recalling their playing days under Bryant at Alabama.

Stabler opened up first. "Looking back, I wish I'd listened to more of what he used to talk to us about. All of those meetings we had, the one-on-one contact. There was so much that he used to teach us about football and about life.

"When I was a junior, before spring practice going into my senior year, Coach and I had a big meeting one day. I had broken some of his training regulations. So we sat down to discuss the matter. There was no question that I was at fault and was deserving of my punishment. But Coach Bryant was more interested in me as a person than my future as a football player.

"When we got through with our meeting, he told me that I was going to be taken off my scholarship, moved out of the dorm and would have to earn my way back onto the team. One of the things Coach told me was 'that playing football at Alabama was a privilege, one that you had to earn and keep.'

"That spring and summer when I was away from the team, I did a lot of soul searching. I became hungry again. I missed what I was once a part of—I wanted to fight, to pay the price, to be a part of the team once again."

Stabler gave a sign of satisfaction. "That summer I worked harder than I've ever worked before. And when we came back for fall practice in August I was ready to lay it on the line. I wanted to contribute to the team, to lead if necessary. Winning was something I had been accustomed to. I wanted to be a winner again."

Pausing for a brief moment, Stabler looked outward toward the military drill fields, allowing his gaze to focus on some distant reminder of an important part of his life. Continuing, he added, "In the long run Coach Bryant was right. He made me grow up. He made me take the responsibility of being a team leader. I'll never forget that."

Dennis Homan, who was sitting with his back to the oak tree picked up on Stabler's point of direction on the conversation. "That same spring, I went in to see Coach Bryant about the wedding plans that Charlotte and I had been discussing. He was on the phone—so I waited outside his office, debating whether to wait or come back at another time.

"Twice in the week before I had come to his office to discuss the matter and couldn't muster enough courage to cross the threshold of his office door to do so. This time I couldn't chicken out. I had to get his permission on our wedding plans.

"So I waited in his secretary's office. And I kept telling myself that there was no way I was going to let him talk me out of the plans that Charlotte and I had made.

"Then a few minutes later he called for me. In his office we briefly discussed the progress of spring practice, how injuries were hampering the team and what I needed to do during the summer to make me a better ballplayer."

Laughing for a moment, Homan continued. "Finally, Coach Bryant looked at me and asked, 'Dennis, what's really on your mind?'

"Knowing that I had something else to discuss with him, I finally spilled the beans and told him of the wedding plans that Charlotte and I had.

"He just looked at me. Staring for perhaps two or three minutes in the way that only he can do.

"Then he opened up to me, kinda like a father would talk to a son when there was something real important that had to be discussed.

"Coach Bryant explained, 'Dennis, when I was a junior, we had Hutson and Howell and a really great team. And getting to play in the Rose Bowl and beating Stanford was something I'll remember the rest of my life.

" 'Then in my senior year they were pushing me to be an All America. As it turned out, I ended up hurting my leg and didn't have the great year it took to be picked.

" 'But I look at you, with all of that speed and those good hands. You deserve it to yourself, to try and make this year the best one possible.'

"Then he stopped for a moment and just looked out of the window of his office. After a moment he turned to me and said, 'Knowing that you gave it your all and not making All America is something you can live with the rest of your life. But not having the chance is something that will linger with you for a long, long time . . .'

"Rising out of my chair I told him, 'Coach, I think I know what you mean.' "

Both Stabler and Homan nodded. They were in agreement to the point which Bryant was trying to make.

"There is one thing I'd like to add," Stabler noted. "During our junior year in 1966, we were undefeated with a 11–0 record and only had 37 points scored on us all year. We were picked to win the championship in 1967, but against Florida State in the opening game we were tied."

Homan then added, "It should have never been close."

We discussed the game in detail, the two of them explaining what had happened, and why the glory never came to the Crimson Tide on that late summer evening in September.

". . . When the gun sounded," Homan told me, "both teams

left the field for their locker rooms. One would be a happy and a loud experience as the victors rejoiced; another would be filled with sadness, tears and eventually silence. A silence that searches within oneself to cope and understand. If you're the right kind of people, however, that silence will humble you and provide a lesson to be learned.

"Watching Coach Bryant leave the field, you could see the naked image of a crumbled man exposed . . . heartbreak in the distorted mouth lines, a wrinkled brow burdened by a head bowed in sorrow, his body resembling a redwood silenced by the storm. This sight explained in a thousand ways why we had come so close, fought so hard, died so violently.

"In his perpetual driving fashion, Coach composed his feelings rapidly. And following a team custom, no matter, win, lose or draw, he led the team in prayer once inside the dressing room. The sobs of our teammates were apparent as Coach fought for tranquility. '*Dear God,*' he said, '*give us the strength in our moment of despair to understand and accept that which we have undergone. . . . Please help mend our wounds and learn the lessons which you would have us to learn. Amen.*'

Stabler picked up on the story. "It was a difficult time, full of tears, full of sobbing young giants. Quietly we suffered. The manly stifled sobs of total despair. Sitting in a corner, I sensed the emotions of my fellow teammates. Before, we had won as an Alabama team, fair, hard and with humility. To be less at this moment, to cry foul, to alibi, would undo much that Coach Bryant had taught us. Eventually the tears would subside, the pain would lessen and the team would leave the locker room, each one lifting his head high in the face of defeat to be an Alabama man.

"Coach Bryant, the teacher, however, sensed the opportunity and began instructing the team on a lesson that could only apply to the situation at hand.

" 'Let's sit down for a minute, just sit down. Get some rest!' Coach asked. He then removed his houndstooth hat and loosened the tie from his shirt collar.

" 'I don't believe we played very well—particularly on defense.'

Walking around with his hands on hips, he continued his talk, 'I don't think anyone went out there and played poorly on purpose. I know that I didn't contribute anything from the bench. All we had really was a lot of confusion over there.'

"Twitching his jaw and still walking, he stopped and stared for a moment. . . . 'I think the reason you didn't win the game— I thought you might have won it anyway—but I think the reason it came out like it did was my decisions last spring, our practices and planning and so forth . . . and I really believe that my decisions last week, not this week, hurt any chances you had of winning, 'cause it's pretty hard to play football if all we do is ask you to stand around, grab one another and holler . . . and that's about all we've asked you to do—I'm not being critical of you.'

"Pausing, then staring at the ground, Coach continued, 'I think this should prove without any doubt that the stuff about great coaches and great defensive coaches is for the birds . . . I've told you a jillion times—the defense or the coaches don't have anything to do with it really—IT'S THE PEOPLE THAT PLAY!

" 'Maybe the Good Lord is kinda testing us to see what we've got in us. I can't tell. If He's testing me then I've been here before!

" 'But the thing we've got to do is forget this one. Like I was telling you this afternoon—I'm not trying to tell you I told you so, but I'll tell you like I always try to tell you and like any coach will tell you—ten minutes after the game it's too late, the next day is too late. So the best thing we can do is to use this as a stepping stone, and if we've got class—we'll be all right. If we haven't then it doesn't matter, does it?

" 'You young people who didn't get to play, I know you feel badly and I feel badly for not playing you, but if you've got *class,* it will work out . . . Keep your heads up, act like a champion!' At that, he began to walk away."

Stabler summed it up. "It was perhaps the most humble moment we would ever know."

# 20

# *Five Disciples*

*"They didn't get me a summer job, so Coach Bryant made me an offer. He said, 'I need a young coach on my staff. You want it?' "*

—Danny Ford

We gathered together in Washington, D.C. in early March 1982, at a cocktail party an hour before Coach Bryant's monumental tribute that Senator Jeremiah Denton had arranged to honor the great gridiron coach for his record breaking feat as football's winningest coach.

It was a special VIP party. Among the crowd were senators, congressmen, generals, chairmen-of-the-board of some of America's giant corporations and many other honored dignitaries. And the gentlemen with whom I was fortunate to visit were without a doubt five of Bryant's most successful pupils.

*       *       *

Danny Ford was a three-year starter and an All-SEC lineman at Alabama for Bryant. Having grown up in Gadsden, Alabama, reading about Bryant's national championship success at Alabama while a youngster, and then playing on the Crimson Tide squad during Kenny Stabler's years, Ford has become very familiar with the definition of the word "winner." Today, he is the youngest head coach in America at Clemson, where he took them to the national championship in 1981, and was named Coach-of-the-Year.

"When I got back from the Orange Bowl, I got a note from him," Ford explained. "He had tried to call. I ain't gonna call him though. I'm afraid to. Heck, he might demand that I give him the national championship that we won this year.

"I guess I'd call him for advice if I had a chance to take another coaching job. He'd probably call me if he knew about it. But he doesn't worry about you until you need him.

"Coach got me my first job when I was starting out. I'd been a graduate assistant, but I wasn't making any money. Eastern Kentucky needed an assistant, and Coach worked it out for me to get the job. I went up there and liked it. They offered me the job, but this was in the spring and I wouldn't go on the payroll until that fall. I was married and needed the money.

"So I went to see Coach Bryant. We talked about it. And he told me to call them and ask for a summer job.

"They didn't get me a summer job, so Coach Bryant made me an offer. He said, 'I need a young coach on my staff. You want it?'

"Heck, I'd have walked through fire for him. He meant that much to me. I stayed at Alabama for two years, then went to Virginia Tech with Jimmy Sharpe before joining Coach Pell at Clemson.

"One of the things that Coach Bryant taught us was to surround yourself with the right kind of people because they know what you want when you want it. That's one lesson that I think about each day."

*     *     *

Jackie Sherrill is without a doubt, one of Bryant's most successful proteges. He is a brilliant young coach who played for Bryant at Alabama during the early sixties when Alabama alums thought that winning national championships were getting to be an annual affair. At the beginning of 1982 he left Pitt (where he had taken them to three straight 11-win seasons) to become the Archduke of Aggieland, and the richest field marshal since Napoleon, having signed a five-year contract worth nearly two million dollars.

Oddly, it is a wonder that Sherrill's and Bryant's paths were able to merge. Sherrill was living in Biloxi, Mississippi and was being heavily recruited by Georgia Tech, Tulane, Ole Miss and Mississippi State.

According to Sherrill, "Alabama was only a vague possibility. Then one day Coach Bryant made a scouting trip to Biloxi preparing for a place to train prior to the Sugar Bowl."

Bryant and Sherrill met at the high school stadium on a day that Sherrill vividly recalls, "because it changed the course of my life.

"We talked for an hour," Sherrill noted. "And not once did he ask me to come to Alabama. He just talked about Alabama and the players on the team. He talked about things he believed in. I was really impressed. After we met there was only one real choice that I could really make."

Sherrill joined an army of 67 freshmen. One of them was Steve Sloan, who was to become Sherrill's roommate, lifetime friend and confidante.

"Only six of us graduated together," Sherrill says today, "but we had enough seniors to win national championships in 1964 and 1965."

Bryant had an inkling that the Biloxi native was going to be an extraordinary chip off the old block. This notion was strengthened one afternoon in 1963, when Alabama was losing an air raid to George Mira and Miami. Mira was hitting everything he threw, especially on a hook route over the middle.

Sherrill played five positions at Alabama, one of them linebacker. He was on the sideline watching Mira strafe the Tide, and he moved into Bryant's shadows.

Others on the sidelines were surprised. Few players had the audacity to offer suggestions at a time like that. They would sooner have put a snake in Bryant's ear than a suggestion.

Soon, though, Sherrill was in the game. And sure enough, he picked one off. Sherrill returned the interception deep into Miami territory. And the Crimson Tide eventually converted for a touchdown, breathed easier, won and lived happily ever after.

Bryant later commented, "Well, obviously, that young man's a winner." It was as close as Bryant gets to pinning a Medal of Honor on a hero's tunic. From that moment, though, Sherrill occupied a high niche on Bryant's All-Alabama team.

"I called Coach Bryant up front, when I was offered the job at Texas A&M," Sherrill explained. "I didn't get him at first, but I talked with him at the tail end of negotiations. He has lots of fond memories from A&M. I've called him every time I made a coaching change.

"It's not like Coach tells you what to do, but you can tell what he thinks by the way he talks to you. Just having him to talk to, to benefit from the experiences he's been through, is what's important. Nobody will ever reach the stature in football that he has. Nobody will ever break his record.

"I remember back in 1970 when I had a decision to make whether to go to Iowa or Oregon as an assistant, I called Coach and asked where he thought I'd have the best opportunity to advance from. He told me Oregon.

He must have started thinking about it and making a few calls. He called me back four hours later and said, 'Don't go.' I said, 'Yes, sir.' I stayed at Iowa State, moved with Coach (John) Majors to Pittsburgh, got my first head job at Washington State in '76 and came back to Pitt when John went to Tennessee the next year.

"Coach helped me with all those decisions. He is my father figure. I put a lot of his ideas into what I do. When I was being recruited, I planned to go to Georgia Tech or Oklahoma. Alabama was playing in the Sugar Bowl and practicing in Biloxi, my hometown. Coach Bryant talked with me two hours and never once asked me to come to Alabama. Now, I never ask a kid to come to Texas A&M. I try to talk with him like Coach talked with me."

\*         \*         \*

Pat Dye grew up in the farming community of Blythe, Georgia, some 20 miles from Augusta. His childhood existence is much like that of Bryant's, except that Dye's family owned nearly 2,000 acres of farmland, Bryant's family was dirt poor.

Dye starred at Richmond Academy in Augusta and later signed a grant-in-aid with Georgia where he became a three-year starter and All America for Wally Butts' Bulldogs. From there he played professionally with Edmonton in the Canadian League and with Ft. Benning while attending to military obligations.

While in Washington to receive the Timmy Award, the equivalent of the Heisman Trophy in the armed forces league, in January 1965, Dye had his first opportunity to meet Bryant, who was there to be honored by the Washington Touchdown Club for fielding the number-one college team. Dye was impressed. He knew he wanted to coach eventually, and he decided if Bryant would give him a job he would pass up returning to the Canadian league. So he asked Bryant for a place on his staff.

Bryant called Butts. "Can Pat Dye coach for me?" he asked. "I don't know whether he can coach for you," Butts replied, "but he could have damn sure played for you." It's a story that Dye tells with obvious pride.

Dye remembers the day he left his family in Atlanta and headed to Tuscaloosa for the interview.

"I had heard about Coach Bryant getting to work early, and I wanted to impress him," he said. "I decided I'd be there when he got to work at 6:30 in the morning. I said, 'Well, it's four and a half hours over there, so I'll leave at 2 o'clock and be sure to get there. I was so excited I didn't sleep anyway. I got up and got dressed and took off.

"I got to Birmingham and it was still dark. I got to Tuscaloosa and it hadn't even begun to break day. I looked around and there wasn't anything open. I finally found a service station and pulled up and looked at my watch and it was 6:30. I looked at their clock and it was 5:30. I had forgotten the time change."

Dye drove to the athletic offices and chatted with the janitor, the only person on the premises, for an hour. Finally, a couple of assistants, Richard Williamson and Jimmy Sharpe, showed up. Bryant arrived at 7:30, told them to go get a cup of coffee while he opened his mail and he'd see Dye later.

"We were walking back from the Student Union, me in my new, seersucker suit that I'd bought in Bremen," Dye remembered. "I was walking beside Jim, and Richard was behind us, and I heard him laughing."

"He said, 'Boy, how long you had that suit?' I said, 'I just bought it. This is the first time I've had it on.' He said, 'I figured that.' I said, 'Why?' He said, 'You haven't cut the tags off of it.'

"I still had the pockets sewed up and tags on both sleeves and on the back pocket and everywhere else and was fixing to go in there and talk to Coach Bryant about a job."

Bryant hired him the next day.

Dye remained an assistant at Alabama nine years, through 1973, teaching four All America linebackers and helping the Crimson Tide to two national titles, five Southeastern Conference championships and three unbeaten seasons. He moved to East Carolina as head coach and compiled a 48–18 record in six years, then head coached Wyoming one season in which the Cowboys' went 6–5. Since then Dye has rebuilt pride, dedication and loyalty into the much divided Auburn alums.

Recently while speaking to a veterinary fraternity at Auburn, Dye mentioned that his daughter, Missy, had shown an interest in the profession. One of those in attendance explained that the profession was getting overcrowded.

Dye's reply was pure Bryant. He told them, "I'll bet it's not overcrowded with people who will work night and day."

The crowd loved it.

\*　　　　\*　　　　\*

Charles "Cholly Mac" McClendon is the only former pupil of Bryant's who has the distinct honor of having defeated his former coach on two separate occasions. All in all Bryant had a 41–6 record against his former pupils.

A native of Lewisville, Arkansas, McClendon attended Magnolia Junior College before serving three years in the Navy and then joining Bryant's postwar movement at Kentucky. Following a stint as an assistant to Bryant at Kentucky, he moved onto Vanderbilt and later to LSU where he assisted another Bryant pupil, Paul Dietzel, in building a national championship team in the late fifties.

Dietzel and Mac built a great program at the bayou school. And when Dietzel was called upon to lead the troops for the Army Academy, "Cholly Mac" was tapped as LSU's head coach where he took them to sensational heights during his 18-year stint which included 13 bowl games, 17 All Americas, 58 All-SEC players, six Academic All Americas, one conference championship, national and conference Coach-of-the-Year honors, numerous Top Ten ratings, and the winningest era in LSU football history.

From there, "Cholly Mac" took the job as executive director of the Tangerine Bowl and quickly turned that bowl into one of the most successful post-season classics. And in 1982, he was tapped by his peers to lead the American Football Coaches Association which is one of the highest honors that a coach could ever receive.

"I remember very well my first visit to Kentucky," he said. "I went there with Joe-Joe Dean, who tried out for the basketball team. Carney Laslie had recruited me from junior college through friends of Coach Bryant in Arkansas. They were holding a football clinic at UK, and Otto Graham was there. My job was to catch the balls thrown by Otto. I can't even remember whether I caught one or not.

"I had a great respect, or perhaps fear is a better word, for 'Wah Wah' Jones. I had read a lot about him. He was a real fine football and basketball player, maybe the last to be that good in both sports. I'll never forget that Pat James entertained me. I still accuse him of keeping that $10 they gave him. I think we got in that picture show for free.

"It didn't take very much to get me to sign because I was awful anxious to play and get an education. I went back home, and they were checking me real close to see if I really wanted to come. I may not have impressed them. There was no reason to think I could play. Looking back, I never played a down of high school football. I was lower than this floor. I went to junior college on a basketball scholarship and ended up playing on the football team.

"My wife had never been away from home. I thought I had made a mistake. She knew I had. I remember she had a hard time getting adjusted. We first lived in a little one-room apartment, and when I walked in after my first day of practice, she was crying. She had tried to fix her first dinner with a hot-plate oven, and nothing had panned out. What she didn't know was that I wasn't hungry. We had worked so hard that I was too tired to eat.

"When we all lived at Cooperstown, the married veterans' housing project, and I didn't have any transportation, William 'Moon' Conde and I would pedal each other on his bicycle as far as we could and then push it the rest of the way home after we got too tired to pedal.

"The work was demanding, but when you deal with numbers, you've got to find out who wants to play. I really didn't think about it as a player. If you're going to win, you've got to give yourself completely. Being older, I understood it. I felt I was so far behind, anyway. There were about 25 of us who stayed out several times and worked after the lights were out. They wanted to find out if we really wanted to play football.

"The thing I remember most about Coach Bryant is when I started work for him as an assistant in 1951, and I would drive him to banquets. We've shed tears together, and you'd think you were as close to the man as a man could be until you met him the next day in the hallway and he didn't know you. I understand now. He had something on his mind and decisions to make to keep him ahead of the game.

"I remember best when we beat Ole Miss, 47–0, and Jim Mackenzie scored a touchdown in that game. The largest crowd that ever met us was at the airport. They were all the way out on the highway. That was really something.

"The Tennessee games were always very much of a frustration for me. In my years there, we did not beat them. I remember the closeness of the games and playing in the snow in 1950 at Knoxville. I coughed all the way home because of the cold in my lungs. It seemed like they were going to come out.

"We had snow on the field before a game with Florida in Lexington, and they burned it off, with gasoline I think. Anyway, it makes a heckuva odor when you hit the ground. I also remember running sprints after a game . . . for conditioning. That would seem a little strange now."

McClendon earned varsity letters in 1949 and 1950 as a defensive end. One of his better games was the 1951 Sugar Bowl, when UK snapped a 31-game Oklahoma winning streak.

According to Bryant, "Early in the game Charlie came off the field with the side of his face torn off. When I turned to call the trainer and looked around he was already going back on the field with the defense. His tackling caused three fumbles that day."

"Billy Vessels was running (with the ball) and I thought I had him," McClendon recalled, "but he had more speed than I thought. He got by me, and his feet hit me in the eye; however, I managed to knock him out of bounds after he got a pretty good gainer. Thank goodness there was a penalty on the play.

"They put cotton on the wound and froze it with whatever they used in those days. I remember so vividly praying, 'Don't let that thing fall down on my eye.'

"Now that I look back on it, Kentucky didn't run all those players off when Coach Bryant first went there. They sort of disqualified themselves. I don't know how it happened that I made it. Maybe I played in fear of not excelling, which is the way I coach . . . with a fear of losing. I realized if I didn't make it, I'd probably be digging the longest ditch in Arkansas."

\*　　　\*　　　\*

If you have the opportunity to meet Bill Battle, you're in for a rare privilege. In all of my travels in which I've met a lot of really great individuals, there are very few who can stand shoulder-to-shoulder with this guy when it comes to the key ingredients of class and character and courage.

A former end for Bryant's first national championship team, Battle grew up in Birmingham, the son of another football celebrity, and prepped at West End High. He played single platoon for the Crimson Tide which meant double duty on offense and defense. Afterwards, he assisted Frank Broyles at Arkansas, under the Bryant-Broyles exchange program for graduate assistants. Later Battle joined Doug Dickey's staff at Tennessee and was tapped to succeed Dickey upon his departure to become head coach at Florida.

Battle built a great program at Tennessee, earning a 59–22–2 record in seven years which included finishing three times in the Top Ten nationally, four wins in five bowl games, and one of those rare wins over his former coach, Bryant. After leaving coaching in 1976, Battle was named president of the very successful corporate conglomerate Circle S Industries, Inc., located in Selma, Alabama, which is jointly owned by industrialist Larry Striplin, Bryant and several other businessmen. Battle's success in the business world is carried over from his success on the football field.

Describing the Bryant mystique, the former Tennessee coach shared with me, "Coach Bryant's impact on college football has been every bit as it has on Alabama football. Everyone in this country has adoped his style. He's a trendsetter. He does the fundamentals, but his flexibility to change has preceded others."

Listening to Battle describe his former coach and the many lessons that Bryant had taught him, especially the ones Bryant explained in his first talk to the freshmen class, I began to recall a similar talk to a latter-day freshmen class. So many of Bryant's boys often referred to this special time in their lives. Here, I believe, is where Bryant begins to motivate them toward national championships, bowl games, gridiron glory and business success.

Remembering back to an August evening in 1976 in a meeting room filled with plaques of former Alabama greats and past bowl game glories, I can recall sitting there with my good friend, Steadman Shealy, waiting to receive the impact of the talk which Battle so vividly described.

Assembled there were thirty incoming freshmen, all eager-eyed, waiting to be initiated, learn the rules and what to expect.

Finally, through the double doors which led into the meeting room, walked the toughest guy in the world, the man they reverently called Coach Paul "Bear" Bryant. He stood there looking over his corps of talent, sizing them up. And after a moment or two, he made his speech, the kind that motivated ordinary young men to do extraordinary things, winning championships and so forth.

It came slowly, deliberately, emphasizing every word and those around listened with earnest.

"I know that your mommas and poppas all sent you here and said to do good in school and practice hard in football. I had a momma once and she said the same things. But I want you to know that your education comes first, then football is second . . . and since it is that way, there's a two-way street. You have a commitment to the University and they have one to you, so take care of your priorities."

Pausing to study his influence among those present, Bryant continued.

"Do any of you know what put us on top when I first came back to Alabama? Well, we didn't have a lot of big people, just a bunch of determined little guys. They worked hard at what they did because they liked what they were doing. They'd been losing so long that they fought to get away from that bad habit. Sure, it took some work, but they knew how to sacrifice.

"But what is sacrifice?" Bryant asked as he pointed at a youngster on the second row.

Pausing as the frightened freshman gave a blank expression, Bryant then continued. "It's having a little pride in yourself to not be like the average student, you gotta outwork him—you gotta have a desire to excel.

"Remember, it takes class to come back in the fourth quarter and win, but if you've sacrificed—you can do it!

"I want you to write home regularly. How many of you have written home since you've been here already? It only takes a few minutes, and it would mean a lot to them, and more to you over the years.

"Secondly, we ask that you attend church regularly. I'm sure that you've had that training at home, and we certainly want you to continue with that."

Coach Bryant spoke with a confidence that comes from success. As Steadman and I watched, we received from Bryant's eyes the full candlepower usually reserved for intense moments. But this was a special time. Bryant, the great coach, was revealing his plan. He will take these young men who appear to be a green and aggressive squad, and change them into a slashing, driving outfit.

"Then there are a whole lot of little things that are real important such as your appearance. I'd like to see you all cleaned and scrubbed and neat and everything. But let me remind you, it doesn't take a man who shaves twice-a-day to play football.

"We'd like to insist on your smiling. I'd like to see a few smiles around the place every once in a while 'cause I'm the world's champion frowner—so I'll do all the frowning. I'd just like to see you smile!

"And then, don't ever get too proud to pray—it'll do you good to go down on your knees and pray."

This seemed to hit home with a lot of kids, a few smiles were the necessary sign of approval.

"Be seen and not heard! The sun is the most powerful thing that there is, yet it doesn't make much noise. The ocean is the deepest thing that there is and it doesn't make much noise, but thunder makes a lot of noise and what does it do?—It makes people run away from you. So do like your parents taught you, be seen and not heard!

"I'd like for you to display a winning attitude. Look and act like an athlete! Recognize the contributions of other students, pat 'em on the back. When you're around school, shake their hand and look 'em in the eye. And, oh yes, don't forget to say 'Yes, sir' and 'No, sir' to your teachers.

"You represent a lot of people now. There's your parents, your family and your friends back home. Don't forget you also represent the University of Alabama—that's your team from now on.

"There won't be many training rules, just use your head. Try to eat and sleep good. Start off your day with breakfast and you'll do all right, that dorm is your home—so keep it clean. Last of all, be on time. If you aren't at practice, THEN BE IN THE HOSPITAL!

"Try to have a goal. Get you one for practice every day—try to get better! If you have a bad day, don't lose your confidence. Just try to improve day-by-day.

"Now finally, I want to point this out to you. YOU'RE NOT

ORDINARY—YOU'RE NOT AVERAGE—YOU'RE SOMETHING SPE-
CIAL—and I don't want you to ever forget that. And since you
are something special, then I know that you can win—if you
put something extra into it every day, and a little bit extra into
a game!"

At that the talk ended. There were many moist eyes on this
evening in August. And as Bryant of Alabama exited through
the massive double doors a great wave of applause began to sweep
across the room, louder, louder, unceasing, on and on. Yet this
applause came not from the clapping of hands, instead, it came
from the expression of these youngster's faces—the sudden swell-
ing of warmth in their hearts.

But that is the Bryant way. The late Benny Marshall, noted
sports writer and Bryant's long time friend, once explained, "From
the day he became a football coach, Bryant has owned the convic-
tion to coach those who follow him that brick walls are not obsta-
cles; they're put up only to be run through."

This I have seen. This I know.

# 21

# *Junction Revisited*

*It was a late autumn afternoon as the small twin-engined* Rio *airplane glided in for its landing at a small west Texas airport near the fabled town of Junction, Texas. This was the same back-country airstrip where thirty years before, a tall, anxious Paul Bryant had arrived to take the reins of a floundering Texas A&M football program. Many times before, I had often wondered how this special time of Bryant's life pieced its way together like it had? Why this place had been so important? And now, as we were making our final descent, those questions were still resting on my mind, they still needed answering . . .*

The morning began with wind and anger. The clouds, low and whirled in a deep gray and blackish blue, cast a pallor over the fertile farmland of the vast region below known as the Mississippi River delta. As our plane continued to journey westward from Tuscaloosa, Alabama, another eventful April day was beginning with gusts of wind suggesting January and flashes of sun promising June. In every way, a season of change had finally come.

The destination of my flight was to be Junction, Texas, a small community in the desolate hill country of West Texas. It had been nearly five years since I had made that first trip to attend the reunion of Bryant and his infamous "Boys of Junction" who had returned, a quarter of a century after the fact, to the place where it had all begun—Junction, Texas.

That first trip had been a sentimental journey down memory lane to visit a fabled war camp in which the grass had once been dead, where the river had been dried up, where the trees didn't give much shade and where the angry red sun had made its rounds every day making the premises hotter and hotter.

Without a doubt, Junction was once a place where only the tough had survived, and a place where an extraordinary bond was formed between a coach and a team that would lose nine times in ten tries and then go in to become in tale and in legend almost larger than life itself. Perhaps, it was a little like having been at the Bataan Death March and survived. Certainly you would not want to have been there. Yet if you had been there at Junction, and stayed, there would be awaiting for you a special badge of courage much like the one reserved for the few coaches, trainers and twenty-seven football players who had decided to ride it not.

Then after all of those years and after all of the torturous hell that they had endured, they returned to Junction on that memorable Friday afternoon, May 18, 1979.

In all, twenty-three of the legendary twenty-seven squad members were to return. Washington Redskins head coach Jack Pardee, and Dallas Cowboys assistant coach Gene Stallings were in pre-season mini-camps and couldn't make it. Neither could Oklahoma Gas and Electric Company vice-president Bobby Drake Keith, nor oil executive Billy Pete Huddleston. However, the remaining games of that spartan affair returned and they came back as big time winners, too—a trademark of the Bryant mold.

Richard Vick, a successful farmer and rich oil tycoon, and Bob Easley, who had made several millions in real estate, were there and so was Joe Schero of Church's Fried Chicken fame. Herb Wolf had left a multi-million dollar construction project in West Africa to be there, and Paul Kennon, the world renowned architect, sneaked in, too. From Chicago, Dallas, Houston, Shreveport and all corners of the United States, these men returned with one common memory, one common bond.

For none of them had known what to expect when first arriving twenty-five years earlier at Junction, a dust bowl town nearly two hundred fifty miles from the Aggie campus and an hour from the nearest neon sign. Many of the original candidates fainted, or were dragged off by their heels, or packed their bags and disappeared into the night from Junction by running, walking, hitch-hiking or, if they were lucky, on an occasional bus to San Angelo, Dallas, San Antonio or El Paso. However, those who stayed became hard as anvils. For this group of youngsters took a large amount of pride in their ability to survive the drills, the dust, the contact, the long hours, the bruises and, yes, the spartan existance. And when the bottom line is drawn, these days will be remembered as ones when life didn't laugh, but weeped instead.

For something must be said of this rare cameraderie among a group of men who had once lost so much and later became such big time winners. And of how they had left for Junction in two buses and returned to a desolate College Station, Texas ten days later in a squeaky, smoke bellowing, old Greyhound bus on September 8, 1954 with Bryant's first Aggie team.

Finally, on that special day in May they came forward, one by one, and spoke of Bryant and what he had meant to them. Don Watson, who had played halfback, remembered how they would hit the field in the morning and look around to see who was missing. Bill Schroeder, a successful lawyer these days, told of the heat stroke he had at Junction, during which he had lost seventeen pounds and played tackle that season weighing 197. He made it sound like fun.

And Elwood Kettler, now the head coach at Angleton High, recalled that five centers quit the team during the Junction camp and how he bruised every knuckle while all of his new centers learned how to swap the ball. Elwood later threw the touchdown pass to Jack Pardee that gave the A&M Aggies their only win that season, 6–0, over Georgia. After the game, Bryant and his trainer, Smokey Harper, danced a jig in the locker room.

A sophomore guard on that team, Darrell Brown, remembered the guy he bunked with and who had sworn he'd never quit. "He was saying that when I fell asleep that night," Brown recalled. "When I woke up the next morning he was gone."

Dennis Goehring, an All America guard who later became the president and CEO of the Bank of A&M in College Station noted, "When we left here we were confident. We knew that we could succeed in any endeavor."

Troy Summerlin, the student manager who was forced to temporarily play center, added, "I was the taxi driver. When somebody was leaving I got the keys from Coach Bryant and drove 'em into town. Finally there wasn't anyone to take. I think the assistant coaches wanted to leave, too, but Coach Bryant locked 'em in at night."

Ten minutes. Twenty. For a half hour, Bryant's boys made their way to the podium. Then, at the close of the ceremonies, Marvin Tate, athletic director at Texas A&M, stood up and said his piece. "I was a senior that year and I was determined not to let him run me off. Now, I guess we all wonder what would have happened if we had quit back then. I'm sure if we did, then we wouldn't be where we are right now, so I have to think that we're all better off for having stuck it out."

Afterwards, when Tate's old coach and teammates had finished, they went down by the river where the townspeople had assembled and had their barbecue, and the Junction High School Band played the *Aggie War Hymn* and Coach Bryant signed autographs and visited with his special friends.

However, before the party broke up and everyone went back home, Bryant, the legendary coach, went over to Tate and told him:

"Over the years, when I've thought about Junction, I haven't been sure that I did the right thing. But now that I've come back and seen how it all worked out, well, I want you to do something for me. I want you to get the names of all the guys who stayed with us and put down what they're doing and send it to me. I'm going to frame it and hang it on my den wall, and when people ask me about Junction and the '54 team, I'm just going to point to what's hanging there on the wall—that will be my proof that we were right, that it was all worth while."

Yes, things were so special then . . .

Looking outward of the plane's cabin window to my right, watching the sun play hide and seek with the billowing clouds between us, my emotions begin to rekindle as certain events of the past five years began to make their way to the forefront of the present.

Time. Yes, it is always the difference, the measuring stick of change. Yet who can clock the time that a man's heart has taken from him?

For nearly five years, I have traveled this long and adverture-some journey. Robert Frost made mention of a similar experience many years ago when he published his memorable poem, *The Road Not Taken.* It has been a journey both demanding and fulfilling, difficult and generous. Most importantly, it has been at time of questioning and a time of learning . . .

Gradually, the plane began to descend. Junction was only min-utes away. The pilots banked the plane to the left to make their preparations for a final approach pattern that would take us through a winding, narrow pass in the barren, sun-scortched foot-hills outside of Junction and onward to our destination—the small back country airstrip at the edge of town.

Glancing once more outside of the cabin window, as the glim-mering sun continued to make its presence known, I began to recall the conversation that my good friend, Jerry Stovall, had shared with me while on that lonely trip, late one evening, travel-ling on Interstate 10 between New Orleans and Baton Rouge . . . *"Mike, in Coach Bryant's way of thinking, the price one must pay for victory is so very expensive that only champions will pay the tremendous price to achieve it."*

I realized then that even though the years may whirl past faster than we can often know or realize, and where we were and where we may one day be, is always seperated by a blurring, fading vortex of half-rememberances and budding dreams of glory, and yes, these images are really colored by sun, not shadow.

Camelot, therefore, is not just a mythical kingdom in some mythical world, instead, it is the gifted ability of inner vision to see what we would rather see and to become what we'd rather be.

But it is that way for all of us and has always been.

Mike Bynum
Tuscaloosa, Alabama
June 4, 1979—July 19, 1984

# *Appendix*

## THE BRYANT RECORD

Winningest Active Coach

National Coach of the Year
1961, 1971, 1973

SEC Coach of the Year
Eight Times

All-Time SEC Coach

Coach of the Decade, voted by
the Football Coaches
Association of America

Past President, American
Football Coaches Association

Career Record of 323 Victories

Best Record for Past Decade
1960s and 1970s

Six National
Championships

Fifteen Conference
Championships

Twenty-Eight Bowl Teams

Forty-One College
Head Coaches

Sixty-Five All America

Fifty-Three Academic
All-SEC Players

One Hundred Twenty-One
All-Conference Players

Four Jacobs Blocking
Award Winners

Twenty-Two Teams in
Nation's Top Ten

Second Total Defense
Past Decade

Third Rushing Defense
Past Decade

National Scoring Defense
Champion for Past Decade

Teams on Television 67 Times

# PAUL BRYANT'S RECORD

## VS.

## ALL OPPONENTS

### (37 Years as a Head Coach)
### WON 323, LOST 85, TIED 17

| Team | Record | Pct. | Team | Record | Pct. |
|------|--------|------|------|--------|------|
| Alabama | 0-2-0 | .000 | Nebraska | 4-2-0 | .667 |
| Arkansas | 4-1-1 | .667 | North Carolina State | 2-0-0 | 1.000 |
| Arkansas State | 1-0-0 | 1.000 | North Dakota | 1-0-0 | 1.000 |
| Auburn | 19-6-0 | .760 | North Texas State | 1-0-0 | 1.000 |
| Baylor | 5-1-0 | .833 | Notre Dame | 0-4-0 | .000 |
| California | 1-0-0 | 1.000 | Ohio State | 1-0-0 | 1.000 |
| Chattanooga | 1-0-0 | 1.000 | Oklahoma | 2-0-1 | .667 |
| Cincinnati | 7-0-0 | 1.000 | Oklahoma State | 0-1-0 | .000 |
| Citadel | 1-0-0 | 1.000 | Penn State | 4-1-0 | .800 |
| Clemson | 6-0-0 | 1.000 | Rice | 3-2-0 | .600 |
| Colorado | 0-1-0 | .000 | Richmond | 2-0-0 | 1.000 |
| Dayton | 1-0-0 | 1.000 | Rutgers | 2-0-0 | 1.000 |
| Duke | 1-0-0 | 1.000 | Santa Clara | 0-1-0 | .000 |
| Evansville | 1-0-0 | 1.000 | South Carolina | 4-0-0 | 1.000 |
| Florida | 12-2-0 | .857 | Southern Cal | 2-2-0 | .500 |
| Florida State | 2-0-1 | .833 | Southern Methodist | 4-2-0 | .667 |
| Furman | 2-0-0 | 1.000 | Southern Mississippi | 11-2-0 | .846 |
| George Washington | 1-0-0 | 1.000 | Tampa | 1-0-0 | 1.000 |
| Georgia | 12-5-0 | .706 | Tennessee | 17-13-4 | .500 |
| Georgia Tech | 10-3-0 | .769 | Tennessee Tech | 1-0-0 | 1.000 |
| Guilford | 1-0-0 | 1.000 | Texas | 1-7-1 | .111 |
| Houston | 9-1-1 | .818 | Texas A&M | 1-2-0 | .333 |
| Illinois | 1-0-0 | 1.000 | Texas Christian | 6-1-0 | .857 |
| Kentucky | 4-0-0 | 1.000 | Texas Tech | 2-1-0 | .667 |
| Louisiana State | 20-5-1 | .769 | Tulane | 8-1-1 | .800 |
| Louisiana Tech | 1-0-0 | 1.000 | Tulsa | 1-0-0 | 1.000 |
| Louisville | 2-0-0 | 1.000 | UCLA | 1-1-0 | .500 |
| Marquette | 2-0-0 | 1.000 | Vanderbilt | 25-2-2 | .862 |
| Maryland | 2-0-0 | 1.000 | Villanova | 5-1-1 | .714 |
| Memphis State | 3-0-0 | 1.000 | Virginia | 1-0-0 | 1.000 |
| Merchant State | 3-0-0 | 1.000 | Virginia Military | 1-0-0 | 1.000 |
| Merchant Marine | | | Virginia Tech | 7-1-0 | .875 |
| Academy | 1-0-0 | 1.000 | Washington | 2-0-0 | 1.000 |
| Miami (Fla.) | 14-0-0 | 1.000 | West Virginia | 2-0-1 | .667 |
| Michigan State | 2-0-0 | 1.000 | Wichita State | 1-0-0 | 1.000 |
| Mississippi | 15-7-1 | .652 | William & Mary | 0-1-0 | .000 |
| Mississippi State | 27-2-0 | .931 | Xavier | 4-0-0 | 1.000 |
| Missouri | 2-2-0 | .500 | | | |

## BRYANT'S RECORD AS HEAD COACH:
## WON 323, LOST 85, TIED 17

| Year | School | W | L | T | Year | School | W | L | T |
|------|--------|---|---|---|------|--------|---|---|---|
| 1945 | Maryland | 6 | 2 | 1 | 1964 | Alabama | *10 | 1 | 0 |
| 1946 | Kentucky | 7 | 3 | 0 | 1965 | Alabama | *9 | 1 | 1 |
| 1947 | Kentucky | 8 | 3 | 0 | 1966 | Alabama | 11 | 0 | 0 |
| 1948 | Kentucky | 5 | 3 | 2 | 1967 | Alabama | 8 | 2 | 1 |
| 1949 | Kentucky | 9 | 3 | 0 | 1968 | Alabama | 8 | 3 | 0 |
| 1950 | Kentucky | 11 | 1 | 0 | 1969 | Alabama | 6 | 5 | 0 |
| 1951 | Kentucky | 8 | 4 | 0 | 1970 | Alabama | 6 | 5 | 1 |
| 1952 | Kentucky | 5 | 4 | 2 | 1971 | Alabama | 11 | 1 | 0 |
| 1953 | Kentucky | 7 | 2 | 1 | 1972 | Alabama | 10 | 2 | 0 |
| 1954 | Texas A&M | 1 | 9 | 0 | 1973 | Alabama | *11 | 1 | 0 |
| 1955 | Texas A&M | 7 | 2 | 1 | 1974 | Alabama | 11 | 1 | 0 |
| 1956 | Texas A&M | 9 | 0 | 1 | 1975 | Alabama | 11 | 1 | 0 |
| 1957 | Texas A&M | 8 | 3 | 0 | 1976 | Alabama | 9 | 3 | 0 |
| 1958 | Alabama | 5 | 4 | 1 | 1977 | Alabama | 11 | 1 | 0 |
| 1959 | Alabama | 7 | 2 | 2 | 1978 | Alabama | *11 | 1 | 0 |
| 1960 | Alabama | 8 | 1 | 2 | 1979 | Alabama | *12 | 0 | 0 |
| 1961 | Alabama | *11 | 0 | 0 | 1980 | Alabama | 10 | 2 | 0 |
| 1962 | Alabama | 10 | 1 | 0 | 1981 | Alabama | 9 | 2 | 1 |
| 1963 | Alabama | 9 | 2 | 0 | 1982 | Alabama | 8 | 4 | 0 |

*National Champions

## BRYANT AS A PLAYER, ASSISTANT COACH AND HEAD COACH

**As a Player**

| | W | L | T | |
|---|---|---|---|---|
| 1933 Alabama | 7 | 1 | 1 | .777 |
| 1934 Alabama | 10 | 0 | 0 | 1.000 |
| 1935 Alabama | 6 | 2 | 1 | .667 |
| Totals | 23 | 3 | 2 | .821 |

**As Assistant Coach**

| | W | L | T | |
|---|---|---|---|---|
| 1936 Alabama | 8 | 0 | 1 | .888 |
| 1937 Alabama | 9 | 1 | 0 | .900 |
| 1938 Alabama | 7 | 1 | 1 | .777 |
| 1939 Alabama | 5 | 3 | 1 | .555 |
| 1940 Vanderbilt | 3 | 6 | 1 | .300 |
| 1941 Vanderbilt | 6 | 1 | 2 | .667 |
| Totals | 36 | 12 | 6 | .678 |

**As Head Coach**

| | W | L | T | |
|---|---|---|---|---|
| Maryland, one year | 6 | 2 | 1 | .667 |
| Kentucky, 8 years | 60 | 23 | 5 | .681 |
| Texas A&M, 4 years | 25 | 14 | 2 | .609 |
| Alabama, 25 years | 232 | 46 | 9 | .808 |
| Totals, 38 years | 323 | 85 | 17 | .797 |
| Composite totals | 384 | 100 | 25 | .754 |

(Player and coach)

National Coach of the Year—
1961, 1971, 1973

SEC Coach of the Year—
1961, 1964, 1971, 1973, 1974,
1977, 1979, 1981

## YEAR-BY-YEAR

### MARYLAND ERA
**1945 (6-2-1)**

| | | |
|---|---|---|
| 60 | Guilford | 6 |
| 21 | Richmond | 0 |
| 22 | Merchant Marine | 6 |
| 13 | Virginia Poly | 21 |
| 13 | West Virginia | 13 |
| 14 | William & Mary | 33 |
| 38 | VMI | 0 |
| 19 | Virginia | 13 |
| 19 | South Carolina | 13 |

### KENTUCKY ERA
**(8 years, 60-23-5)**
**1946 (7-3-0)**

| | | |
|---|---|---|
| 20 | Mississippi | 6 |
| 26 | Cincinnati | 7 |
| 70 | Xavier | 0 |
| 13 | Georgia | 28 |
| 10 | Vanderbilt | 7 |
| 7 | Alabama | 21 |
| 39 | Michigan State | 14 |
| 35 | Marquette | 7 |
| 13 | West Virginia | 0 |
| 0 | Tennessee | 7 |

**1947 (8-3-0)**

| | | |
|---|---|---|
| 7 | Mississippi | 14 |
| 20 | Cincinnati | 0 |
| 20 | Xavier | 7 |
| 26 | Georgia | 0 |
| 14 | Vanderbilt | 0 |
| 7 | Michigan State | 6 |
| 0 | Alabama | 13 |
| 15 | West Virginia | 6 |
| 36 | Evansville | 0 |
| 6 | Tennessee | 13 |

**Great Lakes Bowl**

| | | |
|---|---|---|
| 24 | Villanova | 14 |

**1948 (5-3-2)**

| | | |
|---|---|---|
| 48 | Xavier | 7 |
| 7 | Mississippi | 20 |
| 12 | Georgia | 35 |
| 7 | Vanderbilt | 26 |
| 25 | Marquette | 0 |
| 28 | Cincinnati | 7 |
| 13 | Villanova | 13 |
| 34 | Florida | 15 |
| 0 | Tennessee | 0 |
| 25 | Miami | 5 |

**1949 (9-3-0)**

| | | |
|---|---|---|
| 71 | Southern Miss. | 7 |
| 19 | LSU | 0 |
| 47 | Mississippi | 0 |
| 25 | Georgia | 0 |
| 44 | Citadel | 0 |

| | | |
|---|---|---|
| 7 | SMU | 20 |
| 14 | Cincinnati | 7 |
| 21 | Xavier | 7 |
| 35 | Florida | 0 |
| 0 | Tennessee | 6 |
| 21 | Miami | 6 |

**Orange Bowl**

| | | |
|---|---|---|
| 13 | Santa Clara | 21 |

**1950 (11-1-0)**
**(SEC Champions)**

| | | |
|---|---|---|
| 25 | North Texas St. | 0 |
| 14 | LSU | 0 |
| 27 | Mississippi | 0 |
| 40 | Dayton | 0 |
| 41 | Cincinnati | 7 |
| 34 | Villanova | 7 |
| 28 | Georgia Tech | 14 |
| 40 | Florida | 6 |
| 48 | Mississippi State | 21 |
| 83 | North Dakota | 0 |
| 0 | Tennessee | 7 |

**Sugar Bowl**

| | | |
|---|---|---|
| 13 | Oklahoma | 7 |

**1951 (8-4-0)**

| | | |
|---|---|---|
| 72 | Tennessee Tech | 13 |
| 6 | Texas | 7 |
| 17 | Mississippi | 21 |
| 7 | Georgia Tech | 13 |
| 27 | Mississippi State | 0 |
| 35 | Villanova | 13 |
| 14 | Florida | 6 |
| 32 | Miami | 0 |
| 37 | Tulane | 0 |
| 47 | George Washington | 13 |
| 0 | Tennessee | 28 |

**Cotton Bowl**

| | | |
|---|---|---|
| 20 | TCU | 7 |

**1952 (5-3-2)**

| | | |
|---|---|---|
| 13 | Mississippi | 13 |
| 10 | Texas A&M | 7 |
| 7 | LSU | 34 |
| 14 | Mississippi State | 27 |
| 14 | Cincinnati | 6 |
| 29 | Miami | 0 |
| 27 | Tulane | 6 |
| 27 | Clemson | 14 |
| 14 | Tennessee | 14 |
| 0 | Florida | 27 |

**1953 (7-2-1)**

| | | |
|---|---|---|
| 6 | Texas A&M | 7 |
| 6 | Mississippi | 22 |
| 26 | Florida | 13 |
| 6 | LSU | 6 |
| 32 | Mississippi State | 13 |

| | | |
|---|---|---|
| 19 | Villanova | 0 |
| 19 | Rice | 13 |
| 40 | Vanderbilt | 17 |
| 20 | Memphis State | 7 |
| 27 | Tennessee | 21 |

### TEXAS A&M ERA
**(4 years, 25-14-2)**
**1954 (1-9-0)**

| | | |
|---|---|---|
| 9 | Texas Tech | 41 |
| 6 | Oklahoma State | 14 |
| 6 | Georgia | 0 |
| 7 | Houston | 10 |
| 20 | TCU | 21 |
| 7 | Baylor | 20 |
| 7 | Arkansas | 14 |
| 3 | SMU | 6 |
| 19 | Rice | 29 |
| 13 | Texas | 22 |

**1955 (7-2-1)**

| | | |
|---|---|---|
| 0 | UCLA | 21 |
| 28 | LSU | 0 |
| 21 | Houston | 3 |
| 27 | Nebraska | 0 |
| 19 | TCU | 16 |
| 19 | Baylor | 7 |
| 7 | Arkansas | 7 |
| 13 | SMU | 2 |
| 20 | Rice | 12 |
| 6 | Texas | 21 |

**1956 (9-0-1)**
**(SWC Champions)**

| | | |
|---|---|---|
| 19 | Villanova | 0 |
| 9 | LSU | 6 |
| 40 | Texas Tech | 7 |
| 14 | Houston | 14 |
| 7 | TCU | 6 |
| 19 | Baylor | 13 |
| 27 | Arkansas | 0 |
| 33 | SMU | 7 |
| 21 | Rice | 7 |
| 34 | Texas | 21 |

**1957 (8-3-0)**

| | | |
|---|---|---|
| 21 | Maryland | 13 |
| 21 | Texas Tech | 0 |
| 28 | Missouri | 6 |
| 28 | Houston | 6 |
| 7 | TCU | 0 |
| 14 | Baylor | 0 |
| 7 | Arkansas | 6 |
| 19 | SMU | 6 |
| 6 | Rice | 7 |
| 7 | Texas | 9 |

**Gator Bowl**

| | | |
|---|---|---|
| 0 | Tennessee | 3 |

**ALABAMA ERA**
**(25 years, 232-46-9)**
**1958 (5-4-1)**

| | | |
|---|---|---|
| 3 | LSU | 13 |
| 0 | Vanderbilt | 0 |
| 29 | Furman | 6 |
| 7 | Tennessee | 14 |
| 9 | Mississippi State | 7 |
| 12 | Georgia | 0 |
| 7 | Tulane | 13 |
| 17 | Georgia Tech | 8 |
| 14 | Memphis State | 0 |
| 8 | Auburn | 14 |

**1959 (7-2-2)**

| | | |
|---|---|---|
| 3 | Georgia | 17 |
| 3 | Houston | 0 |
| 7 | Vanderbilt | 7 |
| 13 | Chattanooga | 0 |
| 7 | Tennessee | 7 |
| 10 | Mississippi State | 0 |
| 19 | Tulane | 7 |
| 9 | Georgia Tech | 7 |
| 14 | Memphis State | 7 |
| 10 | Auburn | 0 |
| **Liberty Bowl** | | |
| 0 | Penn State | 7 |

**1960 (8-1-2)**

| | | |
|---|---|---|
| 21 | Georgia | 6 |
| 6 | Tulane | 6 |
| 21 | Vanderbilt | 0 |
| 7 | Tennessee | 20 |
| 14 | Houston | 0 |
| 7 | Mississippi State | 0 |
| 51 | Furman | 0 |
| 16 | Georgia Tech | 15 |
| 34 | Tampa | 6 |
| 3 | Auburn | 0 |
| **Bluebonnet Bowl** | | |
| 3 | Texas | 3 |

**1961 (11-0-0)**
**(National Champions)**
**(SEC Champions)**

| | | |
|---|---|---|
| 32 | Georgia | 6 |
| 9 | Tulane | 0 |
| 35 | Vanderbilt | 6 |
| 26 | N.C. State | 7 |
| 34 | Tennessee | 3 |
| 17 | Houston | 0 |
| 24 | Mississippi State | 0 |
| 66 | Richmond | 0 |
| 10 | Georgia Tech | 0 |
| 34 | Auburn | 0 |
| **Sugar Bowl** | | |
| 10 | Arkansas | 3 |

**1962 (10-1-0)**

| | | |
|---|---|---|
| 35 | Georgia | 0 |
| 44 | Tulane | 6 |
| 17 | Vanderbilt | 7 |
| 14 | Houston | 3 |
| 27 | Tennessee | 7 |
| 35 | Tulsa | 6 |
| 20 | Mississippi State | 0 |
| 36 | Miami | 3 |
| 6 | Georgia Tech | 7 |
| 38 | Auburn | 0 |
| **Orange Bowl** | | |
| 17 | Oklahoma | 0 |

**1963 (9-2-0)**

| | | |
|---|---|---|
| 32 | Georgia | 7 |
| 28 | Tulane | 0 |
| 21 | Vanderbilt | 6 |
| 6 | Florida | 10 |
| 35 | Tennessee | 0 |
| 21 | Houston | 13 |
| 20 | Mississippi State | 19 |
| 27 | Georgia Tech | 11 |
| 8 | Auburn | 10 |
| 17 | Miami | 12 |
| **Sugar Bowl** | | |
| 12 | Mississippi | 7 |

**1964 (10-1-0)**
**(National Champions)**
**(SEC Champions)**

| | | |
|---|---|---|
| 31 | Georgia | 3 |
| 36 | Tulane | 6 |
| 24 | Vanderbilt | 0 |
| 21 | N.C. State | 0 |
| 19 | Tennessee | 8 |
| 17 | Florida | 14 |
| 23 | Mississippi State | 6 |
| 17 | LSU | 9 |
| 24 | Georgia Tech | 7 |
| 21 | Auburn | 14 |
| **Orange Bowl** | | |
| 17 | Texas | 21 |

**1965 (9-1-1)**
**(National Champions)**
**(SEC Champions)**

| | | |
|---|---|---|
| 17 | Georgia | 18 |
| 27 | Tulane | 0 |
| 17 | Mississippi | 16 |
| 22 | Vanderbilt | 7 |
| 7. | Tennessee | 7 |
| 21 | Florida State | 0 |
| 10 | Mississippi State | 7 |
| 31 | LSU | 7 |
| 35 | South Carolina | 14 |
| 20 | Auburn | 3 |
| **Orange-Bowl** | | |
| 39 | Nebraska | 28 |

**1966 (11-0-0)**
**(SEC Champions)**

| | | |
|---|---|---|
| 34 | Louisiana Tech | 0 |
| 17 | Mississippi | 7 |
| 26 | Clemson | 0 |
| 11 | Tennessee | 10 |
| 42 | Vanderbilt | 6 |
| 27 | Mississippi State | 14 |
| 21 | LSU | 0 |
| 24 | South Carolina | 0 |
| 34 | Southern Miss. | 0 |
| 31 | Auburn | 0 |
| **Sugar Bowl** | | |
| 34 | Nebraska | 7 |

**1967 (8-2-1)**

| | | |
|---|---|---|
| 37 | Florida State | 37 |
| 25 | Southern Miss. | 3 |
| 21 | Mississippi | 7 |
| 35 | Vanderbilt | 21 |
| 13 | Tennessee | 24 |
| 13 | Clemson | 10 |
| 13 | Mississippi State | 0 |
| 7 | LSU | 6 |
| 17 | South Carolina | 0 |
| 7 | Auburn | 3 |
| **Cotton Bowl** | | |
| 16 | Texas A&M | 20 |

**1968 (8-3-0)**

| | | |
|---|---|---|
| 14 | Virginia Tech | 7 |
| 17 | Southern Miss. | 14 |
| 8 | Mississippi | 10 |
| 31 | Vanderbilt | 7 |
| 9 | Tennessee | 10 |
| 21 | Clemson | 14 |
| 20 | Mississippi State | 13 |
| 16 | LSU | 7 |
| 14 | Miami | 6 |
| 24 | Auburn | 16 |
| **Gator Bowl** | | |
| 10 | Missouri | 35 |

**1969 (6-5-0)**

| | | |
|---|---|---|
| 17 | Virginia Tech | 13 |
| 63 | Southern Miss | 14 |
| 33 | Mississippi | 32 |
| 10 | Vanderbilt | 14 |
| 14 | Tennessee | 41 |
| 38 | Clemson | 13 |
| 23 | Mississippi State | 19 |
| 15 | LSU | 20 |
| 42 | Miami | 6 |
| 26 | Auburn | 49 |
| **Liberty Bowl** | | |
| 33 | Colorado | 47 |

**1970 (6-5-1)**

| | | |
|---|---|---|
| 21 | USC | 42 |
| 51 | Virginia Tech | 18 |
| 46 | Florida | 15 |
| 23 | Mississippi | 48 |
| 35 | Vanderbilt | 11 |

| 0 | Tennessee | 24 |
|---|---|---|
| 30 | Houston | 21 |
| 35 | Mississippi State | 6 |
| 9 | LSU | 14 |
| 32 | Miami | 8 |
| 28 | Auburn | 33 |

**Astro-Bluebonnet Bowl**

| 24 | Oklahoma | 24 |
|---|---|---|

**1971 (11-1-0)**
**(SEC Champions)**

| 17 | USC | 10 |
|---|---|---|
| 42 | Southern Miss. | 6 |
| 38 | Florida | 0 |
| 40 | Mississippi | 6 |
| 42 | Vanderbilt | 0 |
| 32 | Tennessee | 15 |
| 34 | Houston | 20 |
| 41 | Mississippi State | 10 |
| 14 | LSU | 7 |
| 31 | Miami | 3 |
| 31 | Auburn | 7 |

**Orange Bowl**

| 6 | Nebraska | 38 |
|---|---|---|

**1972 (10-2-0)**
**(SEC Champions)**

| 35 | Duke | 12 |
|---|---|---|
| 35 | Kentucky | 0 |
| 48 | Vanderbilt | 21 |
| 25 | Georgia | 7 |
| 24 | Florida | 7 |
| 17 | Tennessee | 10 |
| 48 | Southern Miss. | 11 |
| 58 | Mississippi State | 14 |
| 35 | LSU | 21 |
| 52 | Virginia Tech | 13 |
| 16 | Auburn | 17 |

**Cotton Bowl**

| 13 | Texas | 17 |
|---|---|---|

**1973 (11-1-0)**
**(National Champions)**
**(SEC Champions)**

| 66 | California | 0 |
|---|---|---|
| 28 | Kentucky | 14 |
| 44 | Vanderbilt | 0 |
| 28 | Georgia | 14 |
| 35 | Florida | 14 |
| 42 | Tennessee | 21 |
| 77 | Virginia Tech | 6 |
| 35 | Mississippi State | 0 |
| 43 | Miami | 13 |
| 21 | LSU | 7 |
| 35 | Auburn | 0 |

**Sugar Bowl**

| 23 | Notre Dame | 24 |
|---|---|---|

**1974 (11-1-0)**
**(SEC Champions)**

| 21 | Maryland | 16 |
|---|---|---|
| 52 | Southern Miss. | 0 |

| 23 | Vanderbilt | 10 |
|---|---|---|
| 35 | Mississippi | 21 |
| 8 | Florida | 7 |
| 28 | Tennessee | 6 |
| 41 | TCU | 3 |
| 35 | Mississippi State | 0 |
| 30 | LSU | 0 |
| 28 | Miami | 7 |
| 17 | Auburn | 13 |

**Orange Bowl**

| 11 | Notre Dame | 13 |
|---|---|---|

**1975 (11-1-0)**
**(SEC Champions)**

| 7 | Missouri | 20 |
|---|---|---|
| 56 | Clemson | 0 |
| 40 | Vanderbilt | 7 |
| 32 | Mississippi | 6 |
| 52 | Washington | 0 |
| 30 | Tennessee | 7 |
| 45 | TCU | 0 |
| 21 | Mississippi State | 10 |
| 23 | LSU | 10 |
| 27 | Southern Miss. | 6 |
| 28 | Auburn | 0 |

**Sugar Bowl**

| 13 | Penn State | 6 |
|---|---|---|

**1976 (9-3-0)**

| 7 | Mississippi | 10 |
|---|---|---|
| 56 | SMU | 3 |
| 42 | Vanderbilt | 14 |
| 0 | Georgia | 21 |
| 24 | Southern Miss. | 8 |
| 20 | Tennessee | 13 |
| 24 | Louisville | 3 |
| 34 | Mississippi State | 17 |
| 28 | LSU | 17 |
| 18 | Notre Dame | 21 |
| 38 | Auburn | 7 |

**Liberty Bowl**

| 36 | UCLA | 6 |
|---|---|---|

**1977 (11-1-0)**
**(SEC Champions)**

| 34 | Mississippi | 13 |
|---|---|---|
| 24 | Nebraska | 31 |
| 24 | Vanderbilt | 12 |
| 18 | Georgia | 10 |
| 21 | USC | 20 |
| 24 | Tennessee | 10 |
| 55 | Louisville | 6 |
| 37 | Mississippi State | 7 |
| 24 | LSU | 3 |
| 36 | Miami | 0 |
| 38 | Auburn | 21 |

**Sugar Bowl**

| 35 | Ohio State | 6 |
|---|---|---|

**1978 (11-1-0)**
**(National Champions)**
**(SEC Champions)**

| 20 | Nebraska | 3 |
|---|---|---|
| 38 | Missouri | 20 |
| 14 | USC | 24 |
| 51 | Vanderbilt | 28 |
| 20 | Washington | 17 |
| 23 | Florida | 12 |
| 30 | Tennessee | 17 |
| 35 | Virginia Tech | 0 |
| 35 | Mississippi State | 14 |
| 31 | LSU | 10 |
| 34 | Auburn | 16 |

**Sugar Bowl**

| 14 | Penn State | 7 |
|---|---|---|

**1979 (12-0-0)**
**(National Champions)**
**(SEC Champions)**

| 30 | Georgia Tech | 6 |
|---|---|---|
| 45 | Baylor | 0 |
| 66 | Vanderbilt | 3 |
| 38 | Wichita State | 0 |
| 40 | Florida | 0 |
| 27 | Tennessee | 17 |
| 31 | Virginia Tech | 7 |
| 24 | Mississippi State | 7 |
| 3 | LSU | 0 |
| 30 | Miami | 0 |
| 25 | Auburn | 18 |

**Sugar Bowl**

| 24 | Arkansas | 9 |
|---|---|---|

**1980 (10-2-0)**

| 26 | Georgia Tech | 3 |
|---|---|---|
| 59 | Mississippi | 35 |
| 41 | Vanderbilt | 0 |
| 45 | Kentucky | 0 |
| 17 | Rutgers | 13 |
| 27 | Tennessee | 0 |
| 42 | Southern Miss. | 7 |
| 3 | Mississippi State | 6 |
| 28 | LSU | 7 |
| 0 | Notre Dame | 7 |
| 34 | Auburn | 18 |

**Cotton Bowl**

| 30 | Baylor | 2 |
|---|---|---|

**1981 (9-2-1)**
**(SEC Champions)**

| 24 | LSU | 7 |
|---|---|---|
| 21 | Georgia Tech | 24 |
| 19 | Kentucky | 10 |
| 28 | Vanderbilt | 7 |
| 38 | Mississippi | 7 |
| 13 | Southern Miss. | 13 |
| 38 | Tennessee | 19 |
| 31 | Rutgers | 7 |
| 13 | Mississippi State | 10 |

| | | | | | | | |
|---|---|---|---|---|---|---|---|
| 31 | Penn State ......... 16 | 24 | Vanderbilt ......... 21 | 10 | LSU .............. 20 |
| 28 | Auburn ........... 17 | 34 | Arkansas State ..... 7 | 29 | Southern Miss. ..... 38 |
| | **Cotton Bowl** | 42 | Penn State ......... 21 | 22 | Auburn ........... 23 |
| 12 | Texas ............. 14 | 28 | Tennessee ......... 35 | | **Liberty Bowl** |
| | | 21 | Cincinnati ......... 7 | 21 | Illinois ............ 15 |
| | **1982 (8-4)** | 20 | Mississippi State .... 12 | | |
| 45 | Georgia Tech....... 7 | | | | |
| 42 | Mississippi ......... 14 | | | | |

## PAUL BRYANT'S BOWL RECORD THROUGH THE YEARS

| Season | Bowl | Results | Record |
|---|---|---|---|
| 1946 | Great Lakes | KENTUCKY 24, Villanova 14 | 1-0 |
| 1949 | Orange | Santa Clara 21, KENTUCKY 13 | 1-1 |
| 1950 | Sugar | KENTUCKY 13, Oklahoma 7 | 2-1 |
| 1951 | Cotton | KENTUCKY 20, TCU 7 | 3-1 |
| 1957 | Gator | Tennessee 3, TEXAS A&M 0 | 3-2 |
| 1959 | Liberty | Penn State 7, ALABAMA 0 | 3-3 |
| 1960 | Bluebonnet | ALABAMA 3, Texas 3 | 3-3-1 |
| 1961 | Sugar | ALABAMA 10, Arkansas 0 | 4-3-1 |
| 1962 | Orange | ALABAMA 17, Oklahoma 0 | 5-3-1 |
| 1963 | Sugar | ALABAMA 12, Mississippi 7 | 6-3-1 |
| 1964 | Orange | Texas 21, ALABAMA 17 | 6-4-1 |
| 1965 | Orange | ALABAMA 39, Nebraska 28 | 7-4-1 |
| 1966 | Sugar | ALABAMA 34, Nebraska 7 | 8-4-1 |
| 1967 | Cotton | Texas A&M 20, ALABAMA 16 | 8-5-1 |
| 1968 | Gator | Missouri 35, ALABAMA 10 | 8-6-1 |
| 1969 | Liberty | Colorado 47, ALABAMA 37 | 8-7-1 |
| 1970 | Bluebonnet | ALABAMA 24, Oklahoma 24 | 8-7-2 |
| 1971 | Orange | Nebraska 38, ALABAMA 6 | 8-8-2 |
| 1972 | Cotton | Texas 17, ALABAMA 13 | 8-9-2 |
| 1973 | Sugar | Notre Dame 24, ALABAMA 23 | 8-10-2 |
| 1974 | Orange | Notre Dame 13, ALABAMA 11 | 8-11-2 |
| 1975 | Sugar | ALABAMA 13, Penn State 6 | 9-11-2 |
| 1976 | Liberty | ALABAMA 36, UCLA 6 | 10-11-2 |
| 1977 | Sugar | ALABAMA 35, Ohio State 6 | 11-11-2 |
| 1978 | Sugar | ALABAMA 14, Penn State 7 | 12-11-2 |
| 1979 | Sugar | ALABAMA 24, Arkansas 9 | 13-11-2 |
| 1980 | Cotton | ALABAMA 30, Baylor 2 | 14-11-2 |
| 1981 | Cotton | Texas 14, ALABAMA 12 | 14-12-2 |
| 1982 | Liberty | ALABAMA 21, Illinois 15 | 15-12-2 |

## COACH BRYANT 41-6 vs. HIS PUPILS

Paul Bryant had a record of 41-6 against his "pupils," including having won 32 games in a row against head coaches who either played for him or coached on his staff.

Individually, here is how Coach Bryant has done against his pupils: 14-2 vs. Charlie McClendon, 6-0 vs. Bob Tyler, 6-1 vs. Bill Battle, 4-0 vs. Jerry Claiborne, 4-0 vs. Steve Sloan, 2-1 vs. Paul Dietzel, 1-0 vs. Charley Pell, 1-0 vs. Howard Schnellenberger, 0-1 vs. Gene Stallings, 1-1 vs. Pat Dye, and 1-0 vs. Larry Lacewell.

## BRYANT'S BOYS WHO BECAME HEAD COACHES
### (College or Professional)
### Total—46

| Name | Head Coach for | Association | Player or Coach |
|---|---|---|---|
| Mickey Andrews | North Alabama** | Alabama | Player |
| Bruce Ariens* | Temple | Alabama | Coach |
| Bill Arnsparger* | LSU** | Kentucky | Player |
| Bill Battle | Tennessee | Alabama | Player |
| Jim Blevins | Jacksonville State | Alabama | Both |
| Clark Boler* | Bloomsburg (Pa.) State | Alabama | Player |
| Charley Bradshaw | Troy State** | Kentucky & Alabama | Both |
| Ray Callahan | Cincinnati | Kentucky | Player |
| Jerry Claiborne* | Kentucky** | Kentucky, Texas A&M & Alabama | Both |
| John David Crow | Northeast Louisiana | Texas A&M & Alabama | Both |
| Phil Cutchin | Oklahoma State | Kentucky, Texas A&M & Alabama | Both |
| Paul Dietzel | South Carolina** | Kentucky | Coach |
| Pat Dye* | Auburn** | Alabama | Coach |
| Bill Elias | Virginia | Maryland | Coach |
| Danny Ford* | Clemson | Alabama | Both |
| Jimmy Fuller | Jacksonville State | Alabama | Player |
| Leon Fuller* | Colorado State | Alabama | Player |
| Bill Hannah (deceased) | Fullerton (Cal.) JC | Alabama | Player |
| Tom Harper | Wake Forest | Kentucky | Player |
| Wilbur Jamerson | Morehead (Ky.) State | Kentucky | Player |
| Al Kincaid* | Wyoming | Alabama | Coach |
| J. T. King | Texas Tech | Texas A&M | Coach |
| Larry Lacewell* | Arkansas State | Alabama | Coach |
| Ken Meyer | San Francisco 49ers | Alabama | Coach |
| Charlie McClendon | Louisiana State | Kentucky | Both |
| Jim McKenzie (deceased) | Oklahoma | Kentucky | Player |
| Bud Moore | Kansas | Alabama | Both |
| Frank Moseley (deceased) | Virginia Tech | Maryland & Kentucky | Coach |
| Bill Oliver | UT-Chattanooga | Alabama | Both |
| Jim Owens | Washington | Kentucky & A&M | Both |
| Jack Pardee* | Houston Gamblers** | Texas A&M | Player |
| Vito (Babe) Parilli | Chicago Wind** | Kentucky | Player |
| Charley Pell* | Florida** | Alabama | Player |
| Ray Perkins* | Alabama** | Alabama | Player |
| Bum Phillips* | New Orleans Saints** | Texas A&M | Coach |
| Don Robbins | Idaho | Texas A&M | Player |
| Howard Schnellenberger | Miami Hurricanes** | Kentucky & Alabama | Both |
| Jimmy Sharpe | Virginia Tech | Alabama | Both |
| Jackie Sherrill* | Texas A&M** | Alabama | Player |
| Steve Sloan* | Duke** | Alabama | Both |
| Gene Stallings | Texas A&M | Texas A&M & Alabama | Both |
| Jim Stanley* | Michigan Panthers** | Texas A&M | Player |
| Loyd Taylor | Tarleton (Texas) State | Texas A&M | Player |
| Bob Tyler | North Texas State** | Alabama | Coach |
| Richard Williamson | Memphis State | Alabama | Both |
| Jim Wright | Wichita State | Texas A&M | Player |

* Denotes current head coach.
** Denotes more than one head coaching post.

## BRYANT'S BOYS WHO WERE LETTERMEN
## UNIVERSITY OF ALABAMA

| Name | Year | Name | Year |
|---|---|---|---|
| Abbruzzese, Raymond | '61 | Brewer, Richard | '67 |
| Adcock, Mike* | '82 | Britt, Gary | '77 |
| Adkinson, Wayne | '72 | Brock, Jim* | '82 |
| Allen, Charles G. | '59 | Brock, Mike | '79 |
| Allison, Scott | '79 | Brooker, Johnny | '82 |
| Allen, Steve | '63 | Brooker, Tommy | '61 |
| Allman, Phil | '78 | Brown, Bill* | '82 |
| Andrews, Mickey | '64 | Brown, Buddy | '73 |
| Aydellette, Buddy | '79 | Brown, Jerry | '75 |
| Bailey, David | '71 | Brown, Larry | '82 |
| Barnes, Ronnie Joe | '74 | Brown, Randy | '68 |
| Barnes, Wiley | '79 | Brungard, David | '70 |
| Barron, Marvin | '73 | Bryan, Richard | '74 |
| Barron, Randy | '68 | Buchanan, Woody | '76 |
| Bates, Tim | '65 | Buck, Oran | '69 |
| Batey, Bo | '76 | Bunch, Jim | '79 |
| Battle, Bill | '62 | Busbee, Kent | '67 |
| Baumhower, Bob | '76 | Busby, Max | '77 |
| Bean, Dickie | '66 | Butler, Clyde | '70 |
| Beard, Jeff | '71 | Callaway, Neil | '77 |
| Beard, Ken | '63 | Callies, Kelly | '77 |
| Beazley, Joe | '82 | Calvert, John | '66 |
| Beck, Ellis | '73 | Canterbury, Frank | '66 |
| Beddingfield, David | '69 | Carroll, Jimmy | '66 |
| Bedwell, David | '67 | Carruth, Paul* | '82 |
| Bell, Stanley | '59 | Carter, Joe* | '82 |
| Bendross, Jesse* | '82 | Cary, Robin | '73 |
| Bentley, Ed | '70 | Cash, Jerry | '71 |
| Berrey, Bucky | '76 | Cash, Steve | '80 |
| Billingsley, Randy | '74 | Castille, Jeremiah | '79 |
| Bird, Ron | '63 | Cavan, Pete | '77 |
| Bisceglia, Steve | '72 | Cayavec, Bob | '82 |
| Blair, Bill | '70 | Chaffin, Phil | '70 |
| Blevins, Jim | '59 | Chambers, Jimmy | '67 |
| Blitz, Jeff | '72 | Chapman, Roger | '78 |
| Blue, Al* | '82 | Chatwood, David | '67 |
| Bolden, Ray | '75 | Childers, Morris | '60 |
| Boler, Clark | '63 | Childs, Bob | '68 |
| Boler, Tom | '80 | Ciemny, Richard | '70 |
| Boles, Duffy | '75 | Clark, Cotton | '62 |
| Bolton, Bruce | '78 | Clark, Phil | '56 |
| Bone, George | '68 | Clark, Tim | '81 |
| Booker, David | '79 | Clay, Steve | '69 |
| Booker, Steve* | '82 | Clements, Mike | '79 |
| Booth, Baxter | '58 | Cline, Jackie | '82 |
| Boothe, Vince | '79 | Cochran, Donald G. | '59 |
| Boschung, Paul | '69 | Cokely, Donald | '71 |
| Bowman, Steve | '65 | Colburn, Rocky | '82 |
| Box, Jimmy | '60 | Cole, Richard | '65 |
| Boyd, Thomas | '81 | Coleman, Michael | '78 |
| Boylston, Bobby | '60 | Coley, Ken | '82 |
| Bradford, Jim | '77 | Collins, Danny | '77 |
| Bragan, Dale | '76 | Collins, Earl | '82 |
| Braggs, Byron | '80 | Cook, Elbert | '62 |
| Braggs, Chester* | '82 | Cook, Leroy | '75 |
| Bramblett, Dante* | '82 | Cook, Wayne | '66 |
| Bramblett, Gary | '82 | Cowell, Vince | '80 |
| Brannen, Jere Lamar | '58 | Cox, Allen | '72 |

| | | | |
|---|---|---|---|
| Hodges, Bruce | '77 | LaBue, John | '76 |
| Holcombe, Danny | '82 | LaBue, Joe | '72 |
| Holoman, Desmond* | '82 | Lambert, Buford | '76 |
| Holsomback, Roy | '60 | Lambert, Rand | '74 |
| Holt, Buddy | '79 | Lancaster, John | '79 |
| Holt, Darwin | '61 | Langston, Griff | '70 |
| Homan, Dennis | '67 | Law, Phil | '71 |
| Homan, Scott | '82 | Lawley, Lane | '70 |
| Hood, Sammy* | '82 | Layton, Dale | '62 |
| Hopper, Mike | '64 | Lazenby, K. J. | '76 |
| Horstead, Don* | '82 | Lee, Mickey | '69 |
| Horton, Jimmy | '71 | Lee, Shon* | '82 |
| Hubbard, Colenzo | '76 | Legg, Murray | '78 |
| Hufstetler, Tom | '78 | Lewis, Al | '63 |
| Hunt, Morris | '73 | Lewis, Walter* | '82 |
| Hunter, Scott | '70 | Lowe, Eddie | '82 |
| Hurlbut, Jack | '63 | Lowe, Woodrow | '75 |
| Hurst, Tim | '77 | Lusk, Tom | '72 |
| Husband, Hunter | '69 | Lyles, Warren | '81 |
| Husband, Woodie | '70 | Lyons, Marty | '78 |
| Ikner, Lou | '78 | Maddox, Sam | '77 |
| Israel, Jimmy | '66 | Mallard, James | '80 |
| Israel, Tom | '69 | Mann, Frank | '70 |
| Ivy, Jim* | '82 | Marcello, Jerry | '73 |
| Jackson, Billy | '80 | Marks, Keith | '79 |
| Jackson, Bobby | '58 | Marshall, Fred | '71 |
| Jackson, Mark* | '82 | Martin, Gary | '63 |
| Jackson, Wilbur | '73 | Martin, Kenny | '67 |
| Jacobs, Don | '80 | Mauro, John | '80 |
| James, Kenneth | '70 | Maxwell, Ray | '75 |
| Jarmon, Rodney* | '82 | Mikel, Bobby | '76 |
| Jilleba, Pete | '69 | Miller, Noah | '73 |
| Johns, Bobby | '67 | Mitchell, Dewey | '77 |
| Johnson, Billy | '67 | Mitchell, John | '72 |
| Johnson, Cornell | '60 | Mitchell, Tank | '64 |
| Johnson, Hoss* | '82 | Montgomery, Greg | '75 |
| Johnston, Donny | '69 | Montgomery, Robert | '70 |
| Jones, Arnos | '80 | Mooneyham, Marlin | '62 |
| Jones, Joe | '80 | Moore, Bud | '60 |
| Jones, Joey* | '82 | Moore, Harold | '66 |
| Jones, Kevin | '78 | Moore, John | '62 |
| Jones, Robbie | '82 | Moore, Mal | '62 |
| Jones, Terry | '77 | Moore, Pete | '69 |
| Jordan, Lee Roy | '62 | Moore, Randy | '73 |
| Junior, E. J. | '80 | Moore, Ricky* | '82 |
| Kearley, Dan | '64 | Morgan, Ed | '68 |
| Kelley, Joe | '68 | Morrison, Duff | '60 |
| Kelley, Les | '66 | Morton, Farris | '62 |
| Kerr, Dudley | '67 | Morton, L. D. | '76 |
| Kilgore, Terry | '67 | Moseley, Elliott | '60 |
| Kim, Peter | '82 | Mosley, John | '66 |
| King, Emmanual* | '82 | Moss, Stan | '67 |
| King, Tyrone | '75 | Mott, Steve | '82 |
| Knapp, David | '72 | Musso, Johnny | '71 |
| Kramer, Mike | '77 | McClendon, Frankie | '64 |
| Krapf, Jim | '72 | McCollough, Gaylon | '64 |
| Krauss, Barry | '78 | McCombs, Eddie | '80 |
| Krout, Bart | '81 | McCrary, Tom* | '82 |
| Kubelius, Skip | '73 | McElroy, Alan | '79 |
| Kulback, Steve | '74 | McGee, Barry | '75 |

| | | | |
|---|---|---|---|
| Shankles, Don | '67 | Thompson, Dickey | '67 |
| Sharpe, Jimmy | '62 | Tillman, Chip | '77 |
| Sharpless, Johnny | '73 | Todd, Richard | '75 |
| Shealy, Steadman | '79 | Tolleson, Tommy | '65 |
| Shelby, Willie | '75 | Trammell, Pat | '61 |
| Sherrill, Jackie | '65 | Travis, Tim | '79 |
| Shinn, Richard | '82 | Trimble, Wayne | '66 |
| Shumann, Eric | '77 | Tripoli, Paul* | '82 |
| Sides, Johnny | '67 | Trodd, Paul* | '82 |
| Simon, Kenny | '82 | Tucker, Mike | '77 |
| Simmons, Jim | '64 | Tucker, Ricky | '79 |
| Simmons, Jim | '71 | Turner, Craig* | '82 |
| Simmons, Malcolm* | '82 | Turpin, John | '78 |
| Sims, Wayne | '59 | Turpin, Dick | '75 |
| Sington, Dave | '58 | Umphrey, Woody | '80 |
| Sington, Fred, Jr. | '59 | Vagotis, Chris | '66 |
| Sisia, Joseph | '60 | Valletto, Carl | '58 |
| Skelton, Bobby | '60 | Varnado, Carey Reid | '70 |
| Slaughter, Derrick* | '82 | Versprille, Eddie | '63 |
| Sloan, Steve | '65 | Vickers, Doug* | '82 |
| Smalley, Jack, Jr. | '77 | Vines, Jay | '78 |
| Smiley, Anthony* | '82 | Wade, Steve | '72 |
| Smith, Barry | '79 | Wade, Tommy | '69 |
| Smith, Bobby | '79 | Wagner, Richard* | '82 |
| Smith, Bobby | '58 | Walker, Hardy* | '82 |
| Smith, Joe* | '82 | Wall, Larry | '64 |
| Smith, Sid | '76 | Washco, George | '75 |
| Somerville, Tom | '67 | Washington, Mike | '74 |
| Spencer, Mike* | '82 | Watkins, David | '73 |
| Spencer, Tom | '79 | Watson, Rick | '76 |
| Spivey, Paul | '73 | Watts, Jimmy* | '82 |
| Sprayberry, Steve | '73 | Weigand, Tommy | '68 |
| Sprinkle, Jerrill | '82 | Welniak, Kevin* | '82 |
| Spruiell, Jerry | '60 | Wesley, Buddy | '60 |
| Stabler, Ken | '67 | Whaley, Frank | '66 |
| Stanford, Bobby | '72 | Wheeler, Wayne | '73 |
| Stapp, Laurien | '60 | White, Darryl | '82 |
| Steakley, Rod | '71 | White, Gus | '76 |
| Stephens, Bruce | '67 | White, Jack | '71 |
| Stephens, Charles | '64 | White, Mike | '82 |
| Stephens, Gerald | '62 | White, Tommy | '60 |
| Stephenson, Dwight | '79 | Whitley, Tom* | '82 |
| Stevens, Wayne | '66 | Whitman, Steve | '79 |
| Stickney, Ravis | '59 | Wieseman, Bill | '63 |
| Stock, Mike | '75 | Wilcox, Tommy | '82 |
| Stokes, Ralph | '74 | Wilder, Ken | '69 |
| Stone, Rocky | '69 | Wilkins, Red | '61 |
| Strickland, Chuck | '73 | Wilkins, Todd* | '82 |
| Strickland, Lynwood | '65 | Wilkinson, Vernon* | '82 |
| Strickland, Ross | '70 | Williams, Charlie | '82 |
| Sullivan, Johnny | '66 | Williams, John | '66 |
| Surlas, Tom | '71 | Williams, Steve | '70 |
| Sutton, Donnie | '68 | Williamson, Richard | '62 |
| Sutton, Mike | '78 | Willis, Perry | '67 |
| Swafford, Bobby | '68 | Wilson, Butch | '62 |
| Swann, Gerald* | '82 | Wilson, Jimmy | '62 |
| Taylor, James | '75 | Wingo, Rich | '78 |
| Thomas, Cliff* | '82 | Wise, Mack | '58 |
| Thomas, Dan | '70 | Wood, Dexter | '72 |
| Thompson, Louis | '66 | Wood, Russ | '82 |

| | | | |
|---|---|---|---|
| Woodruff, Glen | '71 | Yelvington, Gary | '74 |
| Wright, Steve | '63 | *Denotes eligibility remaining after 1982. | |

## UNIVERSITY OF KENTUCKY

| | | | |
|---|---|---|---|
| Adkins, Tommy | '53 | Howe, Jim | '49 |
| Allen, Ermal | '41 | Hunt, Herbie | '53 |
| Babb, Jim | '47 | Ignarssi, John | '51 |
| Bailey, John | '52 | Jamerson, Wilbur | '50 |
| Baldwin, John | '52 | James, Pat | '50 |
| Bassitt, Bob | '52 | Jones, Harry | '52 |
| Bentley, Charles | '49 | Jones, Larry | '52 |
| Bezuk, Bob | '49 | Jones, Paul | '51 |
| Bivin, Arvon | '53 | Jones, Roscoe | '47 |
| Blanda, George | '48 | Jones, Wallace | '48 |
| Boller, Bill | '49 | Kennard, Jim | '46 |
| Bradshaw, Charlie | '49 | Kirk, Harry | '54 |
| Brooks, Bobby | '49 | Kirn, Ted | '51 |
| Browning, Charles | '47 | Klein, Norman | '48 |
| Bruno, Al | '50 | Kock, Joe | '54 |
| Callahan, Ray | '55 | Kuhn, Dave | '56 |
| Carlig, Clyde | '55 | Lair, Matt | '47 |
| Chambers, Bill | '46 | Lawson, Cliff | '51 |
| Claiborne, Jerry | '49 | Leskovar, Bill | '51 |
| Clark, Emery | '51 | Mackenzie, Jim | '51 |
| Conde, Bill | '51 | Martin, Dick | '50 |
| Correll, Ray | '53 | Mason, Max | '51 |
| Cutchin, Phil | '46 | Mayo, Jim | '52 |
| Dawson, Bill | '50 | McClendon, Charlie | '50 |
| Donaldson, Gene | '51 | McDermott, Lloyd | '49 |
| Dyer, Don | '52 | Meeks, Gene | '46 |
| Farley, Bill | '51 | Meihaus, Johnny | '48 |
| Farris, Jack | '47 | Meilinger, Steve | '53 |
| Ferrell, Doc | '48 | Mills, Bradley | '55 |
| Fillion, Tom | '53 | Mingus, Jerry | '52 |
| Ford, Roy | '48 | Mitchell, Dick | '54 |
| Frampton, Don | '49 | Moloney, Dick | '55 |
| Fry, Bob | '52 | Moseley, Bill | '47 |
| Fucci, Dom | '50 | Moseley, Doug | '51 |
| Fuller, Frank | '52 | Netoskie, Don | '56 |
| Gain, Bob | '50 | Netoskie, John | '51 |
| Genito, Carl | '48 | Odivak, Nick | '49 |
| Genito, Ralph | '49 | Parilli, Vito (Babe) | '51 |
| Griffin, Bill | '47 | Phelps, Don | '49 |
| Griggs, John | '52 | Platt, Joe | '53 |
| Gruner, Bunky | '51 | Pope, Bob | '50 |
| Haas, Gene | '46 | Porter, Ray | '49 |
| Hamilton, Allen | '50 | Preston, Leonard | '47 |
| Hamilton, Ed | '51 | Proffitt, Jim | '53 |
| Hanley, Jack | '54 | Rhodemyre, Jay | '47 |
| Hardy, Bob | '55 | Rice, Dennis | '46 |
| Harper, Tom | '53 | Ridge, Don | '47 |
| Heinzinger, Ben | '46 | Rogers, Harry | '50 |
| Hennessey, Larry | '54 | Rushing, Dick | '54 |
| Hensley, Dick | '47 | Sadler, Frank (Mgr.) | '47 |
| Holt, Bobby (Mgr.) | '56 | Saylor, Unis (Mgr.) | '49 |
| Holway, Dick | '49 | Schaffnit, Bill | '50 |
| Hooper, Hayden | '55 | Schenk, Jim | '53 |

| | | | |
|---|---|---|---|
| Schnellenberger, Howard | '55 | Wannamaker, Bill | '50 |
| Sengel, George | '47 | Webb, Clayton | '50 |
| Serini, Wash | '47 | Weinmann, Al (Mgr.) | '51 |
| Shatto, Dick | '53 | Wheeler, Bill | '55 |
| Smith, Calvin | '51 | Wilard, Miles | '53 |
| Strange, Leo | '55 | Williams, Ken | '53 |
| Truman, Lee | '49 | Wooddell, Harold | '50 |
| Tunstill, Jesse | '46 | Yarutis, Leo | '47 |
| Ulinski, Harry | '49 | Yowarsky, Walt | '50 |
| Vance, Wendell | '50 | Zampino, Al | '56 |
| Walker, Charlie Bill | '46 | Zaranka, Ben | '50 |

## MARYLAND

| | | | |
|---|---|---|---|
| Barkalow, Gerald | '45 | Johnston, Richard | '46 |
| Barnes, George | '45 | Kinney, Eugene | '48 |
| Bonk, Harry | '48 | McCarthy, Joseph | '45 |
| Chisari, Thomas | '45 | Morter, LaRoy | '46 |
| Crosland, Robert | '46 | Piker, Robert | '45 |
| Daly, Leslie | '45 | Poling, William | '46 |
| Drach, Joseph | '47 | Schrecongost, John | '45 |
| Evans, Francis | '48 | Schultz, Ferdnand | '45 |
| Fehr, Walter | '46 | Schwarz, Edward | '48 |
| Fritz, Emile | '46 | Smith, Les | '45 |
| Gleasner, Donald | '45 | Toler, Dick | '45 |
| Greer, William | '45 | Turyn, Vic | '48 |

## TEXAS A&M

| | | | |
|---|---|---|---|
| Appelt, Bill | '58 | Goehring, Dennis | '57 |
| Barrett, Ray | '55 | Goff, Richard | '59 |
| Beck, Ken | '59 | Granberry, Billy | '57 |
| Brown, Darrell | '57 | Grant, Don | '56 |
| Browning, Don | '59 | Hale, Lloyd | '57 |
| Burkhart, Jim | '57 | Hall, Charles | '54 |
| Caruthers, Bryon | '60 | Hall, Ken | '56 |
| Cauthorn, Bill | '60 | Hall, Luther | '59 |
| Clark, Henry | '55 | Hamby, Cliff | '58 |
| Clendennen, Bob | '57 | Harvard, Ben | '60 |
| Conrad, Bobby Joe | '58 | Hawthorn, Jackie | '60 |
| Cox, Jimmy | '58 | Henderson, Gene | '56 |
| Crow, John David | '58 | Hobson, Roger | '58 |
| Darwin, Bill | '60 | Howard, Tommy | '59 |
| Dendy, Bill | '55 | Howell, Joe | '60 |
| Daucet, Ray | '59 | Huddleston, Bill Pete | '56 |
| Dudley, Ed | '58 | Johnson, George R. | '56 |
| Easley, Bob | '55 | Kachtik, Don | '55 |
| Elledge, Jerry | '60 | Keith, Bobby Drake | '57 |
| Esquival, Carlos | '57 | Kennon, Paul | '54 |
| Flood, Tommy | '59 | Kettler, Elwood | '55 |
| Franklin, Carter | '60 | Kramer, Jerry | '58 |
| Garner, Bob | '60 | Krueger, Charlie | '58 |
| Gay, Richard | '59 | Langston, Jim (Mgr.) | '58 |
| Gilbert, John | '58 | LeBoeuf, Gordon | '60 |
| Gillar, George | '58 | Lewis, Dick | '61 |
| Gillespie, Bill | '56 | Lockett, Bobby | '57 |
| Godwin, Bill | '60 | Luna, Carl | '59 |

| | | | | |
|---|---|---|---|---|
| Marks, Bobby | '58 | Roper, Stanley | '59 |
| Martin, Gary | '60 | Rowell, Joe | '59 |
| McCandless, Charlie | '56 | Schero, Joe | '55 |
| McClelland, Don | '60 | Schmid, Joe (Mgr.) | '57 |
| McGowan, Billy Joe | '55 | Schroeder, Bill | '54 |
| Meeks, Dean | '60 | Scott, Charlie | '58 |
| Merrill, Carl | '60 | Simmons, A. L. | '58 |
| Milam, Dickie | '59 | Sinclair, Bennie | '55 |
| Milstead, Charlie | '60 | Smithwick, Dick | '58 |
| Moak, Russ | '59 | Sorrells, Dick | '59 |
| Munday, Dick | '57 | Stallings, Gene | '57 |
| Munson, Joe | '60 | Stanley, Jim | '58 |
| Newcomb, Bill | '59 | Stolusky, Bob | '59 |
| Nichols, Grady | '59 | Strait, Tom | '56 |
| Ohlendorf, Norbert | '54 | Summerlin, Troy (Mgr.) | '56 |
| Oliver, Gale | '59 | Tate, Marvin | '55 |
| Osborne, Roddy | '58 | Taylor, Loyd | '58 |
| Pardee, Jack | '57 | Theriot, Sidney | '55 |
| Patrick, Pat | '60 | Tracey, John | '59 |
| Payne, Buddy | '60 | Trimble, Murray | '58 |
| Pearson, Henry | '55 | Vaden, Frank (Mgr.) | '55 |
| Pickard, Bill (Mgr.) | '56 | Vann, Richard | '55 |
| Polk, John | '59 | Vick, Richard | '55 |
| Pollard, Hollis | '57 | Wasserman, Lloyd | '58 |
| Pope, Perry | '60 | Watson, Don | '56 |
| Powell, Dee | '57 | Winkler, Larry | '55 |
| Powell, Jack | '57 | Wolf, Herb | '55 |
| Price, Harold | '56 | Wotipka, Leo | '59 |
| Revellete, Chuck | '58 | Wright, Jimmy | '57 |
| Ridgeway, Jim | '58 | Yeates, Robert | '60 |
| Robbins, Donald | '56 | Zuckero, Al | '56 |
| Rollins, Gary (Mgr.) | '58 | | |

# *About the Author*

Mike Bynum is one of the South's most successful young authors. He is the author of six previous books, all dealing with football, including BOUND FOR GLORY (with Bobby Bowden), WE BELIEVE (with Jerry Brondfield) and NEVER SAY QUIT (with Steadman Shealy), considered by many to be one of the finest inspirational books for young people ever written. Adding to his list of credits, Mike served as "Consulting Producer" to the Mizlou TV special, BEAR BRYANT—COUNTDOWN TO 315, which was produced for NBC.

A former student manager for Coach Bryant's Crimson Tide football team and honor student at The University of Alabama, Mike is presently completing a trilogy of football's three greatest coaches—Bryant, Rockne and Lombardi, after which he will be attending law school.

Mr. Bynum lives in Tuscaloosa, Alabama.